# Trading
# online

**books for the future minded**

## Welcome to the next generation of business

There is a new world which we can look at but we cannot see. Yet within it, the forces of technology and imagination are overturning the way we work and the way we do business.

ft.com books are both gateway and guide to this world. We understand it because we are part of it. But we also understand the needs of businesses which are taking their first steps into it, and those still standing hesitantly on the threshold. Above all, we understand that, as with all business challenges, the key to success lies not with the technology itself, but with the people who must use it and manage it. People like you: the future minded.

See a world of business.
Visit us at **www.ft.com** today.

# Trading online

A step-by-step guide to cyberprofits

*Second edition*

## Alpesh B Patel

PEARSON EDUCATION LIMITED

Head Office:
Edinburgh Gate
Harlow CM20 2JE
Tel: +44 (0)1279 623623
Fax: +44 (0)1279 431059

London Office:
128 Long Acre
London WC2E 9AN
Tel: +44 (0)20 7447 2000
Fax: +44 (0)20 7240 5771
Website: www.business-minds.com

..............................................

First published in Great Britain in 2000

© Pearson Education Limited 2000

The right of Alpesh Patel to be identified as author
of this work has been asserted by him in accordance
with the Copyright, Designs and Patents Act 1988.

ISBN 0 273 65041 6

*British Library Cataloguing in Publication Data*
A CIP catalogue record for this book can be obtained from the British Library.

10 9 8 7 6 5 4 3 2 1

Typeset by Northern Phototypesetting Co. Ltd, Bolton
Printed and bound in Great Britain by Biddles Ltd, Guildford & King's Lynn

*The Publishers' policy is to use paper manufactured from sustainable forests.*

# About the author

## Alpesh B Patel LLB, BA (Oxon), AKC, barrister-at-law

Alpesh is a graduate in the joint honours school of Philosophy, Politics and Economics from St Anne's College, Oxford University, and has a degree in Law from King's College, London University. As a barrister, Alpesh was involved in advising banks, building societies and pension funds on financial services. He left practice as a barrister to trade full-time and founded TraderMind Derivatives Ltd. The company has acted as consultant up to CEO level of multi-billion-dollar online trading companies, advising on market entry and expansion strategy, site content and design.

Alpesh, through TraderMind, provides online trading content to TV, radio, the internet and newspapers, and strategy advice on using online trading content to increase sponsorship and advertising on their particular media and through strategic alliances.

Alpesh has been interviewed on CNN, Sky Business News, CNBC, Bloomberg TV, the Money Channel, the BBC World Service, BBC TV and BBC radio as well as numerous US radio shows, to discuss internet issues. He has also been profiled in the *Asian Age*, the *Times of India*, the *Hindustan Times* and the *Independent* and quoted in *Bottom Line* (whose circulation exceeds one million), *Tornado-Insider*, *India Today* the *Guardian* newspaper among many other publications.

## TV, radio and print

Alpesh also:

- is the co-founder of Pathburner.com – providing top-end investment tools for the private investor
- writes the popular and prominent 'Diary of an Internet Trader' for the weekend *Financial times*
- appears weekly on two shows on Bloomberg TV
- is editor of *e-Shares* magazine, a monthly part of *Shares* magazine – UK Launch Magazine of the year 1999

- writes two weekly columns for UK-iNvest, owned by Freeserve (the UK's largest ISP), and does a twice daily report about his own trading day for them, 'Patel on the Markets'
- writes 'Patel on Tech Stocks' for E*Trade UK, part of the world's second-largest online brokerage company
- writes 'Alpesh Patel's Essential Trading Books' for Amazon UK's business books section
- broadcasts about internet issues on Talk Sport Radio
- writes for European Investor – investor web site aimed at all major euro markets
- is contributing editor to *Bridge Trader* (a US markets paper with 60,000 circulation), and
- writes for FTMarketWatch.com weekly.

### Books

Alpesh is the author of *Net Trading* (FT.com 2000), *Trading Online: A Step-by-Step Guide to Cyberprofits* (FT Pitman 1999), *The Mind of a Trader: Lessons in Trading Strategy from the World's Leading Traders* (FT Pitman 1998) and *Your Questions Answered: Money, Savings and Financial Planning* (Rushmere Wynne 1997). *Net Trading* is to be translated into Spanish, French and German.

*Trading Online* is the number one bestselling investment book on Amazon UK and reached number two on the overall bestseller list. It was listed as one of the top ten investment books of 1999 in the *Independent* newspaper and as one of the top ten business books of 1999 by Amazon UK and by BOL.co.uk.

### Trading

Alpesh started buying stocks sixteen years ago at the age of twelve, moving on from privatization stocks to penny shares. Today he concentrates on US and UK stocks as well as futures and options trading, making extensive use of the internet for research since he was a Congressional Intern in 1994 and combining this with his own technical analysis systems.

### Lectures

Alpesh lectures on online trading, trading psychology and technical analysis around the world and at the time of going to print has in the next six months fifteen speaking engagements, including the Charles Schwab Private Investor Conference, the On Money Conference, engagements in Central America and the Middle East, and a six-city tour of the UK.

## Governmental

At the invitation of the UK Foreign Secretary, Alpesh is a member of a UK–India round-table to discuss ways in which UK and Indian companies might work together on the world stage. He has provided evidence to the UK Parliamentary Select Committee on Trade and Industry's report on e-commerce and has also given a speech about trading psychology to the Centre for the Study of Financial Innovation, a think-tank supported by leading City institutions and the Bank of England.

As part of his Oxford degree Alpesh was a Congressional Intern for the Hon. Eliot Engel in Washington DC for four months.

## Associations

Alpesh is:

- a member of the Bar Association of Commerce, finance and Industry

- an associate of the Society of Technical Analysts

- a colleague of the International Federation of Technical Analysts

- a member of the Global Association of Risk Professionals

- an Oxford University Business Alumnus, and

- a chartered member of the Indus Entrepreneurs UK (www.tie.org).


alpesh-patel@msn.com

# Contents

## SECTION 3   The truth is out there

## SECTION 4 Appendices

ॐ

Ba
Sushilaben Rambhai Patel

Papa
Bipinchandra Rambhai Patel

Mummy
Ramilaben Bipin Patel

I watched a small man with thick calluses on both hands work fifteen and
sixteen hours a day. I saw him once literally bleed from the bottoms of his feet,
a man who came here uneducated, alone, unable to speak the language, who
taught me all I needed to know about faith and hard work by the
simple eloquence of his example.

Mario Cuomo (Mayor, New York)

United your resolve, united your hearts;
United be your mind, Thus you live long together.

*Rig Veda*, 10.191.4
(c. 2000 BC, trans. from Sanskrit)

# Acknowledgements

For this Version 2.0 I grow ever more indebted to the team at ft.com – Richard Stagg and Jacqueline Cassidy – for 'fast-tracking' and putting everything on internet time.

Thank you again to Richard, my editor, for confirming that the market needed such a title, for your help and advice in what should be included and the e-mails and photocopies of relevant articles. (Looking back, we should have started an internet company instead – you were well ahead of the pack. Hope those Pearson stock options compensate.)

A book is always a mammoth partnership, yet no author ever complains that it is his name alone that appears on the cover. To reverse in some small way this injustice I must thank the following at Pearson Education for their essential help in making this book a success: Elie Ball, Sarah Harper and Angela Lewis in Marketing; Geoff Chatterton in Production; Pen Allport, Helen Baxter, Jacqueline Cassidy, Martin Croft, Collette Holden, Amanda Thompson and Susan Williams in Editorial. I hope to meet in due course those individuals whose names are not included – I trust they will forgive the omission.

# Preface

*Private information is practically the source of every large modern fortune.*

Oscar Wilde

There can scarcely be an individual in the industrialized world that does not have, or at least know someone who has, an online trading account. With online trading moving at internet speed, this book addresses and provides insight into the major issues of online trading from the perspective of an author who has been trading since the age of twelve and trading online for six years.

- *What is the best way to trade online* **in terms of choosing brokers, getting prices, doing fundamental and technical analysis, getting stock picks, and from the point of view of every other major online trading issue?**
- **Find out not just which are the best online trading sites, but which are the hidden gems and – most importantly –** *how I use them in my trading to make money.*
- **And how do I get profitable trading ideas without spending my life in front of a PC?**

This second edition of the massively successful *Trading Online* probably differs from the first by about 70–80 per cent. Indeed it could have been a wholly new book, but we could not then have used the excellent title or the 'brand awareness' for this edition. Most people will not recognize it as the same book; think of Windows 3.1 and Windows 2000, or young Elvis and old Elvis – it's that different. The focus has shifted to *how to use the net to make online trading profits* – it is more analytic; it is detailed rather than descriptive.

## The trading online revolution

'Cost of online share deals falls', 'Investors get live to attactions of internet groups', 'New electronic wizardry in the marketplace', 'E-commerce booms', 'Future at your fingertips'. These are just some recent headlines about internet trading and investing.

*What's all the fuss about?*

Well, imagine trading and investing without having to speak to a broker, no more scouring newspapers, journals and tip-sheets or plotting charts or updating portfolios by hand. No more rummaging for opinion and analysis. No more wishing there were someone you could bounce ideas off or wondering if you have missed some late-breaking pertinent information. Instead, imagine everything available on your desk from one morning to the next – up-to-the-minute, real-time, all the time.

Would it be a quicker, cheaper, easier and more profitable way to trade and invest? You better believe it! It will become as common as having a bank account or a mortgage.

## Why you need to read this book

To avoid being overwhelmed by the information, you need clear, simple 'how-to' directions to quickly *finding* the type of information YOU need, and then managing it effectively for profit as well as showing you how to use it best. The competitive advantage that the internet offers will be rapidly eroded without such an efficient professional approach.

*Brokerage commissions to top $5.3 billion*

| Online-trading forecast | 1998 | 2002 |
| --- | --- | --- |
| Commission revenues | $1.3 billion | $5.3 billion |
| Accounts | 6.4 million | 24.7 million |
| Individual investors | 5.6 million | 22.7 million |
| Percent of total investors | 8% | 30% |

Source: International Data Corp.

Without information, at best you will waste hours tied up in the net jungle; at worst you will lose money. After all, access to a law library does not make you a lawyer any more than access to the latest financial information makes you a profitable trader. You need the guidance of someone who has been there, done that and done it profitably. Introducing *Trading Online*.

One final reason to get into online trading – have a look at the following graph. Those are the potential gains that await the online trader – but only the skilled, knowledgeable one.

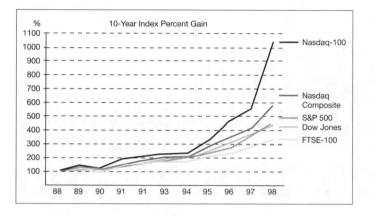

Alpesh Patel
July, 2000

# Key to countries

# Stop Press

These sites just made it before the publication date. They are predominantly European since it is Europe that tends to be catching up with the US and thus producing the newest sites.

## Financial Sites

## FTMarketWatch ✱✱✱

www.ftmarketwatch.com

### How to use this site and what for

This is the latest offering from the FT camp. The site's focus is European, with a team providing up-to-the-second news and thoughtful columns providing market analysis, as well as more detailed stock analysis.

Use it for stock analysis but not quite stock picks. Their analysis can give you an insight which may then trigger more research on your part.

## FBC24 **

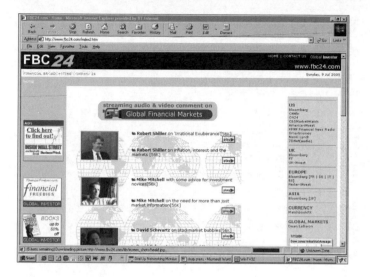

www.fcb24.com

### How to use this site and for what for

This site focuses on audio visual content. It not only conducts its own interviews with investment specialists but also usefully points to other sites that carry audio and video content – for those of us who are tired of reading. All in all, very useful and refreshing.

## ThisisMoney **

www.thisismoney.co.uk

### How to use this site and what for

Use this site for its 'companies mentioned today' which lists companies and stories in the press today. You could then see if there are any positive stories and maybe use those to trade off (after further research) or just put them on your watch list.

Also use their 'Ask the Experts' section to get free advice.

## Sharewatch **

www.sharewatch.com

### How to use this site and what for

The most useful features of this one are:

- US stock upgrades and downgrades from major brokerage houses
- The Sharewatch wire which lists, by the minute, the latest corporate news
- News archive for historical news and research
- UK and US industry news

## Multex.com

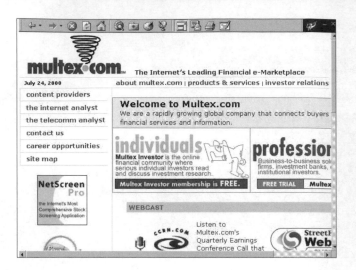

`www.multex.com`

### How to use this site and what for

Multex takes institutional stock research and offers it to private investors. Use the site to find research about stocks you are interested in from such companies as Salomon Smith Barney, Lehman Brothers and the like.

The cost of the research however varies from the free to the expensive. I only use it for the free research otherwise the costs can be too great. Also, the unfortunate thing is that the free research often requires long registration processes. However, since it is free I can't complain.

Also use them just to find out about sectors you are interested in or want to find more about, even if you do not have a stock in mind. For instance, say you want to know more about internet networking, or the sector Cisco is a part of. Then you would look for research on Cisco in the knowledge it will usually discuss the stock and the sector, future directions and ideas.'

## Brokers

## iDealing **

www.idealing.com

### How to use this site and what for

A new ultra-cheap execution-only broker. Their selling proint is £10 for any trade. They provide market information and virtual portfolios by linking you to other sites – which is cheating, but hey, £10 flat fee is great if you are likely to trade higher value trades and actively.

# www.Comdirect.co.uk **

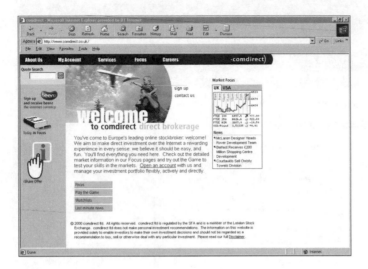

www.comdirect.co.uk

### How to use this site and what for

The UK version of Comdirect follows from its success in its native Germany. Even if you are not a customer, use the free Market Focus section to get a very useful graphical summary of how major European indices are doing. It is useful for drilling down between the main index to see which sectors are performing well within that index.

The site organization makes individual stock research very easy because you can, at the click of few buttons, see stock news. The site covers international and US shares too.

## Deal4Free ***

`www.deal4free.com`

### How to use this site and what for

Yes, commission free trading. Use this if you are active trader. They offer commission free trading because it trades CFDs (contracts for differences) which mimic the underlying shares but are not shares. You need never know it is a CFD. Visit the site to learn more about CFDs. Free software from the company sits on your PC and dynamically provides you streaming real-time prices. Executions are very quick because they are direct to market not via the internet as with browser-based brokers.

## FastTrade *

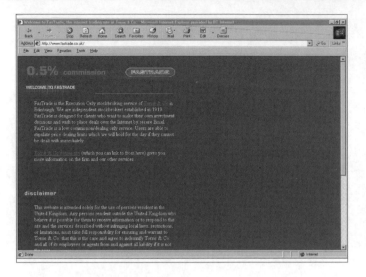

www.fasttrade.co.uk

### How to use this site and what for

Another discount broker – with 0.5% commission – offering trading in European, UK and North American securities. Other than that how do you differentiate it?

## IGIndex **

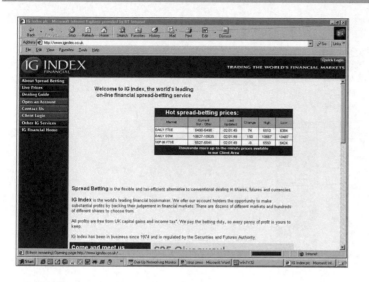

www.igindex.com

### How to use this site and what for

Spread betting is unheard of in the US. In the UK it has a large following. Since it is betting, wins carry no capital gains tax. Share dealing can be great if you are looking to trade on margin.

The site provides online dealing, real time prices as well as a useful share dealing screen. It is best suited for the active experienced trader.

## InvestIN **

www.investin.com

### How to use this site and what for

Fancy day trading? Use this site. They provide an execution only service for NASDAQ and NYSE stocks at a flat rate of $19.95 per trade. Since it is direct, access executions are very quick. The trading platform has level II prices.

## Sharepeople **

www.sharepeople.com

### How to use this site and what for

This site brings the convenience of global trading from one account at £17.50 per trade. Also use this for its 5.6% p.a. gross interest rate (at the time of writing). It provides a host of portfolio tools.

## The Share Centre *

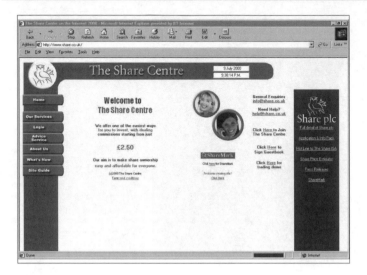

www.share.co.uk

### How to use this site and what for

Commissions start at £2.50! However, they are actually 1% of the deal size with a £2.50 minimum. So this is best if you have to sell some small holdings, not for bigger value trades. Also watch out, the company aggregates orders and executes them at fixed daily times to save costs – so it is not for the active trader.

## Direct Trader ***

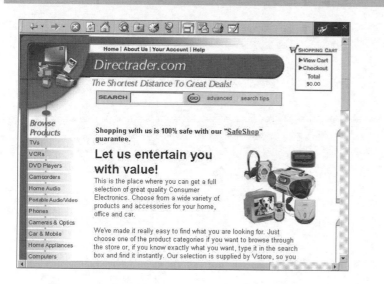

www.directtrader.com

### How to use this site and what for

This one is for the active serious short-term trader and day trader. Good trading platform and speedy direct market access make it a treat to trade through. But it is for the experienced trader.

## Nothing-Ventured **

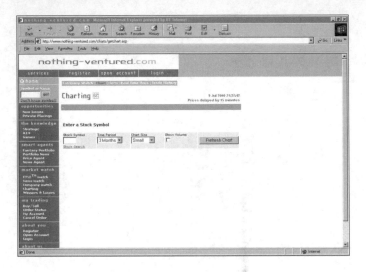

www.nothing-ventured.com

### How to use this site and what for

A well designed site. Use it for breaking news and access to new issues and private placings. However, beware they are all from Durlacher (the brokers behind the site) but nevertheless they have been very good at picking winning offerings.

Although it has charting, online trading and other services, I would recommend using other dedicated sites for these services.

## Pathburner ***

www.pathburner.com

### How to use this site and what for

Lots of free investment tools here, from chat to company research. The site is partic-ularly for those seeking top quality advice from advisory brokers. But then again, as site co-founder, I would say that wouldn't I. Check it out for yourself.

- the current real-time price (for free please) (so you know what you may be paying or receiving and can decide if it's worth it)
- the preceding trades (so you can see how high or low things look at the moment)
- the volume sizes they took place at (so you see if it has been a heavy-volume day to give you some idea of whether this is an abnormal trading day for the stock or if the price is fluctuating as part of its normal trading activity)
- the time the trades took place (to give you a feel of what the trading day has looked like)
- how the quotes have been moving all day (e.g. steadily upward, or downward)
- plus total volume today
- percentage change today
- last trade
- the normal trade size (so you know if you are going to have problems buying or selling however much you want)
- the 52-week high and low
- level II quotes (if you don't know what these are, you can think of them as showing you who else is looking to buy or sell and at what prices)
- can I get multiple quotes (i.e. type in a string of stock symbols and have the quotes listed)?

Not all of this information may be relevant to making a decision. Sometimes it is just hypnotic. However, whether I ultimately use it or not, I want the five-star quote information if it's out there; I want to see what the professionals see. Oh, and I want it for free if possible.

Plus, since I may not be in front of the PC 24-7, I want sites that allow me to enter price alerts and then page me or send a mobile phone alert – nifty eh?

## Price data

Price data can be real-time, delayed (e.g. 20 minutes), end-of-day or historical (e.g. daily data going back two years). Which one of these would be most useful to you depends on several factors, as shown in Table 2.1.

*Table 2.1 Comparison of types of price data*

| Type of trader | Most useful form of data | Methods of viewing |
|---|---|---|
| Open and close position in 48 hours | Real-time quotes | Internet site or software on PC |
| Open and close position in 7–14 days | Real-time or delayed quotes | Internet site or software on PC |
| Technical analyst (see later) | Historical and end-of-day charts | Internet site or software on PC |

Before you can analyze any product you need to have some way of examining its price. For this, three components are essential and the skeleton plan provides lists of sites for accessing each:

**1** a data provider that can provide the price data daily or intra-daily, and provide historical prices

**2** some way of viewing the prices, whether at the data provider's internet site or on software downloaded on your computer

**3** software which can convert the data into graphical format and chart them over time.

Sometimes, internet data providers also provide charts online, reducing the need for separate software on your PC (see Illustration 2.1). However, as these charts are held by the site itself, there is far less you can do with them than with actual software. Nevertheless, they are a cheap alternative to software and worth considering. Consequently, the skeleton plans refer to some of these sites as well.

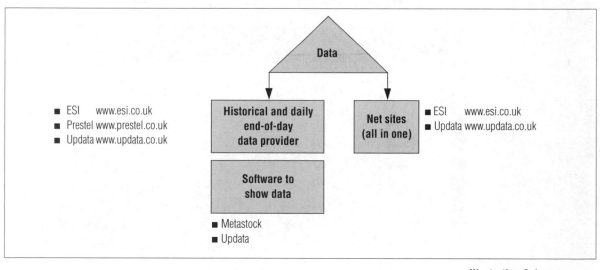

*Illustration 2.1*
*Internet data providers*

## Data providers

When you are choosing a data provider, whether real-time, delayed, end-of-day or historical, to provide prices for futures, options or stocks, that provider ought to meet certain criteria. All the recommended sites in the skeleton plans meet these criteria:

■ accurate

■ cost-effective

- readily accessible data formats for a wide range of software
- several modes of delivery, e.g. internet delivery may be supplemented with satellite, or radio signal or phone line delivery of data.

## Software charting and analyzing data

Most trading software companies provide ample illustrations of their software on their sites. Some permit demo downloads and online ordering. These sites are good places to shop around in from the comfort of your PC monitor. The skeleton plans for each product recommend software that meets certain criteria that ought always to be your minimum requirements when trading:

- cost-effective – preferably a one-off fee and not an annual licensing fee
- value for money – as many functions per dollar as possible
- easy to use – user-friendly intuitive displays (Diagram 2.1).

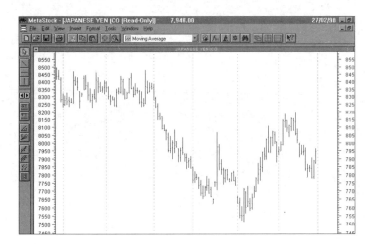

Diagram 2.1
Typical charting and
analysis software

## Some killer quote sites

These are my picks of the bunch and how I use them, as well as their strengths and what *not* to use them for.

## Bigcharts ***

www.bigcharts.com

### How to use it and what for

Okay, if you haven't heard of this one – where have you been? It is one of the best charting sites around, but more of that in a later chapter. We are here for quotes and quote-related features. Most online traders don't realize it is excellent for quotes because their layout is so good.

The site has the 'my favourite quotes' feature making it easier to keep tabs on your top picks – use it for that. The downside is it does not cover Bulletin Board stocks like Upgrade or PayforView.com. But it does allow charting straight from the quotes – dead easy to use.

## BullSession **

www.bullsession.com

### How to use it and what for

You would want to use this for its dynamic (i.e. automatic) real-time quote updating. The other key features are that you can have lots of portfolios on it and see how your profits (or maybe even your losses) look in real time. The downside – yup, there is a subscription fee. It starts at $25.95, and I would have given it three stars if it were free. However, it does provide about as much quote-related info as you could hope for for the price, including:

- bid and ask
- bid and ask sizes
- last trade
- close
- open
- volume
- tick
- price alerts
- daily high and low
- 52-week high and low
- price/earnings (p/e) ratios
- earnings
- ex-dividend rate
- yield
- number of trades.

## Barchart **

www.barchart.com

### How to use it and what for

This one is useful if you are looking to trade options, futures and commodities and need quotes for those. It is useful for the charts and analysis of those too. Given the lack of sites dealing well with derivatives data, this is a good one and the layout is pretty easy to navigate.

Although it covers stocks, don't use it for those.

## Datalink ***

www.datalink.net

### How to use it and what for

The excellent magazine *SmartMoney* rated this service the number one alert service. The key reason to consider using this service is that it can notify you of real-time quotes and other market information on a pager. But what sane person wants to be away from their PC during market hours anyway?

Use this one also if you are a mutual fund junky.

As they explain, you are alerted via your pager or PCS phone whenever your stocks exceed the 'alert' criteria you've set. These 'alert' criteria include:

- fixed increases or decreases in the price of a stock, such as MSFT shares going up or down by more than $3.00
- relative high and low market price thresholds of a particular stock, such as MSFT exceeding a high of $145.00, or going below $105.00
- daily trading volumes for a particular stock, such as a daily volume of more than 1,000,000 shares.

When one of the stocks you are monitoring exceeds one of your set thresholds, QuoteXpress automatically sends you an alert.

## eSignal ***

www.esignal.com

### How to use it and what for

This site is part of the Data Broadcasting Corporation, one of the most reliable names in the quote and market information industry. Use this one to effectively get top-of-the-range real-time quotes so your PC or laptop basically becomes a ticker-tape machine. As well as quotes you can of course get news charts and research. But you would really use this if you were going to be trading quite intensively and also wanted quotes for options and commodities.

It is internet delivered and you are using eSignal because it is a reliable brand that should not have any down-time! The downside is it costs – from $79 upwards per month (although this can vary).

## Free Real Time ***

www.freerealtime.com

### How to use it and what for

The site name tells you exactly what you may want to use this one for – the quotes are real-time and they are free. A lot of traders still think you have to pay for online real-time quotes. This site proves you don't. It is useful and easy to use. I find it most useful when the markets are moving quickly or I am monitoring several positions, any one of which I may be looking to enter or exit imminently, and so timing is of the essence. Don't use it for delayed quotes – you can get those anywhere, like on some of the other sites we are going to mention.

## Island ***

www.isld.com

### How to use it and what for

There are those people who know what Island is and what an ECN is. If you are one of the unlucky few who don't, then here goes – Island is an electronic communications network (ECN). Think of it as a trading network through which you can place trades, or, as they put it: 'Island is a computerized trading system that gives brokerages the power to electronically display and match stock orders for retail and institutional investors.'

Use their Top 20 list to find the quotes for the most popular stocks on their ECN and therefore which ones Island users are most focused on. This gives an indication of where the action is and what may be the most volatile stocks of the day and possibly the next few days. Of course that leads you on to more research. Nothing on this site is enough to base an investment decision on, but you get to see close-up what is happening.

You get free level II quotes to see what the demand is for a particular stock. I find this both really informative and hypnotic. They are telling you how strong the under-lying demand is, albeit only on their own ECN; the quotes show you the levels at which buyers and sellers want to buy and sell and at what price and what size.

| Buy orders | Sell orders |
|---|---|
| *Shares price* | *Shares price* |
| $\dfrac{1,000}{8\frac{5}{8}}$ | $\dfrac{200}{13\frac{1}{2}}$ |
| $\dfrac{370}{8\frac{9}{16}}$ | $\dfrac{100}{13\frac{3}{4}}$ |
| | $\dfrac{105}{14}$ |
| | $\dfrac{100}{14}$ |
| | $\dfrac{1,000}{15}$ |
| | $\dfrac{1,000}{15}$ |
| | $\dfrac{125}{15\frac{1}{2}}$ |
| | $\dfrac{100}{19\frac{1}{4}}$ |
| | $\dfrac{1,300}{21\frac{3}{8}}$ |
| | $\dfrac{500}{22}$ |

## Market Eye **

`www.market-eye.co.uk` UK

### How to use it and what for

Use this one for UK stocks. Again, unlike most quote services, this one comes with bells and whistles. As well as giving you the buy and sell quotes, it gives you the buy size and sell size, the volume-weighted average (VW av.) price, the last price traded and the mid-price. What is the VW av. price? It is the average price the stock has traded that day allowing for weighting for the volume it traded at each price. So for instance the last traded price may show 100 because one stock was traded at that price, but the VW av. price would usually be different from that and can give a feel for where the bulk of the trades have really taken place.

This can be useful because a stock may look like it is up or down for the day but it may in reality be trading away from that price most of the time. So if you think your stock is falling, it may not be a genuine heavy fall. This is a service you can live without, but it can be useful if you want a different take on what may 'really' be happening behind a stock.

## Interactive Investor International ***

www.iii.co.uk    UK    US

### How to use it and what for

The quotes on iii are pretty run of the mill but the thing to use this one for is to set e-mail alerts to yourself if a stock price reaches a certain level. That way even if you are at work and can't constantly receive real-time price because of firewalls or because of company policy, you can at least still get your e-mail alert. What is even more useful is that you can set those alerts on UK and US stocks from the same single site.

## UK-iNvest ***

www.ukinvest.com    UK    US

### How to use it and what for

This one has a pretty plain vanilla quote service. However, what is good is that you can access UK, US, Canadian and Italian quotes from the one site and it has a great little streaming live quote service like the CNBC or Bloomberg TV ticker. Plus use it for live UK share prices (free registration).

## EuropeanInvestor ***

www.europeaninvestor.com *EU*

### How to use it and what for

The great thing about the quotes on this site is that it covers from one place every single major European market plus the US. In the world of global online trading where more people are considering trading foreign stocks, this is a great site to get quotes – very convenient. The layout and design are also excellent.

It is a site for more than quotes, of course, including European corporate news – after all they are based in Brussels. More of that later when we look at excellent news and research sites.

## Summary

- There are real-time, delayed, end-of-day and historical data.
- Data are needed for quotes and for charts.
- The main choices involving data relate to how they will be viewed and their source.
- In terms of viewing, software offers more flexibility than the internet.
- The internet is ideal for cheap real-time or delayed quotes, with some sites offering charts as well.

With data sorted we next move on to doing something with it: analysis, getting ever closer to making the fateful trading decision.

# 3

# Getting trading ideas

> **"** *Don't be scared to feel you don't know anything, because you don't know anything until you learn* **"**

**Brian Winterflood**  Managing Director, Winterflood Securities

## In this chapter

In this chapter we cut to the chase. We want to generate trading ideas and so we start with filters, screens and lists.

## Objectives

- Find out how to use the best online filter sites for trading ideas.
- Make the most of tips on screening for stocks.

## How people choose what to buy: some popular methods

Most people, whatever they trade, have several tried and tested methods they use to conjure the inspiration in deciding what to purchase.

## Filters, screens and lists

So many stocks, so little time. That is where stock filters and screening sites come in handy.

They all work on similar criteria and that is why I have grouped them all together. For instance with some you can enter certain criteria you want stocks to match, e.g. earnings per share under 30 and revenue growth above 25 per cent, and the filter returns a list of stocks matching your criteria.

They are a very quick and useful way of getting trading ideas because the computer does most of the hard work for you.

*Example*

## A typical stock screen

When screening or filtering for stocks (Diagram 3.1) you may decide that you want a company with strong earnings likely to keep a cash reserve (through paying low dividends) which it may use to return value to shareholders by share buy-backs or acquisitions or mergers, in which case you may look for a stock with the following characteristics:

**1**  a three-year historical earnings growth rate of 20 per cent or more

**2**  a return on equity (ROE) of 25 per cent or more

**3**  stocks providing annualized total returns over the past 5 years of 20 per cent or more

**4**  companies with payout ratios (dividends as a percentage of earnings) of 15 per cent or less and dividend yields (dividends as a percentage of stock price) of 1 per cent or less.

What would you get? Well, one of the companies listed was Intel. You could then undertake further research.

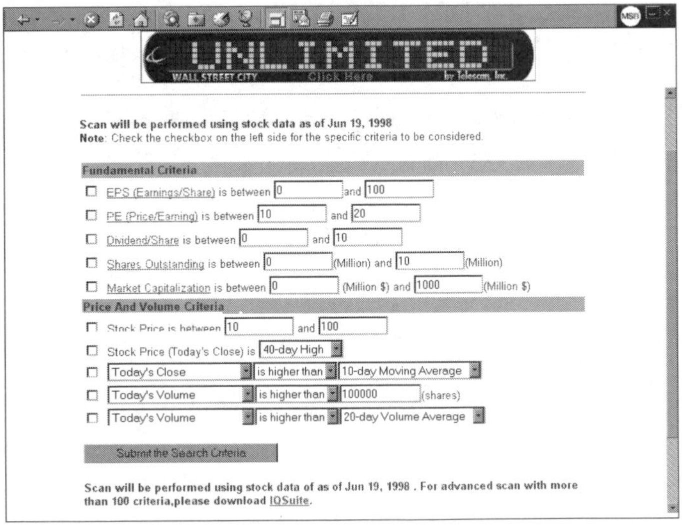

*Diagram 3.1*
*Stock prospecting using a screen*

## How do you know what criteria to use?

Most good sites will have some pre-programmed filters already incorporated which will fill in the gaps for you. For instance if you click on 'Growth Criteria' a set of values may get filled into the screening boxes. You could then leave them as they are or add your own. Other common searches have such names as (I have included in brackets a summary of why we would want to look at stock lists generated by those screens or filters):

- high earnings growth stocks (strong earnings should translate into strong stock-price growth)

- lowest p/e ratio stocks (low stock price to earnings should mean the price of the stock rises to reflect the earnings generated)

- attractive gross margin stocks (the greater the profit margin presumably the greater the profits, which in turn should reflect in increased stock prices)

- high sales growth (sales are the input for earnings, which in turn affect the stock price)

- high insider buying (if the company's directors are buying then the stock should be a good purchase relative to one where the company insiders are not buying, all other things being equal)

- strong stocks recently weak (if the stock has been having a strong run except for just the short term then it may well present an opportunity to buy it cheap before it resumes its longer-term strong trend)

- undervalued (those stocks that are relatively low in price and so should rise, relative to the earnings, cash flow or book value they hold, when compared to the other stocks in the same industry).

The sites explain the rationale behind why someone would want to do such a search.

Other sites will provide lists based on pre-programmed criteria allowing no user changes to those criteria. You would still get a list of stocks and then continue from there with the type of further research we are going to talk about. You can easily spend hours playing around with these prospecting for some gems – and indeed finding them.

Since many sites include filters, I have gone for the sites I consider the most useful, hidden gems on the web, with the most 'bells and whistles'.

## WallStreetCity ***

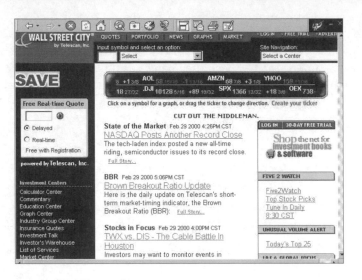

www.wallstreetcity.com

### How to use the site and what for

This is a gem of a site and if you haven't discovered it yet you have been missing out big time! In fact you could easily spend a whole day on this one and still not have found everything that is on it.

As far as screens, filters and lists go this is how I suggest using it:

1   Under **Site Navigation** go to **Search for an Investment.** From here you can use the ProSearch criteria to find stocks, e.g. small cap, high growth, high projected earnings. This will then produce a list.

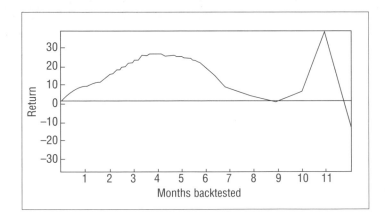

- The great thing is that the site will display how this search has performed over the recent past by doing a backtest – useful.

- But be careful: it is telling you how your portfolio would have done if you had bought all these stocks in the list. Of course you wouldn't do that, and a couple of poor performers in an otherwise excellent search may make the search performance look poor. But nevertheless it is a useful way to get some stock names out.

- However, the problem with this way of searching is that you really want the site to go through all the various combinations of search criteria and then tell you which search criteria would have provided the best returns and the stocks in that list – we'll get to that in a moment.

- Another deficiency is that you still want to do more research, e.g. examine the technical graphs, valuation criteria etc. We will get to that later. For now you can make a note of the stocks listed.

2  Another useful way to generate lists on the same site is to do the following. Still from **Search for an Investment** click on **What's working now.** This tells you which search produced the best 12-month returns of all the searches possible and then lists the stocks generated. Of course, past performance is no guarantee of future performance.

- Here are the criteria of the one example at the time of writing. However, the criteria themselves aren't important. All that is important is the return and the list of stocks of course.

| **Search components:** | |
| --- | --- |
| *Rel performance 6 wk* | |
| High as possible | 100% |
| *Return on sales* | |
| Low as possible | 100% |
| *Company growth ratio* | |
| High as possible | 100% |
| *Chaikin oscillator* | |
| Low as possible | 100% |
| *Sales increase last qtr* | |
| Low as possible | 100% |
| *Sales increase 2 qtr ago* | |
| Low as possible | 100% |
| *Stock exchange* | |
| All US markets | |
| Copy this search into ProSearch | |

**3**  To get a bit more control over your searches go to the **Best and Worst Lists** under the **Search for an Investment** page.

■ These will allow you to search under certain special areas. For example, if you only want to search stocks based on a lot of specialist earnings-based criteria then this is the place to do it. For instance, this is what some of the specialist earnings criteria look like – you can enter your own figures.

– EPS %Change 2 Qtr Ago
– EPS %Change 3 Qtr Ago
– EPS %Change 4 Qtr Ago
– EPS %Change Last Qtr
– EPS Average %Change
– EPS Consistency 5 Yr
– EPS Consistency 10 Yr
– EPS Earnings/Share
– EPS Est Date Next Release
– EPS Growth 1 Yr
– EPS Growth 3 Yr
– EPS Growth 5 Yr.

■ The ones I like best are the fundamental list and the basing pattern breakout lists. One of the searches I did on the three-week basing breakouts produced a 12-month historic return of 280 per cent on telecoms stocks!

■ The fundamentals criteria include the following:

– Book Value Growth 5 Yr
– Capital Spending Growth 5 Yr
– Cash Flow Growth 1 Yr
– Cash Flow Growth 3 Yr
– Cash Flow Growth 5 Yr
– Cash Flow/Share Free
– Cash/Price Ratio
– Current Ratio
– Debt Service/EPS
– Debt/Equity Ratio
– Gross Profit Margin
– Interest Coverage.

■ Don't worry if you don't know what all of these mean (e.g. the current ratio and interest coverage): you can leave them blank.

**4**  A slightly different way to produce great lists from the same **Search for an Investment** page is to click on **Best Stock Prospects**. This produces a list of the best search performance results, e.g. the *Strongest 6-week stocks* search's pre-programmed search criteria produced an 86 per cent 12-month return. The average percentage gain or loss for the top 25 stocks is shown next to each search. The results are also broken down by market capitalization, since different-sized companies vary in performance depending on market conditions.

**5**  Yet another list can be generated by clicking on the **Pre-built Searches** from the **Search for an Investment** page. These save you the trouble of entering your own criteria, but do not have the advantage of having the site search for the best of all the searches. I like it for focusing on certain criteria such as **Undervalued stocks**, generally based on the criteria the site has pre-entered. This can be time-saving.

- The site does a great job of explaining the reasoning behind each criterion. For example it explains why you would want to search for stocks showing **breaking out of basing position**: 'this search finds stocks that have broken out of basing patterns. That is, the stock has been trading in a flat trading range and the stock has broken out of this range. A positive breakout indicates a breakout to the upside, a negative breakout indicates a breakout to the downside. A general rule of thumb on breakouts is the longer the trading range the greater the move on a breakout. This search produces a fine selection of potential new investments but, as always, a breakout does not guarantee the stock will keep moving in the same direction.'

**6**  Another way to use this site is to undertake industry analysis. Click on **Industry Group Analysis** on the site. Next, clicking on the following links gets you different lists – each useful for a separate reason as explained below:

- **Analysts' Ratings.** This displays each industry group and the average of all the analysts' buy-to-sell recommendations for the stocks in that industry. This is useful as you can tell immediately which industry groups analysts consider the best buys – then click on that industry group to see the stocks in it and which of those are the best buys. Of course on the downside, analysts can be wrong and some stocks may only have one or two analysts covering them.

- **Best and Worst Industries.** This tells you which industries produced the best returns over certain time frames, which you can select. So, once you know for instance that Foreign Telecommunications is one of the best-performing industries over a six-week period, you can go on to find which stocks are driving that growth.

■ **Insider Buying.** This ranks all the industries according to the extent of insider buying of stocks they are composed of. So if you can see that the leisure industry has the most insiders buying its stocks, you may be inclined to have a list of those stocks and see which one of those has the most insiders buying them. The rationale is that the more insider buying there is, the better the prospects will be. It is a little simple, but can throw up some stock names you might not otherwise come across – and that is the whole idea.

7   Aside from industry analysis, there is one other excellent source of stock lists on this site: **Over/Undervalued stocks**.

■ This lists stocks according to which are the most over- or undervalued. It does this by examining the following valuation criteria:

UNDERVALUED                           OVERVALUED

– price/sales ratio
– p/e ratio
– relative p/e ratio
– projected p/e ratio
– price to book ratio
– price to cash flow ratio
– growth ratio
– debt to equity ratio
– current ratio.

■ Again it is not foolproof and there is no guarantee that undervalued stocks are more likely to outperform overvalued ones, but the rationale is a popular and sound one.

# Zacks Investment Research ***

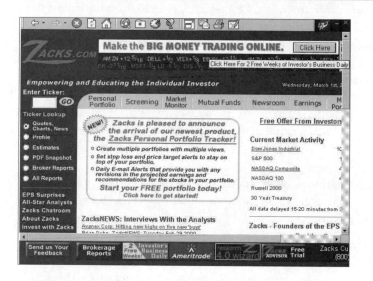

www.zacks.com

## How to use the site and what for

The problem with WallStreetCity can be that you have too many choices and are left asking 'What do I use?' Zacks can be a bit simpler. Use Zacks for its two types of screens: the pre-defined one and the custom one (where you enter your own screening criteria). The problem with the custom screen is that I find it more cumbersome to use on Zacks than in WallStreetCity and therefore prefer the pre-defined ones. These are the pre-defined screens and my views on them.

**Top Value.** This is a value-based screen relying on price to earnings ratio and the expected growth rate of earnings. The problem with it is that value-based screens have not been producing good results for IT and internet companies which may have negative earnings, or for short-term trading which has less to do with value. Use this screen for non-IT or technology searches and for longer-term investments.

**Top EPS Growth Stocks.** This is looking for growth stocks with high projected earnings per share, a sound criterion to use to hunt for stocks. The downside is that even growth stocks with strong projected earnings miss their earnings expectations and can then plummet. Unisys and Lucent are classic examples. So I use this one and then do more research on the stocks listed.

**Highest Dividend Yield.** This one is strictly for those looking for income from their stocks by way of dividend payments and who are not necessarily concerned about capital appreciation.

**Top Percentage Price Movers.** Use this for shorter-term trading. You can use it in two ways. The stocks with the biggest recent moves are likely to continue and you can then buy into them to ride the wave. Or they are going to drop back after their most recent rise and so you may want to short them.

But how do you know what the most likely scenario is? Do further research. The ones likely to continue upward are usually in an uptrend, have good newsflow and are up on an announcement likely to affect the long-term future of the company, e.g. a new ten-year alliance with Microsoft.

The ones which are likely to fall back after an announcement are those that are in a longer-term downtrend, have generally bad news each week and may have moved up on a speculative piece of news, e.g. 'Oil company has strong hopes of discovering fields in Sri Lanka.'

You get a feel for these things with experience, but the key thing is to interpret news objectively and put yourself in the shoes of other investors and get a feel for what they might do to the price.

**Best Change in Average Broker Recommendation.** Again a good and sensible screen. The screen lists those stocks which had the biggest change of opinion by brokers, e.g. if all ten brokers went from sell to strong buy on a stock then this screen would tell you.

You don't *need* me to explain why that is a useful list – but just in case you do: it is because if analysts, who are paid to monitor a stock full-time, agree *en masse* that the stock deserves to be upgraded, then maybe we should take heed. Additionally those same brokers may well then instruct their clients to buy the stock and the price will go up.

## Stockpoint ✱✱✱

www.stockpoint.com  UK

### How to use this site and what for

Click on **Investing Tools** from the home page of this site to get to the stock screens. Again these are useful for their pre-defined screens. The following are the types of screens you can use this site for and my view on the screens. The most sophisticated screens use Java and applets and so this is going to be a problem for people using older browsers. Get your hands on the latest Internet Explorer or Netscape Navigator, though even then it can be a bit slow. I leave the site if I get fed up and go to other screening sites.

**Top 25 Stocks.** Top 25 Stocks quickly returns to you the top 25 stocks traded on US exchanges in a sector or industry. Each stock is ranked by performance. You can choose the return period to sort by and whether you would like to restrict your sort to American Depository Receipts (ADR). The ADR feature I found especially useful for diversifying my holdings to include foreign (i.e. non-US companies).

After you receive the results, you can view the Market Guide company profiles or Stockpoint's Quick Charts for a particular stock by clicking on the appropriate link.

**StockFinder.** The StockFinder will search the major exchanges (NYSE, AMEX, Nasdaq) to find the stocks that match your criteria. For example, if you are looking for an airline stock that has a p/e ratio below 10, enter your specific stock criteria in the StockFinder and press 'Search'. You will then receive a list of the stocks that match your request. To see more detailed data on a particular stock, click on the ticker symbol in the results table.

This search is the simple customized one and I suggest you don't use it because WallStreetCity is better. But it can be useful if you want a quick and simple customized search without all the complexity of the WallStreetCity site.

**StockFinder Pro.** Use StockFinder Pro to search multiple data sources of nearly 10,000 publicly traded companies. StockFinder Pro returns a list of up to 100 stocks that match your customized search criteria based on over 26 data fields, such as price, volume, p/e ratio, four-week price change percentage and industry sector. Results are presented in a spreadsheet format. Because StockFinder Pro is built with Java, you can interact with the results, add customized data fields and reorder columns according to your personal preference without conducting another search.

**Top 25 Funds.** Top 25 Funds quickly returns the top 25 mutual funds in each category to you. Each fund is ranked by performance. You can search your return period and load/no-load. After you receive the results, you can view the Value Line Mutual Fund Survey information for a particular fund by clicking on the symbol. This will show the fund's investments and relevant performance data, as well as administrative information.

**FundFinder.** With FundFinder, you are able to concentrate on the mutual funds that match your personal search criteria. For example, you may be looking for an income fund that has a low minimum initial investment and has performed in the top quarter of income funds over the last five years. Simply enter your criteria and press the 'Search' button. After you see the results, proceed as for Top 25 Funds above.

**FundFinder Pro.** FundFinder Pro allows you to examine the Value Line mutual fund Survey information for funds that meet your criteria using Stockpoint's Java-based analysis tool. Again, because FundFinder Pro is built with Java, you can interact with the results, add customized data fields, and reorder columns according to your personal preference without conducting another search.

## UK-iNvest ★★★

www.ukinvest.com  UK

### How to use the site and what for

Use the stock screen on this site for UK stocks. It is powered by Stockpoint and so if you use the US version it should be straightforward. The downside is that the screen is actually hidden away in the site; click on **Tools** on the home page then on **Stock Screener**.

There are nowhere near as many stock screening sites for UK stocks as there are for US ones, and so this places UK-iNvest near the top of the pack. If you have gone through all the explanations of the other sites above then this should be easy to use.

## DigitalLook ★★★

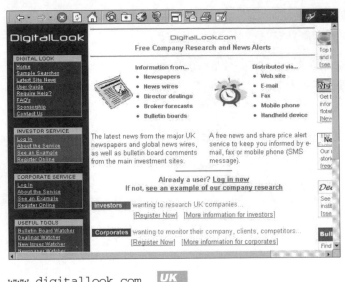

www.digitallook.com    UK

### How to use the site and what for

Again one of the few sites offering screening for UK stocks. Some of the criteria by which you can filter include:

- high dividend yield
- low p/e or PEG (price earnings to growth)
- low price/sales per share
- high consensus broker recommendation
- price risers/fallers today/over last 7/30 days
- most popular (i.e. most watched in DigitalLook)
- recently in the news
- active on the bulletin boards.

What is different and useful is the search on the most recently in the news, and most active on the bulletin boards. Use this for stocks which may be about to have short-term pops irrespective of their longer-term prospects. Often a buzz on the bulletin board translates into an opportunity for a stock pop – but this is a riskier trade. See Chapter 15 on bulletin boards.

## Share scope ***

www.sharescope.co.uk    UK

### How to use this site and what for

This is not internet-based stock filtering but software-based. This is the website from which you can order the software. It is cheap and probably the best filter service for UK stocks online or offline because of the convenience and easy-to-use graphical interface. Because it is offline software it is lightning-fast. Among many other things, it can sort according to stocks in a particular industry with the highest to lowest:

- price changes
- PEGs (ideally you want this to be as low as possible to indicate a stock likely to be undervalued and to grow over the medium to longer term)
- p/e ratios
- earnings per share
- dividend yield
- insider buying.

*Table 3.1 Stock and stock option traders*

| Item | What signifies positive for the security* |
|------|------------------------------------------|
| *Price and volume* | |
| 52-week high | A new high |
| *Growth* | |
| Revenue percentage change | An increase (acceleration) |
| Sales growth rate | An increase (acceleration) |
| Earnings per share growth rate | An increase (acceleration) |
| *Dividend information* | |
| Dividend yield | An increase (acceleration) |
| Dividend rate | An increase (acceleration) |
| *Institutional ownership information* | |
| Institutional percentage owned | An increase (acceleration) |
| Institutional net shares purchased | An increase (acceleration) |
| *Financial strength* | |
| Long-term debt to total equity | A decrease (deceleration) |
| *Profitability* | |
| Gross margin | An increase (acceleration) |
| Operating margin | An increase (acceleration) |
| Net profit margin | An increase (acceleration) |
| *Valuation ratios* | |
| Earnings per share | An increase (acceleration) |
| Price to earnings ratio | A decrease (deceleration) |
| Cashflow per share | An increase (acceleration) |
| *Insider trading* | |
| Insider shares purchased | An increase (acceleration) |
| Insider ownership percentage | An increase (acceleration) |
| *Management effectiveness* | |
| Return on assets | An increase (acceleration) |
| Return on investments | An increase (acceleration) |
| Return on equity | An increase (acceleration) |
| *News* | |
| Company in the news | Unexpected positive story |
| Sector in news | Unexpected item not in price of individual stocks |
| Broker report | Upgrade; positive news |
| *Income statements* | |
| Total operating expenses | A decrease (deceleration) |
| Free cashflow | An increase (acceleration) |
| *Efficiency ratios* | |
| Sales per employee | An increase (acceleration) |
| Income per employee | An increase (acceleration) |

\*  Conventionally, all other things being equal, compared to similar companies in same sector and compared to self 1/3/5 years earlier and not already incorporated in market expectations.

*Table 3.2  Mutual fund traders*

| Item |
| --- |
| Management performance over short, medium and long term |
| Changes in management (could signify changes in performance) |
| Fees (high fees reduce performance) |
| Risk profile (is it a high-risk fund?) |
| Performance relative to market and other funds |

*Table 3.3  Futures and options on futures traders*

| Fundamental factor | Fundamental factor |
| --- | --- |
| *Agricultural* | *Oil* |
| Weather | Weather |
| Planting intentions | Quota agreements |
| Price of substitutes | Production levels |
| Current stocks | Political unrest |
| Yields | |
| Probability of crop disease | |
| *Meats* | *Copper* |
| Expected litter sizes | Mining activity |
| Farrowing intentions | Housing starts |
| Prices of competing goods | Stocks at the London Metal Exchange |
| Consumption trends | Probability of unrest in production areas |
| Present stocks | |
| *Platinum* | *Gold* |
| Automobile production | Political unrest |
| Mining levels | Jewellery consumption |
| Jewellery consumption | Inflationary pressures |
| | Prices of alternative stores of value |
| *Financial futures* | |
| Economy (see later) | |

*Table 3.4  All traders – the macroeconomy*

| Macroeconomic statistic | Probable effect |
| --- | --- |
| *Interest rates* | If increase (acceleration) better returns in deposits than stocks, commodities or bonds – so their prices fall; exchange rate appreciates (see below) |
| *Exchange rate* | If high, exports expensive so demand decreases (decelerates). Foreign imports more competitive |
| *Balance of payments* | If deficit widens, interest rates may be reduced so exports increase (accelerate) |
| *GDP* | If high, possible inflationary pressures so possible rise in interest rate (see above) |
| *Foreign markets* | If foreign economies sluggish, foreign demand low |
| *Capacity utilization* | If high, possible inflationary pressures so possible rise in interest rate (see above) |
| *Jobless claims* | If low, possible inflationary pressures so possible rise in interest rate (see above) |
| *Existing home sales* | If high, possible inflationary pressures so possible rise in interest rate (see above) |
| *Mortgage lending* | If high, possible inflationary pressures so possible rise in interest rate (see above) |
| *Consumer confidence* | If high, possible inflationary pressures so possible rise in interest rate (see above) |
| *Construction spending* | If high, possible inflationary pressures so possible rise in interest rate (see above) |
| *Factory orders* | If high, possible inflationary pressures so possible rise in interest rate (see above) |
| *Non-farm payroll* | If high, possible inflationary pressures so possible rise in interest rate (see above) |
| *Retail sales* | If high, possible inflationary pressures so possible rise in interest rate (see above) |

This is a very simplified illustration; macroeconomic policies vary from country to country and a lot depends on expectations (i.e. was the data in line with what was expected?). This is a basis, however, to help the beginner understand the news stories better and get a firmer feel for fundamental analysis and the fact that everything is connected to everything else – the only issue being how strongly it is connected. See the recommended reading and internet sites for further investigation.

Note, also, that what may be considered potentially inflationary factors, such as relatively lower jobless claims, will have the opposite effect in an economy coming out of a recession compared to one which is near the peak of the economic cycle. Therefore, the background economic picture has also to be borne in mind.

## Summary

I have tried to provide you with a detailed method of how to get stock ideas from the top filter sites. The tips I offer are based on years of experience, and if you make any money from this, send a cheque to …

# 4

# Charts, technical analysis and momentum indicators

*❝ October. This is one of the peculiarly dangerous months to speculate in stocks. The others are July, January, September, April, November, May, March, June, December, August and February❞*

**Mark Twain**

## In this chapter

Using technical analysis (price charts and indicators) is probably the quickest and easiest way to evaluate the short-term prospects of a stock. If you do it well you can scan through lots of stocks and get a good idea not only of what to buy and when, but of when to sell. For those new to technical analysis (TA), we go through the basics before we go to the killer sites and see how to use them to generate profitable trading ideas.

## Objectives

- What is this thing 'technical analysis' people keep talking about?

- Key things we need to know about TA to get trading ideas.

- Using the hidden gems that lie behind the top TA sites in order to get profitable trading ideas.

- Knowing which securities to buy.

- Even if I know what to buy, when is the best time to buy it, so I reduce the chances of the stock going down right after I have bought it?

- What are the signs that a security is 'tanking', i.e. ripe for a fall?

- I can't be bothered reading a load of accounts, analysts' reports and dull stuff like that before deciding what to buy: what should I do?

- How do the big institutions use technical analysis?

## Technical analysis

Vast books have been written on TA (check out the reading list for some of the best). This is a refresher chapter for people who may need reminding of some of the key concepts of technical analysis, but it is also for all those newbies who need to get up to speed about TA. I am not going to go through every single analytic method known to man and beast. I am going to focus on the techniques I use, those that are the most popular and those the major institutions use. There will be no discussion of the latest esoteric method developed by some overgrown maths professor out of Lima who swears that TA, mixed with a bit of sun-spot gazing, produces great trading results. No. You only get the good stuff here.

I love TA, and trust me, this stuff is so straightforward once you get the hang of it. I have explained it to Oxford professors and 14-year-old students. Remember throughout that TA is simply a way of trying to find out when to buy low and sell high.

## The rationale for technical analysis

To repeat, the reason for using TA is to know when to buy low and sell high. It tends to work best over a time frame of a few days to a few weeks, so is ideal for short-term trading. Many of the indicators and methods of analysis we will examine are trying to determine when traders may have overreacted and have sold too much stock too quickly or vice versa, therefore affording us the opportunity to enter or exit the market at the best time to maximize profits.

But TA does not always work. Nothing in the markets always works – as far I know, although I understand that George Soros may have a better idea than most of what often works. Whenever we use TA, or any other form of analysis, we are in fact looking for points where there is an increased *probability* of a price move. Let us then look at some tools to determine high-probability price-move areas.

## Charting

Let us start at the beginning, as simply as possible. The first thing all technical analysts will do is put up a price chart. There are many, many types. Check out for instance Diagrams 4.1–4.3.

*Diagram 4.1*
*Bar chart*

*Diagram 4.2*
*Japanese candlesticks*

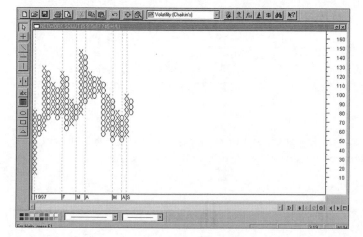

*Diagram 4.3*
*Point and figure chart*

Bar charts are the most popular ways of depicting prices. The length is determined by the extremities of the high and the low. The horizontal line on the left of each vertical line represents the opening price, and the horizontal line on the right represents the close.

In Japanese candlesticks there is a 'body' and a line (like a wick). The body is a rectangle drawn between the open and close of the day. It is shaded black if the close is lower than the open, and white if the close is above the open. The wick is added to join the high and low of the day. Of course if there is no price movement after the open then there will be no body or wick, and just a horizontal line.

I won't bore you with point and figure charts, or for that matter Renko or Kagi – bar charts and candlesticks are by far the most popular and all we need to know before we undertake a PhD in TA.

## Trendlines

A trendline simply joins a series of higher lows or lower highs. Uh? Look at the Diagram 4.4. We see the line joining higher lows. Drawing trendlines is best treated as an art and you should not look for exact points, but get a feel for where prices are hitting the approximate narrow area around the line and then moving back up. What trendlines try to represent are areas where there is a relatively increased probability of a price move off the trendline.

**Diagram 4.4**
**Trendlines**

You would not trade off the trendline, but rather use it as one piece of evidence when determining likely price moves – more of how to do this later.

## Support and resistance

You will often have read or heard something like 'Prices met stiff resistance today and could not break through the 60 barrier.' By drawing support and resistance levels we are again trying to determine areas where prices are *probably*, but not certainly, going to behave in a particular way. See for instance Diagrams 4.5 and 4.6. They depict support and resistance levels respectively. So, when the price approaches the resistance area it has greater difficulty getting past that area, and you may decide you want to exit your position (if you are holding one) at that point.

**Diagram 4.5**
**Support**

**Diagram 4.6**
**La résistance!**

Like trendlines, they must not be thought of as set in stone. They are liable to move and can be penetrated intra-day or maybe even over a couple of days. They should perhaps be thought of as zones of probable price action. In a moment we will look at how to use this to actually trade.

With trendlines and supports and resistances, the probability of a price move in a particular direction increases the longer the trendline has been in 'force', i.e. not penetrated but merely had the price touch it and then bounce off it. So if a trendline has six points over a six-month period where the price did not pass through it but instead touched and moved in the opposite direction, that will be a strong signal that the price will do this on the seventh approach. Have a look at Diagram 4.7 which should remove the clouds of foggy ambiguity from your mind.

**Diagram 4.7**
**Trendlines**

With supports and resistances what we are seeing is a battle between buyers and sellers. For instance, at a resistance level sellers may have decided they will start selling a security at that level because it is overpriced, and buyers are too few to do much about it. So the price has to retreat as selling increases. If the buyers increase in number and size at the crucial point (i.e. go for a push through the line of resistance with reinforcements) then the price may break through with the force of a broken dam, with maurauding buyers pushing the price up higher and short sellers who had not anticipated the breakthrough now having to buy back their positions to limit their losses, thereby becoming buyers and pushing the prices even higher.

This is one reason why the price often jumps at breakouts with a sharp rise, a gap up in price, and increased volume. Watch for these things and you will soon get a feel for price action around supports and resistances.

## Support and resistance trading strategies

One strategy traders use with, say, resistances is to wait to see if the resistance is broken, and if it is then – on the basis that all those people who did not expect it to be broken would be wrong and now have to go with the side of the break – prices should break through resistances and when they do break through, with a significant rise. So, first look for a penetration or breakthrough of the resistance; if there is one, then it should be followed by a big move (i.e. a breakout).

So what counts for penetration? Given market volatility you could get prices piercing a trendline or support or resistance but then closing back above it. For this reason some technical analysts only draw trendlines and support and resistance levels based on closing prices, because intra-day prices are too erratic to mean a real penetration has occurred. Others say the price must close for two or three days in a penetrating position. (I hope none of you are reading this chapter in bed: there is a danger your concentration may be distracted.)

An alternative method of trading is to wait and see if the trendline is *not* broken, and then to trade in the direction of the rebound.

## Role reversal

When a support or resistance level is broken it tends then to reverse its role and to become a resistance level or support level respectively (see Diagram 4.8). This is a common occurrence and the same rules about resistances and supports apply as before.

**Diagram 4.8**
**Move trends**

Trendlines, supports and resistances can be drawn on any time frame, whether the charts you are using are three-minute or weekly ones. You would first determine the time frame you intend to trade in and choose the bar charts appropriate to that. For instance if you intend to hold a position for only a few days then you would use the daily charts.

*Hot tip*

**Always more**
*Always use more than just trendlines in making trading decisions, unless you have a liking for losing money. Remember too, trading using TA is an art and should not be thought of as providing scientific entry and exit points. You cannot without psychic abilities get in at exactly the very best price – all technical analysts try to be as good as possible and that means being merely good enough. With the markets there is no 100 per cent perfection. Again, you are not dealing with certainties but with probabilities and that is why you need stop losses.*

## Pullback

After the breakthrough of a support or resistance the price will often 'pull back' to the trendline it just broke through (Diagram 4.9). You have to be careful of this because you may think the move has ended, in which case you may exit an otherwise profitable trade prematurely. Unfortunately you will not know if it is a pullback (which could also be used as another opportunity to enter the trade if you missed it first time) or a false breakout until it is too late. So the key is to set stop losses and watch the prices like a hawk. If the price breaks through and then pulls back to near the support line again, is it now starting to go back through the support line and continuing on as if it had never broken through (i.e. a false breakout) or is it starting to return in the direction of the breakout? Feel free to take a break, look at the charts, think it over, have a snooze, and return to this.

*Diagram 4.9*
*Pullback*

# Reversal pattern strategies

Reversal patterns are chart patterns which historically have tended to precede a reversal in prices. Again, they are added to our overall evidence of what the price may do, which then gives us a better idea whether we should exit a position or enter one. So let's do a rundown. If you like what you see then you should definitely learn more before trading by picking up some of the technical analysis books in the recommended reading.

## Head and shoulders strategies

An anatomical pattern, this. Have a look at Diagram 4.10 for a nice example. It is not always as clear cut.

*Diagram 4.10*
*Head and shoulder*

This is a common pattern on bar charts and is fairly reliable. The horizontal line represents the 'neckline' and you must always wait for it to be broken for it to be a head and shoulders position. The pattern can occur on a slope. The price is supposed to reach as far below the neckline as the top of the head is from the neckline.

The position can also occur as a bullish pattern if it appears as an opposite mirror reflection. In that case, the price would break up through the neckline. In many ways you can think of the neckline as a support and trade the pattern like a trendline break as mentioned above.

## Tops and bottoms strategies

A bottom is the opposite of, wait for it, a … top (Diagram 4.11). The top occurs where the price rises to a resistance level, falls back, rises and again falls back. The volume on the rise to the second peak should be lower than the volume on the rise to the first peak. This is because buyers are getting weaker at pushing the price up. The valley to peak should be at least 15 per cent to represent a proper top. As buyers lose numbers and heart, the sellers push the price down and a reversal occurs.

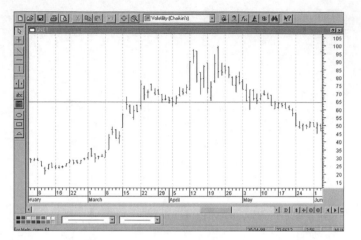

*Diagram 4.11*
*You're the tops*

## Triangle strategies

Diagram 4.12 shows a triangle. For a price reversal on the upside the horizontal line appears above the ascending diagonal line. We are then looking for a breakout through the horizontal line. To trade the pattern you can treat it very much like a breakout pattern from a resistance level.

*Diagram 4.12*
*A triangle*

The example above is an ascending triangle; the descending triangle is an exact mirror reflection and that would represent a price breakout to the downside. In the ascending triangle pattern, buyers are willing to pay increasingly higher prices but at the resistance level their willingness subsides and sellers come in. Near the pinnacle of the triangle, the buyers overcome the sellers and a breakout occurs.

Volume should be decreasing to the apex and then increase on breakout as the marauding purchasing invaders breach the sellers' line of defence. The triangle pattern occurs quite frequently, and the price target is as far above the horizontal as the mouth of the triangle is wide! Why that should be the price target is a bit of a mystery.

## Saucer strategies

The pattern for this is shown in Diagram 4.13. It represents a gradual change in opinion about a stock. Although saucers are rare, if you can spot them as the price is rising they can be an additionally confirmatory indicator of a trend change. There are no price targets for this pattern, so exit needs to be determined more by rising stop losses or by the other technical methods we discuss below.

*Diagram 4.13*
*A flying pattern – the saucer*

# Continuation patterns

These patterns confirm that the current direction of price movement will continue. They can represent a pause in price and so can be used as a good point to step on before the escalator starts moving up again.

## Rectangles: not a square strategy

The rectangle is simply where the price action moves sideways between a support and resistance level after a rise (see Diagram 4.14). It can be thought of as a resting place where buying and selling troops stop for a moment to reconsider price levels; some start profit, while other latecomers get on board.

A strategy for this is to trade it in the same way you would any other breakout through a resistance (forgotten? – we discussed it above). Once the breakout occurs

**Chart 4.14**
**Rectangle**

prices should continue onwards and upwards. Unlike just a plain breakout through a resistance level, the fact that there has been a rectangle formation first and a price rise before it adds to the likelihood of a breakout from the resistance.

## Flag strategy: flying the flag for more of the same

A flag can appear in an uptrend or downtrend. See Diagram 4.15 for an example. The flag looks like a rectangle rotated diagonally upward and is preceded by a downtrend. The flag is where instead of a sideways move after a downturn, buyers for a while outgun sellers and cause prices to rise as they believe prices have oversold, but the sellers soon return as prices rise. The flag is important only after the bottom of the flag is pierced – so wait for that. Then you know the market will fall further and you see a flag. If it is not pierced you simply have a reversal.

**Diagram 4.15**
**The price continues**
**to flag**

## Pennant strategy

The pennant is like other continuation patterns in that it forms as a breathing space in the battle between buyers and sellers. In Diagram 4.16 you can see a clear example.

*Diagram 4.16*
*A pennant*

The pennant in the example shows a rising trend followed by a price move where two boundary lines converge, representing the battle between buyers and sellers. Volume should decrease to the apex and increase on the breakout through the upper boundary.

You can treat the breakout through the upper boundary in the same way for trading as we said before when discussing trading breakouts generally. The pennant just makes a breakout more likely to result in a continuation than a simple breakout without a pennant.

## Momentum-based strategies

Momentum is a generic term I am using here to discuss four similar indicators: stochastic, momentum, MACD (see later) and RSI (an indicator is basically a plotted line based on a mathematical formula and the stock price).

The reasoning behind all momentum indicators is that a security price moving in a particular direction tends to slow before reversing direction. Therefore if we can pinpoint where it has started slowing, we can be ready for the reversal and plan our strategies accordingly. Think of prices as a ball thrown in the air; before the ball reverses it tends to slow down. Indicators try to depict that in a graphical format.

### Time frames

All the above indicators are based on mathematical operations undertaken on price. You do not need to worry about what the specifics are, but for those interested the reading list is the best place to find out. These formulae have one or two, sometimes three, variables that affect how the indicators are displayed and the time frame for which they will give the best signals. Most software and sites already incorporate as default settings the most popular values for the variables and so again you do not need to worry about that. You can just experiment with different variable values to see what produces the best results. So, onwards now to the issue of how to interpret these indicators so that you can base some strategies around them.

You would rarely base a buy or sell decision on just one of the following indicators. We are always looking for as much evidence as possible about a price move in a particular direction and towards the end we shall see how a professional TA would do it.

## Overbought/oversold strategies

All the momentum indicators can be used to indicate how overbought or oversold a security is. For illustration let us stick to oversold, which is the opposite of overbought. We say a security is oversold when selling has forced the price down so much that it should bounce back. So how do the momentum indicators measure this?

Looking at Diagram 4.17, which plots the momentum indicator, we would say that the security is oversold when the momentum indicator is near its extreme lows relative to its other lows. Now you can get more precise and say that the security is oversold if the momentum is below a specific figure.

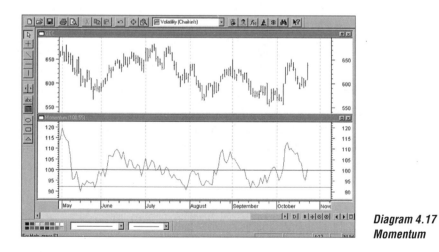

*Diagram 4.17*
*Momentum*

### Trading strategy

One way to trade oversold signals is to buy the security when the momentum indicator moves up from being oversold. Now this is way too simple a strategy to be consistently profitable. So why am I telling you and why is it too simple?

Even though it is too simple a strategy in itself, it is a useful piece of evidence to add to the whole melting pot of which way we think prices may go. It is too simple because momentum indicators often go oversold, go up a little out of oversold territory and then become oversold again. Also, we must remember, price has to be our ultimate indicator and we must wait for the price to move up as well, because the momentum indicator could continue up, but prices continue down.

One way to use this evidence in conjunction with any other evidence of an impending price move may be if the momentum is oversold and just starts moving up and the price is in a rectangle formation and just starts a breakout. You would have more confidence in the move because you have two independent strategies confirming that the move is less likely to be a false move. (See Diagram 4.18).

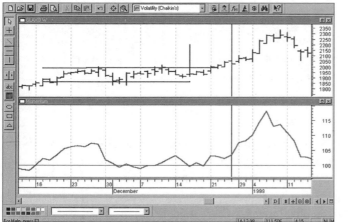

*Diagram 4.18*
*Trading strategy*

## Positive divergence

Improving on oversold signals is positive divergence. Check out Diagram 4.19. A positive divergence occurs when the momentum indicator (whether the momentum, stochastic, MACD or RSI) makes a higher low, but the price does not make a corresponding higher low, instead makes a lower low.

*Diagram 4.19*
*Positive divergence*

### Trading strategy

One popular strategy is to buy as the momentum and the price rise after the price makes its higher low. This is not foolproof but is more reliable and more favoured by technical analysts than simply oversold signals.

## Negative divergence

Diagram 4.20 illustrates a negative divergence. The momentum indicator makes lower highs while the price does not, or even higher highs. As the momentum indicator then starts to fall from its high (which should be in overbought territory) so should the price. Again this is a stronger signal of an impending price fall than just a straightforward oversold signal.

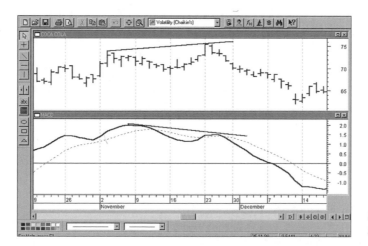

*Diagram 4.20*
*Negative divergence*

**Trading strategy**

Go short or exit a long position as the price and momentum start to dip. To avoid a bad signal, you could incorporate a rule like 'The momentum has to fall from an oversold position and the price has to break the previous day's low before you exit or go short.'

# Reverse divergence

The reverse divergence is a variation on the above theme. It occurs when the price makes lower highs but the momentum makes higher highs deeper into oversold territory. Diagram 4.21 shows an example. The price should fall with the momentum indicator now.

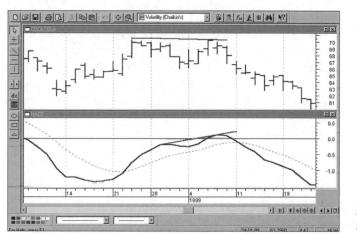

*Diagram 4.21*
*Reverse divergence*

**Trading strategy**

You can decide to exit or go short as the momentum and price both move downwards from the momentum's oversold position.

## Momentum trendlines

Trendlines on momentum indicators as in Diagram 4.22 can sometimes give clues to possible price movement where no trendline can be drawn on the price chart.

*Diagram 4.22*
*Mo' better trendlines*

### Trading strategy

The trendline on the momentum can be used in the same way as in normal price indicators. So for instance a resistance level on the momentum indicator may give a good indication that an imminent price reversal is about to occur. The same cautions with corroborating indicators and price confirmation apply as before; i.e. make sure you have another indicator or chart pattern confirming the bearishness (see Gann studies) and wait until prices fall.

## Stochastics

Whilst the stochastic is a momentum-based indicator and the above interpretations and strategies can be applied to it, there are also some specific to it because of its design. Diagram 4.23 shows a stochastic and price chart.

### %K crosses %D

With the stochastic you can see there is a solid line (%K) and a dotted line (%D). Don't worry about the mathematical formulae that generate them. Stochastic followers will consider a buy signal when the %K crosses up through the %D in an oversold territory as in Diagram 4.23. A sell signal is when the %K crosses down through the %D and both are in overbought territory. When combined with the other pattern above, such positive divergences can be quite a powerful indicator.

### False divergence

This pattern occurs when the %K approaches the %D and looks like it is going to cross it and be a buy signal, but instead it just teases us by kissing it and rebounding off it. This can be a strong signal of a price continuing to fall. Diagram 4.24 shows an example of this. It can also occur as a bullish pattern (see Gann studies later) as in Diagram 4.25.

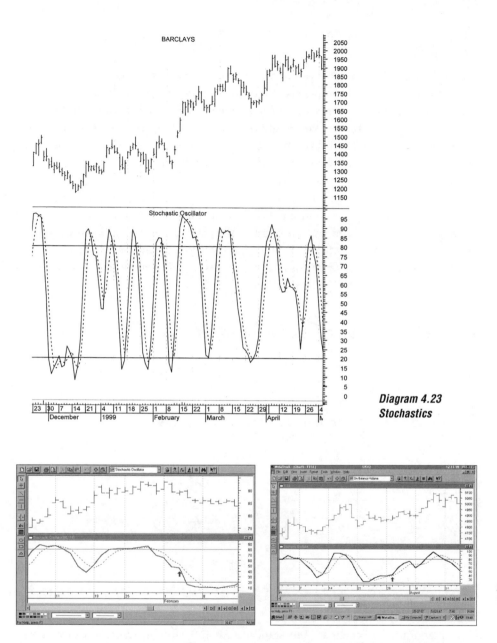

Diagram 4.23
Stochastics

Diagrams 4.24 and 4.25
Teasers

## Stochastic compared to the RSI and momentum indicators

I tend to find the stochastic less prone to false signals which see me enter, only to have the price then not do as expected. The stochastic is not a volatile indicator and gives smoother, easier-to-read lines. I like it.

# The weaknesses in stochastics, momentum and RSI

If we understand the weaknesses of certain indicators we can then hopefully avoid traps of poor trades and compensate for those weaknesses by adding new indicators which do not suffer the same weaknesses. The stochastic, momentum and RSI can all waver in the oversold or overbought regions for prolonged periods of time when a trend is continuing onwards in the same direction. So you could get a false signal to sell prematurely during an uptrend as the oversold indicator suggests a sell signal. Diagram 4.26 illustrates this problem.

The question then arises of how we can solve the problem. One way is not to act on a signal until the price confirms it. So for instance you would not act on a sell signal from the momentum indicator unless the price closes lower than the previous day's low and then opens the next day and moves lower. Another way to avoid the premature signal is to observe both the momentum indicator and the MACD. So let us turn now to the MACD. (Not a bad link, eh?)

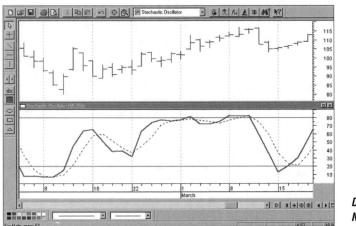

*Diagram 4.26*
*New indicators*

# MACD (pronounced Mac-D like the famous chain of burger joints)

Not named after a Scotsman, but standing for the Moving Average Convergence Divergence, the MACD by its mathematical construction does not tend to suffer from the problems of the other momentum indicators. Diagram 4.27 illustrates this.

The dotted line is the moving average of the MACD and is called the signal line. A crossing of the solid line from above in the overbought region can be interpreted as a sell signal, and a move up of the dotted line through the solid line when in the oversold region is a buy signal.

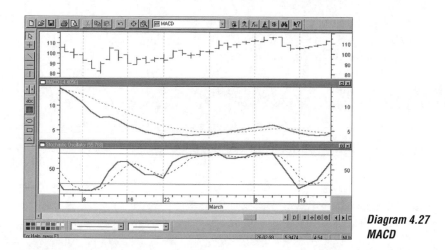

*Diagram 4.27*
*MACD*

## Trading strategy

The MACD tends to give fewer buy or sell signals than the other momentum indicators. I tend to use it to avoid the problems with the momentum indicators giving premature signals. So for instance in Diagram 4.28 we see the momentum indicator suggest a buy signal but the MACD is dropping so sharply that it overrides the momentum signal.

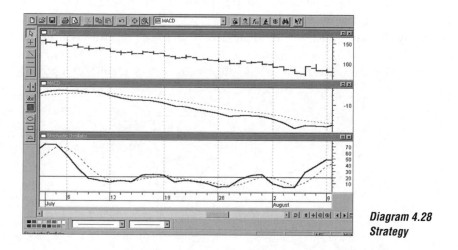

*Diagram 4.28*
*Strategy*

Why not use MACD all the time? Well, I think it works best when combined with the momentum indicators because the MACD is a little bit slow and tends to give buy signals a bit too late. So a better strategy is to buy based on the momentum indicators as long as the MACD is not falling sharply, and possibly has even just started moving sideways. See Diagram 4.29 for an illustration.

Hence we can use the stochastic and the MACD together.

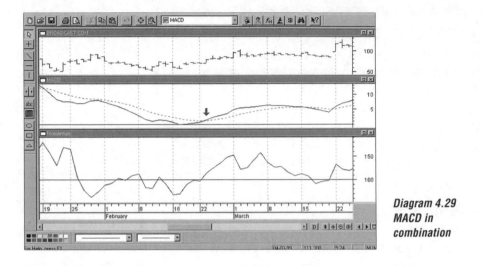

*Diagram 4.29*
*MACD in*
*combination*

The MACD is better used as a longer-term indicator. It reveals more about the market background and the broader trend. Once we are convinced the trend is upward as indicated by the MACD and by looking at the price diagram we can turn to the stochastic to give us some indication of the shorter-term price move.

Great buying opportunities stem from when a stock is oversold in the short term, as indicated by the stochastic, but in a longer-term uptrend, as indicated by the MACD.

So to summarize, it is a good time to buy into a security if we identify an uptrend

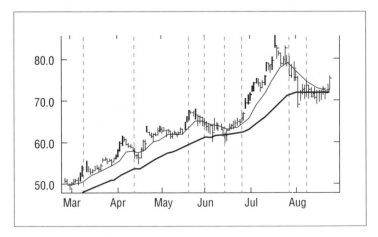

*Diagram 4.30*

and then buy on weakness on the uptrend – for instance as the momentum indicators fall to an oversold position on the uptrend. As the uptrend resumes, the stock price will move up and you will have got in at a relatively cheap price.

Diagram 4.31 (look at where I have inserted the horizontal line) the MACD is trending upward and so is the stock, suggesting medium-term strong buy or hold opportunity. However, in the short term it is oversold. The price has dipped. This is where the stochastic comes in. It is telling us that the short-term situation is oversold and we may want to buy in at that relatively cheap level.

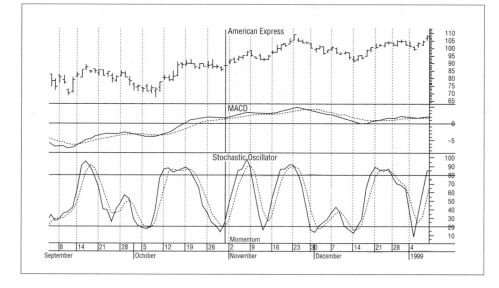

*Diagram 4.31*

# Ways of displaying prices

When a price chart is constructed, time is always plotted on the x-axis and price levels on the y-axis. The line chart simply joins each consecutive day's closing price to produce lines.

A bar chart displays the asset's open, high, low and close. A straight vertical line is drawn joining the low to the high of the day and the open and close are displayed by having a tiny horizontal line to the left (for open) or the right (for close) of the said vertical line.

There are numerous other ways to draw prices, two of the most popular being Japanese candlesticks and point and figure (see earlier and recommended reading).

# Bollinger bands

Bollinger bands are plotted at certain standard deviations above and below moving averages (see later). They bind the price charts like tunnels or envelopes (see Diagram 4.32).

### Interpretation

Generally they are interpreted so that

- price tends to move from one band to the opposite band
- sharp price changes are indicated as imminent once the bands contract.

# Correlation

Correlation measures the extent to which one variable, e.g. a securities price, is connected to another variable, for example the price of another security. The aim is to predict movements in one, given movements in the other.

### Interpretation

If we know that one set of variables is highly correlated to another we can use that to predict movements in the latter after movement in the former.

# Ease of movement

This calculates how easily prices are moving, on the basis that the larger the price move, and the lighter the volume, the more easily prices are moving (see Diagram 4.32).

## Interpretation

A buy signal is indicated when the ease of movement indicator line crosses the zero centre line upwards because the security is moving upward easily. A sell signal is indicated when the indicator line crosses the zero centre line downwards.

*Diagram 4.32*
*Ease of movement,*
*Bollinger bands*

## Envelopes

The envelope is two moving averages (see later), one shifted above and one shifted below the price by a certain percentage (see Diagram 4.33).

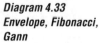

*Diagram 4.33*
*Envelope, Fibonacci,*
*Gann*

### Interpretation

The idea is that the envelope lines are boundaries of the price range. So, if the price hits its lower range it is relatively unlikely to go lower. The thinking is that prices revert to more 'normal' levels after reaching extremities.

## Fibonacci numbers

Fibonacci numbers (named after the 12th-century Italian mathematician) are numbers starting with 1 followed by 1 which are the sum of the two previous numbers. The Fibonacci sequence begins: 1, 1, 2, 3, 5, 8, 13, 21, 34, 55. They exist in nature. On this basis, traders have adopted the relationships for interpreting price charts (see Diagram 4.33).

### Interpretation

In technical analysis, Fibonacci fans, arcs, lines and time zones are but four indicators using this numerical relationship. Fibonacci lines for instance are drawn by first marking a line between two extreme price points, and then your software will draw in the remaining lines at Fibonacci levels above and below this level. Prices will often retrace to a Fibonacci support level after a significant move.

## Gann studies

These are named after one of the most famous market technicians of all time, W.D. Gann (1878–1955). Gann believed that the best relationship between prices and time occurred when the angle at which prices rose or fell was that of 45 degrees to the horizontal time axis.

### Interpretation

Very simply, if prices are above the 45-degree line then they are bullish, and if they are below the 45-degree line then they are bearish. Gann also gave the values of other angles at which prices ought to find support or resistance, namely 7.5, 15, 18.75, 26.25, 45, 63.75, 71.25, 75 and 82.5 degrees (see Diagram 4.33).

Gann developed Gann lines, Gann fans, Gann grids, and most technical analysis software which deals with Gann will also include these.

# Linear regression

A linear regression line can be considered a line of best fit around a set of prices. It is drawn by the computer so that on average the distance between the price and the line is the narrowest in comparison to any other line over the same period for the same price (see Diagram 4.34).

## Interpretation

If we consider the linear regression line the 'equilibrium' price then if prices move too far from the linear regression line they ought to return to it. A buy signal is generated when prices move relatively far from the linear regression line to the bottom and a sell signal is when prices move relatively far above the linear regression line.

# Moving average convergence divergence (MACD)

This indicator line is plotted by subtracting the value of one exponential moving average (see later) from that of another exponential moving average. Another exponential moving average signal line is then drawn on top of this (see Diagram 4.34).

## Interpretation

The simple rule is to buy when the signal line crosses above the indicator line, and sell when it goes below it.

# Momentum

The momentum exhibited by an asset's price is measured by the ratio of today's price compared to the price a certain number of days ago (see Diagram 4.34).

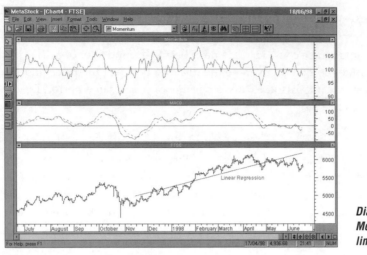

*Diagram 4.34*
*Momentum, MACD,*
*linear regression*

### Interpretation

There are many ways to interpret the momentum indicator. Some of the most popular are:

■ Buy when it hits an extreme low value (oversold). Sell when it hits an extreme high value (oversold).

■ Buy when the momentum indicator crosses above a moving average of itself. Sell when the momentum indicator crosses below a moving average of itself.

## Moving averages

A moving average is calculated by taking the average of an asset's price over the last *x* days. It is 'moving' because as each day progresses you can determine what the last *x* price changes are.

As well as this type of moving average – a simple moving average – there is also an exponential moving average. This is calculated so that more weight is given to the latest price and so on until least weight is given to the last price being considered.

### Interpretation

There are several popular methods of interpreting moving averages, a buy signal being generated when the price moves above the moving average and a sell signal when it moves below (see Diagram 4.35).

Another popular method is to display two moving averages of different time periods and buy when the shorter time period's moving average crosses above the longer time period's moving average.

The important thing is to experiment with various time periods of moving average and attempt to find one that is consistently good at predicting moves.

# On-balance volume (OBV)

This indicator attempts to depict the relationship between volume and price. If the asset's price rises then the day's volume is added to a cumulative total. If the asset's price falls then that day's volume is subtracted from the cumulative total. Therefore, when there is a price rise, the whole day's volume is assumed to have contributed to it by being up-volume. When there is a price fall the whole day's volume is assumed to have contributed to that by being down-volume (see Diagram 4.35).

## Interpretation

OBV is designed for short-term trading. The OBV can be considered to be in a rising trend when each successive low is higher than the previous low and each new high is higher than the previous high. A sell signal is generated when the trend is broken.

Similarly, the OBV can be considered to be in a falling trend when each successive low is lower than the previous low and each new high is lower than the previous high. A buy signal is generated when the trend is broken.

*Diagram 4.35*
*On-balance volume,*
*moving average*

## Open interest

This is only applicable to futures. It measures the number of open transactions in a particular contract.

### Interpretation

If open interest and prices rise then that tends to indicate new buyers. Similarly, if open interest and prices move in opposite directions or if open interest and prices fall then that tends to show a warning signal.

## Parabolic stop-and-reverse (SAR) indicator

This indicator is in fact a moving stop that rises with prices (see Diagram 4.36).

### Interpretation

This indicator is popularly used so that if the price is above the SAR then you buy or stay long; if the price is below the SAR then you sell or stay short.

## Price rate of change (ROC)

This indicator is calculated by dividing the price change over the last $x$ periods by the closing price of the security $x$ periods ago (see Diagram 4.36).

### Interpretation

The price ROC tends to be interpreted in the same manner as the momentum indicator. Namely:

- Buy when it hits an extreme low value (oversold); sell when it hits an extreme high value (overbought).

- Buy when the price ROC indicator crosses above a moving average of itself; sell when the price ROC indicator crosses below a moving average of itself.

## Relative strength index (RSI)

The RSI measures the current price against the price $x$ periods ago. It is similar in that respect to the other oscillators such as the momentum indicator, price ROC and stochastic (see below). It is based on comparing the average of upward price changes with that of downward price changes (see Diagram 4.36).

### Interpretation

This indicator tends to be popularly interpreted in the same way as the momentum, price ROC and stochastic indicators.

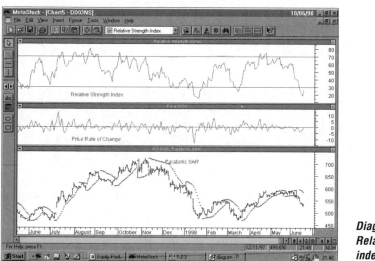

**Diagram 4.36**
**Relative strentgh**
**index, price ROC, SAR**

## Standard deviation

The standard deviation (Diagram 4.37) is a mathematical notation. In oversimple terms it is the average by which the price moves from its own average. It is therefore a measure of volatility.

### Interpretation

Relatively low standard deviation values, i.e. low volatility, tend to warn of an imminent price move on the basis that volatility will increase and revert to its longer-term average.

## Stochastic oscillator

This oscillator (Diagram 4.37) compares today's price with the trading range over the past $x$ days (%K line). A moving average of this line is also taken (%D line).

### Interpretation

As with the other oscillators we have discussed, buy signals are generally considered to occur when the main line (%K) rises above the %D line. A buy signal can also be indicated when the %K hits a relatively extreme level. If it is a high level then this indicates a sell signal on the basis that the asset is overbought; if the %K hits a relatively low level then this indicates a buy signal on the basis that the asset is oversold.

## Trendlines

A trendline is a line between two points in a chart drawn so that it also touches at least one other. Its purpose is to illustrate areas of price support and resistance. An up trendline is drawn so that it touches three successive rising price troughs. A down trendline is drawn so that it touches three successive price peaks.

### Interpretation

The common assumption with trendlines is that prices will bounce off them, unless they don't, in which case they will not! Isn't technical analysis wonderful? Although this appears frustratingly nonsensical, it makes sense when we consider probability. The idea is that there is a probability greater than 1/2 that the price will rebound off the trendline. Therefore the odds are slightly in your favour when trading off a trendline.

## William's %R

The William's %R is another oscillator and is similar in construction to the stochastic oscillator (see Diagram 4.37).

### Interpretation

This oscillator is interpreted in much the same manner as the other oscillators. In particular a buy signal is generated by a relatively low extreme reading of the indicator and a sell signal by a relatively high reading of the indicator.

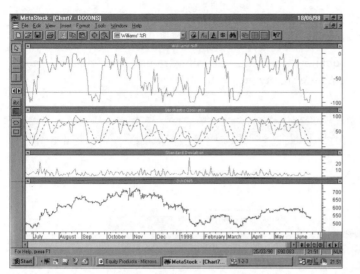

*Diagram 4.37
William's %R,
stochastic oscillator,
standard deviation
price*

## The most popular indicators

Popular among most technical analysts is the use of at least one oscillator indicator, such as the price ROC, momentum, stochastic, William's %R and MACD. Of these the most popular is probably the stochastic. However, since the way in which the MACD is calculated is different from the other oscillators it is often used in conjunction with the stochastic.

In terms of displaying charts the old bar chart method remained most popular, with Japanese candlesticks a close second.

Trendlines and moving averages are 'meat and veg' for the technical analyst and although few rely on them exclusively, they will consider them in their overall analysis of an asset.

Of the volume indicators, the on-balance volume is probably the most popular, although many technical analysts will simply examine a histogram depicting daily volume to get a feel of what volume is doing.

## The sites

So now we have to find out how to use the best online trading sites which will allow us to do all of the above. These are my pick of the bunch.

## ClearStation ***

www.clearstation.com

### How to use this site and what for

This is probably the best site for quickly displaying momentum information. Use this for short to medium-term trading (up to three-month hold) although if your pick keeps rising you may well just keep with it for longer.

**To plot momentum charts.** Entering the stock symbol and clicking on the **Get Graphs** button (one of the most useful on the site) displays the price diagram plus the momentum and stochastic diagrams, making the application of what we learnt about momentum indicators very easy. We don't need to do *any* additional tinkering.

**Comparisons.** Also use the site to quickly compare the technical momentum patterns on a host of stocks by entering their tickers in the **Get Graphs** box and then clicking on **Get Graphs**. That way they will all be displayed in sequence and you can scroll down and make a note of the ones with the best momentum outlook and ditch the others.

So if for instance you were choosing between four stocks which had been provided, say from the WallStreetCity site's lists, then enter those ticker codes to see which has the best diagram based on MACD and momentum.

**Lists.** Clear Station provides lists of stocks based on the following criteria – the great thing is that by clicking on **Graph in Bulk** you can immediately compare the technical diagrams of each of the stocks:

- record price breakout
- MACD bullish
- stochastic bullish
- earnings surprise
- analyst upgrade.

Then there are those stocks which are gleaned from members' own comments, listed under:

- member recommendation
- community favourite stock
- top community pick
- active community discussion.

You can see why for each one it may be an indication of how well the stock might do. But of course that does not always follow. Under 'MACD bullish' I found the following – would you want to buy these stocks based solely on the MACD's being bullish?

Use the ClearStation lists such as 'MACD bullish' to give you one positive reason to enter the stock and, needless to say, after that examine the diagram to see the stock trend, the company profile, recent news, EPS, PEGs etc. to make a fuller decision as to whether you want to buy the stock or not. Is it one of the top 25 must-haves likely to have the best reward-to-risk ratio? If not, move on.

**Even more technical-based lists.** To get some more excellent lists click on **Technical Events**. ClearStation then lists all stocks according to which meet certain bullish technical criteria such as those shown below. It is pretty clear that in isolation each can seem quite a useful list to have, e.g. record volume – we may want to know which stocks have just broken the 52-week highest volume they have traded in a single day, because this may tell us about increased outside interest in the stock, and that could herald a buying spree which the news story people may not yet know about.

However, each of the criteria in isolation is not enough to base a buying decision on. Whilst each one may make sense, I would only be reassured I am making a good trading decision by looking at the price diagram, the other technical indicators and fundamentals relating to the stock and then comparing this to other stocks:

- **Record activity**
  - **Record breakouts** – stocks that hit a 52-week price high (with no prior price high within the last month)

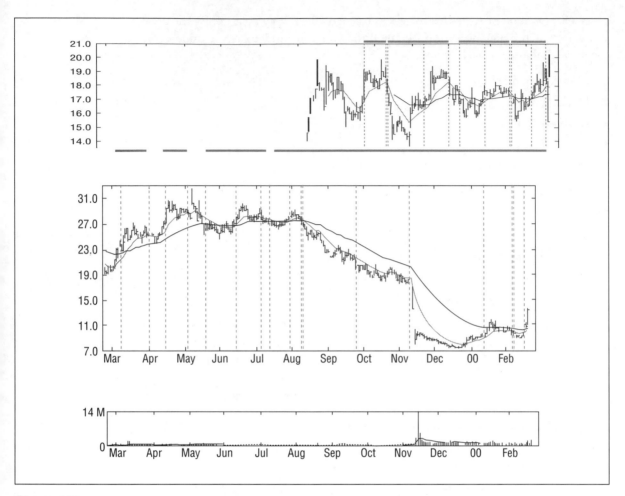

*Diagram 4.38*

> – **Record price high** – stocks setting 52-week record price highs
> – **Record volume** – stocks setting 52-week volume highs
> – **Record price low** – stocks that have fallen to a new 52-week low price.

- **Most actives and price movers**
  - **Most active** – the 50 stocks with the highest volume on each exchange throughout the day
  - **Percentage gainer** – stocks exhibiting the highest percentage gain
  - **Percentage loser** – stocks exhibiting the highest percentage loss
  - **Price gainer** – stocks experiencing the greatest price gain
  - **Price loser** – stocks experiencing the greatest loss in price
  - **Gap up** – stocks with an opening price higher than the preceding closing

price (a stock which closed at 10 and opened the next trading day at 12 is said to have gapped up 2)

- **Gap down** – stocks with an opening price lower than the preceding closing price (a stock which closed at 10 and opened the next trading day at 8 is said to have gapped down 2).

■ **Price action events**
- **Close below 50-day EMA** – stocks with closing prices below the 50-day EMA
- **Close above 50-day EMA (a bullish sign)** – stocks with closing prices above the 50-day EMA
- **Close below 13-day EMA** – stocks with closing prices below the 13-day EMA
- **Close above 13-day EMA (a bullish sign)** – stocks with closing prices above the 13-day EMA
- **13-day EMA cross below 50-day EMA** – stocks whose fast moving average line (the 13-day line) has just fallen below the slow moving average line (the 50-day line); this occurrence can signal the beginning of a downtrend
- **13-day EMA cross above 50-day EMA (a bullish sign)** – stocks whose fast moving average line (the 13-day line) has just risen above the slow moving average line (the 50-day line); this occurrence can signal the beginning of an uptrend.

■ **Continuing trends: bullish** – three separate lists of stocks exhibiting the strongest bullish trends of the week, month and year.

**Even more fundamentals-based lists.** Not seen enough lists yet? It makes sense at least to have a closer look at the diagrams of stocks that have undergone the following *prima facie* bullish fundamental events:

■ **Fundamental events** – news and events that can affect the price action of a stock
- **Earnings surprise** – stocks whose earnings are exceeding or falling short of market expectations
- **Dividend declaration** – stocks for which dividends have recently been announced
- **Stock splits** – stocks which have recently split (a split is an increase in a corporation's outstanding shares of stock without any change in the shareholders' equity. In a split, the share price declines. If a stock at $100 splits two-for-one (2–1), the number of authorized shares doubles and the price per share drops by half to $50)
- **Report earnings** – companies whose earnings have just been reported
- **Analyst upgrade**

- **Analyst downgrade**
- **Stock splits pending** – stocks for which a split has been announced but not yet effected.

ClearStation lists stocks which fall into each of the above classes. I suggest using the **Graph in Bulk** link again to compare their technicals.

**Industry lists.** Another useful way to use the ClearStation charting functions is to note that when you graph a stock the site lets you see the list of all other stocks in the same industry. You can then sort them according to various criteria, e.g. percentage price change, price, market cap, volume etc. After that click on **Graph in Bulk** to see how each compares to the next one.

This is useful if you know you want to invest in a particular industry, e.g. the software industry, but are not sure which stocks to go for. Here are some useful shortcuts to generate great stock ideas:

■ Go for stocks which have just made a new high and are in a smooth uptrend, not exhibiting great volatility.

■ Make sure the stock has doubled over the past 9–12 weeks (that ensures a strong return trajectory).

■ Go for a stock between $10 and $20.

■ The MACD cannot be too overbought.

■ The stochastic was oversold on an uptrend and is now just starting to perk up.

Using the **Graph in Bulk** link should make all this a doddle and be very quick to achieve. You are essentially expecting strong returns because the trajectory of the trend to date projects them.

# Equis **

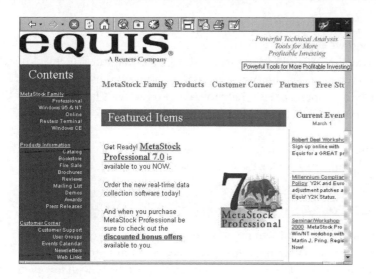

`www.equis.com`

## How to use this site and what for

The best thing about this site, other than as a place from which to buy the excellent Metastock software (more on that later) is the interactive charting part of the site. Again, most people do not realize it exists because it is a little hidden away but click on **Online Charting** to get to it.

Use it for a more sophisticated charting package than at ClearStation; you can zoom in and out very easily, plot Japanese candlestick diagrams, plot more technical indicators and plot trendlines. All this for free.

# TradingCharts *

`www.tradingdiagrams.com`

## How to use the site and what for

Use this if you really don't want all the complex technical anaysis stuff cluttering up your screen and you are looking for a crisp, clean, easy-to-see diagram for simplicity's sake. It is best suited to a fundamental analyst who wants to look at diagrams.

The **MyDiagrams** function is really useful for storing the stocks for which you are regularly going to want to see the diagrams. It would be even better if you could scroll from one to the next, but it is still helpful.

## Bigcharts ***

www.bigdiagrams.com

### How to use the site and what for

The quick diagram function is straightforward. It draws the diagram quickly, but that is not why we want to use this site. You can get diagrams anywhere – we want the good stuff for the best people. That is where the free **Interactive Charting** button comes in. Use that for comparison of stock performances to other stocks, to indices, to plot indicators.

It is particularly useful because you can choose the indicators and can have more than one. Note: ClearStation limits you on the former and Equis limits you on the latter.

## Other good sites you are likely to come across

In this section I want briefly to run down my view on some other charting sites that you may come across but which I am not necessarily recommending for regular use – I feel those listed above do the job better or are more comprehensive. However, here's my opinion on some of the rest:

## E*Trade UK ***

www.etrade.co.uk    UK

### How to use it and what for

I told you I would try to find the hidden gems. If you are looking for diagrams on UK equities and want indicators such as momentum and comparison of securities' performances plus easy educational material on how to interpret all this, then this is the place for you.

## UK-iNvest ***

www.ukinvest.com  UK

### How to use it and what for

Use the standard diagrams for plotting technical indicators on these crisp, clear diagrams. Use the **Javadiagram** function for interactive diagrams where you can zoom in and out and put in momentum and stochastic indicators. It could be a bit clearer and can be improved but is one of the more useful charting sites for the UK investor.

## Wright Research Center **

http://profiles.wisi.com  UK  EU  INT

### How to use this site and what for

This site is useful for finding diagrams of stocks of different countries all from the same site. If you are a fundamental analyst you will like this too because as well as the diagram it gives a host of fundamental data about the stock on the same page, but what I really like is that it plots earnings and dividends on the same diagram so you can see how they are doing too.

Use this to judge any company whose stock prices seem to be taking off relative to their earnings; it may be a quick visual guide to overvaluation. Diagram 4.39 shows how earnings (represented by the top line) have not been increasing at the same rate as the stock price. While that is not a buy or sell signal, it puts you on notice that the company will have to make great strides to meet the expectations that have built up in the company.

It would be even better if it plotted EPS or p/e and PEG ratios too.

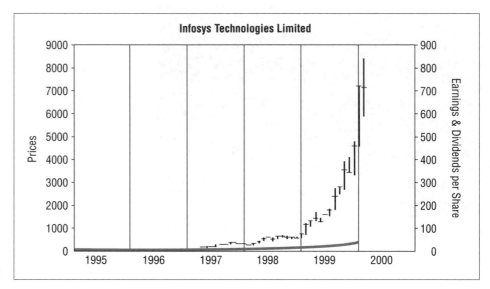

**Diagram 4.39**

## Chart Trend

www.diagramtrend.com

### How to use this site and what for

This site gives daily e-mail trading tips for a monthly charge. I feel this is simply not good value given that other sites out there provide ideas for free through lists.

## DecisionPoint

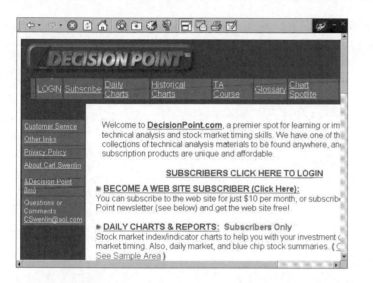

www.decisionpoint.com

### How to use this site and what for

DecisionPoint offers extensive technical analysis charting functions and indicators as well as historical diagrams. All for a fee.

My view is that I don't want to pay for these things if a lot of them can be found free elsewhere. Also, if I am into the really heavy-duty technical indicators why not just buy software such as Superdiagrams?

## IQC

www.siliconinvestor.com

### How to use this site and what for

IQC is a great little site – now part of Silicon Investor – but again the same story; I won't pay for something I can get from software or free sites already recommended in this book.

## MarketEdge

www.stkwtch.com

### How to use this site and what for

Other than the stupid web address, this is not too bad. You would use it if you want to pay for quite detailed stock picks based on technical analysis from an experienced money manager. I prefer my own research – maybe I am either too cocky or too cheap to pay for someone else's advice!

## Interactive Investor International

www.iii.co.uk    UK

### How to use this site and what for

Although this site gets a lot of publicity due to its marketing effort after flotation, its strong point is not its charting, which could be improved.

## Market-Eye

www.marketeye.co.uk    UK

### How to use this site and what for

The charting here is too basic and the interactive charting only allows you to zoom in or out or rebase and you have to pay for bar diagrams in place of line diagrams. Who are they kidding? All that is free on the other sites I have mentioned, plus the background makes it difficult to use.

## Educational sites

The sites listed in Table 4.1 are useful for the information they provide on technical analysis for those interested in learning more. These together with the recommended reading should be more than adequate for most technical analysts, and should get you well on the way to becoming an expert.

*Table 4.1  Educational sites*

| Name | Address | Comment |
|------|---------|---------|
| Bridge | news.bridge.com | Specialists in data and news but some useful information |
| DecisionPoint | www.decisionpoint.com | Specialists in technical analysis |
| Equis | www.equis.com | Specialists in charting software |
| Market Technicians Society | www.mta-usa.com | The technical analysts society |
| *Stocks & Commodities* Mag | www.traders.com | The specialist technical analysis magazine |

For other sites, don't forget to check out Chapters 15 and 18.

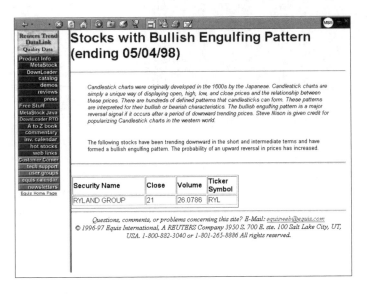

www.equis.com

*Diagram 4.40*
*The traders'*
*magazine*

## Software

There are numerous companies that provide computer software which can then be used to download quotes from quote vendors and perform technical analysis. Few permit you to download their software from their web sites but you can preview and download demos and find out what they do. Table 4.2 lists some of the best technical analysis software vendors. All should work on UK or US price data.

*Table 4.2 Technical analysis software sites*

| Product | Company | Address | Ranking |
|---------|---------|---------|---------|
| Metastock 6.5 | Equis | www.equis.com | *** (Recommended) |
| OmniTrader 3.1 | Nirvana | www.nirv.com | *** |
| SuperDiagrams | Omega | www.omegaresearch.com | ** |
| TeleDiagram 2000 | Worden Bros | www.worden.com | ** |
| TradeStation | Omega | www.omegaresearch.com | ** |
| Window on Wall St | Window on Wall St | www.wallstreet.net | ** |

*** Very good software, excellent value for money and recognized as a market leader.

** All-round good software, value for money with some features not found elsewhere.
   Software lower than ** is not included because the standard of software is so high.

# What to look for

Whatever software you choose look for the following features.

## Data included

Are data included in the cost or do you need to go to a supplier – if so which ones? (If only a few suppliers supply data then the hidden cost of getting data could be prohibitive.)

## Data downloader

Do you need extra software to download data from a data provider and get them into your software? If so, what is the cost of that?

## Data cleaner

Does the software come with a feature that scans all downloaded data for errors such as dates out of sequence, highs lower than lows, etc.?

## Data format

Can you convert different data formats, thereby increasing your choice of data provider and so of data costs?

## Display types

How many indicators and types of diagrams can be drawn?

## Alerts

Can you set price alerts?

## System development

Is there a programming language permitting you to produce your own system?

## Screening

Can you use the software to screen through all data according to a system (Diagrams 4.41, 4.42)?

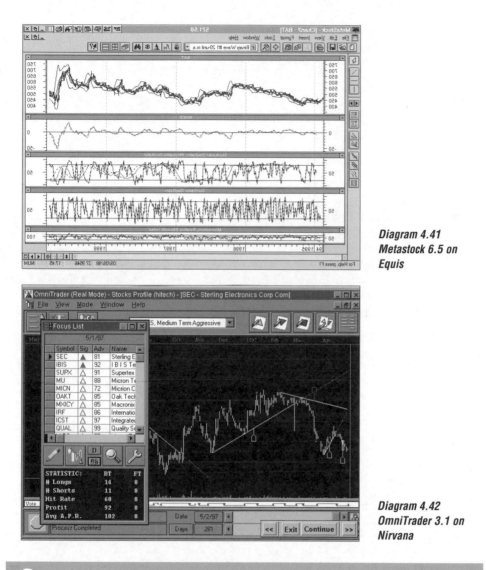

*Diagram 4.41*
*Metastock 6.5 on*
*Equis*

*Diagram 4.42*
*OmniTrader 3.1 on*
*Nirvana*

## Summary

There are numerous technical analysis resources on the web. The major choice is between using software and a data download or using an online charting service. The latter, with its inherent limitations, is the better choice for the fundamental analysts and/or dabblers in technical analysis. The former is the choice of the serious technical analyst.

To summarize this very briefly, we have looked for indicators of relatively high probability that the stock price is going to move one way and not another, and the rest is detail. It is something you should re-read, as one read is unlikely to be enough. Now you deserve a break.

## 5

# Fundamentals

*The real measure of your wealth is how much you'd be worth if you lost all your money*

Anon.

## In this chapter

Let's have a look at a whole host of popular methods for trading ideas. We will want to examine the company's balance sheet for a start and get a feel for how the company is doing. Trading around an earnings announcement is also a popular way of trading for some people and we'll see how that is done and how to use specific sites to do it. Similarly, when upgrades or downgrades are issued on a stock, we want to know where we can find these announcements and how we can use them for our trading to find lower-risk, higher-return trades. Some traders like to see if the company's inside officers, such as directors, are trading its stock – we need to examine how that works and how to use it. And potential stock-split candidates and post-split stocks can also be an interesting way of trading – again, we'll look at which the sites are, exactly what the thinking is behind this trading method and how we can join in.

## Objectives

- Broadly understand how to read fundamental information about a stock.
- Get an idea about how to find upgrades and earnings information, how to find out the level of insider trading and if there are stock splits and how to use that information as a basis of gaining stock ideas.

## Using fundamental profiles

Market Guide (*www.marketguide.com*) provides probably the quickest and easiest way to get a feel for a company. For UK stocks Hemmington Scott not only provides its own company profile sheets to numerous web sites but also provides similar comprehensive information about companies' fundamentals. There are other sites providing comparable information and you can apply what you see on Market Guide equally well to those if you find them easier to use. So let's get an idea of what we are looking for:

■ Firstly I want to know what the company does. Sounds pretty basic but the business must make sense to me. Is it in a sector that I can see from my reading and analysis elsewhere is something I want to be involved in? For instance, is it a telecommunications infrastructure company or an application services provider?

■ The report shows the year-to-date operating results compared to the same period a year ago and then discusses reasons for the increase or decrease in recently reported revenues and income. Here it will tell me whether there are any one-time events affecting the announced results, such as a gain on the sale of a division or a write-off, or whether the changes in the results are part of an ongoing, sustainable trend. Personally, I look for good, sound, upward-improving trends or if there are one-off impacts on the balance sheets then I want to make sure they are going to be positive for the next set of results. For instance, is the one-off expense due to a revenue-generating acquisition or investment in research and development?

■ Market Guide explains how to use the earnings information:

You won't find an Earnings Announcement on every Snapshot Report, but it is very important that you take note of its presence or absence. If it's present, it will be there to alert you to the fact that the company has issued a 'flash' report announcing earnings for the latest quarter.

Suppose, for example, twenty days have passed since the end of the company's most recent quarterly reporting period. Companies aren't legally required to announce the quarter's results that quickly, but many choose to do so anyway. This is often accomplished by the issuance of a 'flash' earnings report (a news release explaining the latest quarterly results accompanied by summary financial data). It isn't quite as detailed in every respect as the official 10-Q document that is usually filed later on, but flash reports issued nowadays do still contain quite a bit of information; enough to justify major investment decisions by all segments of the Wall Street community.

This is important information, because it gives you a sense of the 'freshness' of the information you'll be seeing when you study the company in greater detail. Starting on the Snapshot itself, and throughout the other components of the Market Guide Reports, you'll see the abbreviations TTM, which stands for 'trailing twelve months', and MRQ, which means 'most recent quarter'. The presence or absence of an Earnings Announcement will tell you precisely how to interpret those concepts.

Market Guide believes that the latest information must be made available to its clients. So if a 'flash' Earnings Announcement press release is issued, Market Guide collects the latest revenue, net income, Earnings Per Share (EPS) and shares outstanding values. All relevant ratios such as trailing 12-month EPS or Net Profit Margin affected by preliminary earnings announcements reflect these latest reported numbers, and are identified as such by an asterisk.

In other words, suppose it's July 20th. If the Snapshot tells you that there is a June period Earnings Announcement, you can assume that all TTM data identified by an asterisk is for the 12-month period that ended in June. All other data (TTM items not accompanied by an asterisk and, generally, all MRQ data) would be as of March. You'll see this confirmed on the Snapshot in an entry called Complete Financials, which can be found to the right of the price chart.

■ The **Key Ratios and Statistics** section is my favourite. Here is an example of what is in there:

*Key ratios and statistics*

| Price & volume | | Valuation ratios | |
|---|---|---|---|
| Recent price $ | 43.63 | Price/earnings (TTM) | 39.55* |
| 52-week high $ | 47.38 | Price/sales (TTM) | 4.93* |
| 52-week low $ | 25.00 | Price/book (MRQ) | 6.60 |
| Average daily volume (Mil.) | 4.09 | Price/cash flow (TTM) | 24.61 |
| Beta | 0.97 | **Per share data** | |
| **Share related items** | | Earnings (TTM) $ | 1.10* |
| Market capital (Mil.) $ | 59,029.73 | Sales (TTM) $ | 8.85* |
| Shares out (Mil.) | 1,353.12 | Book value (MRQ) $ | 6.61 |
| Float (Mil.) | 1,339.60 | Cash flow (TTM) $ | 1.77 |
| **Dividend information** | | Cash (MRQ) $ | 0.23 |
| Yield % | 0.46 | **Management effectiveness** | |
| Annual dividend | 0.20 | Return on equity (TTM) | 17.34* |
| Payout ratio (TTM) % | 87.43 | Return on assets (TTM) | 8.30 |
| **Financial strength** | | Return on investment (TTM) | 9.45* |
| Quick ratio (MRQ) | 0.39 | **Profitability** | |
| Current ratio (MRQ) | 0.58 | Gross margin (TTM) % | 36.16 |
| LT debt/equity (MRQ) | 0.71 | Operating margin (TTM) % | 23.20 |
| Total debt/equity (MRQ) | 0.79 | Profit margin (TTM) % | 12.48* |

Let's go through some of these and see what we may be looking for (take a deep breath … and exhale …).

## Price & volume

The **Snapshot Price & Volume Table** shows the recent stock price and the 52-week high and low. I tend to look for companies near their highs. That suggests to me stocks that are in favour with the market.

Next, there is the stock's average daily trading volume. If trading volume is low and a large investor wants to acquire or sell a position, then they will be faced with buying or selling shares over time or risking a material impact on the price of the stock. Since unexpected developments can precipitate the need to quickly buy or sell, this measure of liquidity helps to identify risk. I, however, rarely look too closely at this although many traders do, to get a feel for how big or popular the stock and its following are.

The average daily volume for all stocks in the Market Guide database is presently about 200,000 shares (rounding that figure to the nearest million, as we do in the Snapshot report, would result in the number being shown as .20 Mil.). The large capitalization stocks included in the S&P 500 index trade are, on average, about

1,600,000 shares per day (1.6 Mil.). The biggest and most liquid issues within the S&P 500 trade more than 4 Mil. shares per day. Meanwhile, 'small cap' stocks (those with market capitalizations ranging from $100 million to $500 million) presently average .10 Mil. shares per day. If a stock's daily volume is less than .01 Mil. you need carefully to assess the liquidity risks.

Next there is beta, a measure of the volatility (risk) of a company's stock price relative to the overall volatility of the stock market. Again, I tend not to look at this, but here is an explanation of how to use it: 'A stock that is no more or less volatile than the overall stock market will have a beta of 1.00. Stocks that are more volatile than the stock market will have a beta greater than 1.00, whereas stocks less volatile than the market will have a beta of less than 1.00. Aggressive investors looking for growth companies should be willing to buy stocks with higher beta values. Income oriented, or risk-averse investors should look for lower beta stocks. The beta value used here is measured over a five-year time frame.'

You can get a utility stock with a dividend yield in the 5–7 per cent range. You can buy a risk-free US Treasury bond yielding in the neighbourhood of 5.5–6 per cent. Or you can buy non-utility stocks, many of which sport yields in the range of zero–1.5 per cent. Why would anyone ever choose the latter? The answer: growth. This is perhaps the single most important consideration for the typical equity investor. Indeed, it's the reason why shares of healthy firms usually sell at prices that are far above their here-and-now liquidation values. Investors don't generally buy companies with the idea of realizing cash from liquidation; they buy companies based on their appeal as businesses, capable of growing in the years ahead. Accordingly, the Market Guide **Growth Rates Comparison Table** is a very important one for you to consider.

## Growth rates

*Growth rates (%)*

| Company | Industry | Sector | S&P 500 |
|---|---|---|---|
| Sales (MRQ) vs qtr 1 yr ago | 9.08* | 7.92 | 19.47 |
| Sales (TTM) vs TTM 1 yr ago | 8.88* | 8.30 | 26.89 |
| Sales – 5-yr growth rate | 9.85 | 13.15 | 22.43 |
| EPS (MRQ) vs qtr 1 yr ago | −13.79* | 5.39 | 25.44 |
| EPS (TTM) vs TTM 1 yr ago | −3.92* | 3.84 | 23.49 |
| EPS – 5-yr growth rate | 12.66 | 14.13 | 21.84 |
| Capital Spending – 5-yr growth rate | 14.20 | 15.81 | 28.30 |

## Sales growth

A company can perform well over the short term with rising earnings even if sales are dropping. This can occur if profits (earnings) are being increased due to cost-cutting. However, there will come a time when costs cannot be lowered any further and decreasing sales growth feeds back into lower earnings. For that reason examining sales growth is important.

## Earnings per share growth

EPS growth is a key factor feeding into company growth.

The year-to-year comparison for the most recent quarter (MRQ) represents the most up-to-date growth information available to the financial community and is always an important determinant of near-term stock-price performance. Assume that strong MRQ growth rates will be accompanied by strong stock-price performance and vice versa. If that is not the case then examine the **News** reports to find out why.

Market Guide explains that when examining company-to-industry capital spending comparisons, remember that it is normal for a business to spend at least some money for capital projects year in, year out. But at times capital spending can mushroom to especially high levels as a major project ramps up and then slide to a lesser pace as the newly completed project allows the company to trim down to basic 'maintenance' levels. If you see that a company's capital spending growth was significantly higher than that of its industry, that could suggest that the company's needs should moderate, relative to its peers, in the next few years. That would give the company more flexibility regarding the use of its cash flow (dividends, share buybacks, acquisitions, etc.). If you see that growth in spending trailed the industry average, that might suggest pent-up capital needs (and increased spending) in the years ahead.

Finally, compare the five-year growth rates for capital spending and sales. This can be important since there's usually a relationship between the value of a company's assets and the amount of sales that those assets can generate. A rate of sales growth that exceeds the rate of capital spending growth might indicate that a company is finding new ways to generate more revenues from existing plant. But it could also mean that capacity is getting tight and that capital spending increases are just around the corner.

# Valuation ratios

These are essential. They give me an idea of whether I am picking up a bargain, a fairly priced stock or an expensive one. For me the key is price trend, so valuations do not veto a stock selection but if all other things were equal, I would want a lower-valued stock. Alternatively some investors focus purely on valuations and this can be a useful gauge of a company's potential.

## Price to earnings

The p/e ratio shows you the multiple you're paying for each dollar of earnings of the company. One would normally prefer a company with a lower p/e to one with higher p/e. However, note that there can be little wrong with paying a higher p/e multiple for a rapidly growing company because you expect its future earnings rate to be higher. A good rule of thumb is that a stock is attractive if its p/e ratio is lower than its long-term compound growth rate in EPS. Conversely, a company with a low p/e ratio is not necessarily a good thing. It may be because its outlook is more uncertain due to factors such as competition, a lawsuit, or a cyclical downturn. I tend to look for p/e lower than the industry average.

As well as p/e, examining other similar ratios is always very useful (and definitely impresses the opposite sex at bars – go ahead and try it); these are *price to sales* (which is especially useful for early-stage growth companies that might not have reached profitability), *price to book value*, and *price to cash flow*. Each provides a slightly different perspective and I look on them as an artist not as a scientist; in other words, I try to get a broad, general feel for the figures rather than requiring them to be very exact.

## Beta

Beta measures stock price volatility relative to the overall stock market. So, for instance, if we use the S&P 500 as a proxy for the market as a whole and we automatically define its beta as being 1.00, then a higher beta indicates that a stock is more volatile while a lower beta indicates stability. For example, a stock with a beta of 0.90 would, on average, be expected to rise or fall only 90 per cent as much as the market. So if the market dropped 10 per cent, such a stock might rise or fall 9 per cent.

## Price to sales

Price to sales is generally used to evaluate companies that don't have earnings and that don't pay dividends – in recent times that has often meant internet companies. For these companies, you may consider that high multiples of sales and high growth rates suggest optimistic future earnings expectations on the part of investors. Where earnings have wild swings in any particular year, for instance due to one-off items, price to sales can be a good indicator of the underlying health of the company.

## Price to book

Price to book is a theoretical comparison of the value of the company's stock to the value of the assets it owns (free and clear of debt). This is probably of less importance in practice than in theory. The idea behind it is that book value is a proxy for the proceeds that would be realized if the company was to be liquidated by selling all its assets and paying all its debt.

In reality, though, assets are valued on the books at the actual prices the company paid to acquire them, minus cumulative depreciation/amortization charges. The idea behind these costs is gradually to reduce the value of the assets to zero over a period of use in which they approach obsolescence. However, this is based on specific accounting formulas that may not resemble 'real world' time to obsolescence. And remember that for a services company the 'book value' does not produce the revenue. So all in all, I tend to ignore this.

## Cash flow and net income

Net income gives us some idea of 'how much money the company is generating' which in turn may give us an idea of the health and wealth of the company. To calculate net income, we subtract all expenses from revenues. Unfortunately things are never quite that simple. For instance, a manufacturing firm spends $10 million to build a factory that will help it create products for a period of ten years. We would recognize factory construction expenses of $10 million in year one, and zero in each of years two to ten. This would suggest one unusually poor year for profits, followed by nine very good ones.

The preferred practice is to match revenues as closely as possible to the expenses incurred to generate those revenues. In our example, we assume that the $10 million factory generates ten years' worth of revenues so we apportion one-tenth of the $10 million outlay in each of those ten years. This one-tenth charge is known as depreciation (amortization is a similar annual charge for a different sort of one-off expenditure that is matched against more than one year's worth of sales).

So, how should an investor assess all of this? Well, keep on reading. As well as net income we would want to look at cash flow as an indicator of corporate health and strength. If you want to know how much the company can afford to pay in dividends or use for other investments, you would look to the cash flow, which is calculated by adding non-cash depreciation and amortization charges back to net income.

But cash flow alone doesn't give us the full story. Free cash flow looks at the cash the company's operations actually generated in a given year and subtracts important 'non-operating' cash outlays, capital spending and dividend payments. Accordingly, free cash flow is the purest measure of a company's capacity to generate cash.

Cash flow is a less pure number, but also less susceptible to wide year-to-year swings as capital programmes periodically build up and wind down.

Clearly, we are looking to compare price to cash flow and price to free cash flow relative to other companies in the same industry and also to see how cash flow and free cash flow change year on year for the company in order to gauge a measure of its growth and valuation. We want price to cash flow ratios to be low relative to other companies in the same industry and we want cash flow to be rising year on year.

Let's take a *closer* look at cash flows (yes, it may feel tedious – but it's good for you).

*Selected statement of cash flow (CF) items (indirect method)*

| | Annual | | | Year to date | |
|---|---|---|---|---|---|
| | 12 months ending 31/12/95 | 12 months ending 31/12/96 | 12 months ending 31/12/97 | 9 months ending 30/09/97 | 9 months ending 30/09/98 |
| Net income | 1,427,300 | 1,572,600 | 1,642,500 | 1,231,600 | 1,201,600 |
| Depreciation & amortization | 709,000 | 742,900 | 793,800 | 557,000 | 648,300 |
| Non-cash items | −4,200 | 32,900 | −110,700 | 0 | 0 |
| Other operating CF | 164,100 | 112,600 | 116,700 | −68,400 | 147,500 |
| **Total operating CF** | **2,296,200** | **2,461,000** | **2,442,300** | **1,720,200** | **1,997,400** |
| Capital expenditures | −2,063,700 | −2,375,300 | −2,111,200 | −1,444,000 | −1,350,100 |
| Other investing CF | −45,300 | −195,000 | −106,000 | −102,200 | −50,100 |
| **Total investing CF** | **−2,109,000** | **−2,570,300** | **−2,217,200** | **−1,546,200** | **−1,400,200** |
| Dividends paid | −226,500 | −232,000 | −247,700 | −186,300 | −179,500 |
| Sale (purchases) of stock | −314,500 | −599,900 | −1,113,100 | −568,400 | −1,049,100 |
| Net borrowings | 445,100 | 779,300 | 1,001,500 | 415,000 | 390,100 |
| Other financing CF | 63,600 | 157,000 | 145,700 | 146,000 | 204,200 |
| **Total financing CF** | **−32,300** | **104,400** | **−213,600** | **−193,700** | **−634,300** |
| Exchange rate effect | 0 | 0 | 0 | 0 | 0 |
| **Net change in cash** | **154,900** | **−4,900** | **11,500** | **−19,700** | **−37,100** |

**Note:** Units in thousands of US dollars

The above *Statement of Cash Flow* from Market Guide is divided into three sections. As Market Guide explains:

The *operating* section tells you how the company's basic business performed. The *Investing* section will highlight capital expenditures, purchase of investment securities, and acquisitions. This is how the company has invested its money for the future. The *financing* section shows if the company borrowed money, or if the company issued or repurchased shares. The *net change in cash* is equal to the net effects of what the company generates in operations, spends to invest for the future, how it finances itself, and the impact of foreign currency adjustments.

You want to see a company in which *net income plus depreciation are greater than capital expenditures plus dividend payments*. This is the definition of *free cash flow*. If a company has free cash flow, then it can finance its growth and finance its dividend payments from internal sources. If a company doesn't have a positive free cash flow, it may have to sell equity which will dilute your holdings, borrow money, sell assets, or use its working capital more efficiently.

The cash flow statement provides insight into which of these sources funded the company's activities in the period(s) in question.

Some of the items to look for in the statement of cash flows include:

- Positive and growing cash from operations.

- Large and growing capital expenditures meaning that the company is investing in its future.

- Repurchase of stock represented by a negative number (as it is a use of cash) is generally positive. Sales of stock (positive values) are generally negative unless explained by rapid growth which often requires additional equity capital.

- A negative number for net borrowings indicating a repayment of debt is generally positive. A profitable company with low financial leverage taking on some new debt may also be positive. A highly leveraged company taking on more debt can be dangerous.

## Share related items

For me *market capitalization* just provides an idea of how big the company is that I am investing in: it is not a trade-breaker. It is the stock price multiplied by the number of shares outstanding. This is the benchmark upon which a company is classified as:

- large cap (capitalization greater than $5 billion)
- mid cap (capitalization between $1 billion and $5 billion)
- small cap (capitalization between $300 million and $1 billion), or
- micro cap (capitalization below $300 million).

Larger companies tend to be safer to invest in than small companies, although several studies indicate that while riskier, the smaller companies as a group tend to outperform larger companies over long periods of time. I tend to focus more on smaller and some micro cap companies, sprinkled with a few safer large caps like Telecom Italia, Cisco, Sun, Oracle, TelMex, Apple and Nokia.

The shares outstanding is the number of shares issued by the company less any shares the company has bought back. The float indicates the number of shares held by everybody other than officers, directors and 5 per cent or more owners. If there is little float, there's generally very little trading volume and anybody wishing to buy or sell the stock may impact the price significantly.

# Dividend information

The annual dividend is the total amount of dividends you could expect to receive if you held the stock for a year and there was no change in the company's dividend payment. It is based on the current quarterly dividend payment rate projected forward for four quarters. Since I look for growth companies I prefer it if the company reinvests its dividend rather than paying it to shareholders. There was a time when a company not paying a dividend could expect to have its share price punished by virtue of the fact that many conservative funds looking for income rather than capital growth from their stocks would steer clear of such companies. Higher yields on stocks can suggest Wall Street expectations of sluggish growth.

The dividend yield is the indicated annual dividend rate expressed as a percentage of the price of the stock, and could be compared to the coupon yield on a bond. It allows you to see how much income you can expect per $ or £ investment from this stock, so allowing you to compare it with other stocks you may be looking at. Some prefer high yield, others low. If you are looking for high growth companies as a general rule, all other things being equal, you will prefer low yield companies.

The *payout ratio* tells you what percentage of the company's earnings have been given to shareholders as cash dividends over the past twelve months. I look for stocks with a low payout ratio, which indicates that the company has chosen to reinvest most of the profits back into the business.

There are a few sectors whose stocks are regarded as income vehicles – utility and real estate in particular. Investors in these sectors focus more on yields than those in other sectors.

# Management effectiveness

The management effectiveness is about return on capital. If you invest in Government bonds, you would know you are going to get a certain return: the 'risk-free rate of return'. Since investments in businesses are riskier you would be expecting a better return than the risk-free one.

## Return on equity

The shareholders of a company can be thought of as having given a company capital – or equity. The return on equity (ROE) is a measure of how effectively the company has managed this equity. Equity represents that portion of the company's assets that would be distributed to shareholders if the company were liquidated and all assets sold at values reflected on the company's balance sheet, so it is what the company itself and therefore the shareholders own and does not include, for instance, money loaned from a bank.

## Return on investment

Since return on investment (ROI) only relates to capital provided by shareholders, it is a limited measure of management effectiveness since we also want to know how the company is performing with the other sources of money at its disposal. Return on investment shows how effective management is in utilizing money provided by the company's owners (equity) and long-term creditors.

## Return on assets

As well as shareholder capital and long-term money granted to the company there are also shorter-term loans of capital, and so return on assets (ROA) is a broader measure than the above two of how a company is handling funds provided to it. For example, an internet company may borrow money to purchase some Sun Microsystems routers for its web site. The lender may be providing short-term (i.e. less than one year) credit. Return on assets measures management's effectiveness in using everything at its disposal (equity, long-term credit and temporary capital) to produce profits.

# Profitability

Profitability ratios relate to how much of the revenue the company receives is being turned into profit.

*Gross margin* shows you what percentage of each revenue dollar is left after deducting direct costs of producing the goods or services which in turn bring in the revenue. For a services company, the most common direct costs would be the salaries of the employees. The money left at this stage is called *gross profit*. Gross margin expresses the relationship between gross profit and *revenues* in percentage terms. For example, a gross margin of 10 per cent means that ten cents out of every revenue dollar are left after deducting direct costs.

*Operating profit* and *operating margin* follow the progress of each revenue dollar to another important level. From gross profit we now subtract indirect costs, often referred to as overheads. Examples of overheads would be the costs associated with headquarters operations: costs that are essential to the business, but not directly connected to any single individual product manufactured and sold by the company.

Finally, *net profit* and the *net margin* show you how much of each revenue dollar is left after all costs, of any kind, are subtracted, such as interest on corporate debt and income taxes. High margins are better than low margins, and this applies equally when comparing companies in the same industry.

## Tax rates

Profitability is also affected by tax rates. A company may have an unusually low tax rate because of losses carried forward or other temporary issues. These will vanish in the future and could sharply affect the profitability of the company. Consequently it is a good thing to see if the company has an unusually low tax rate.

# Recommendations

Ultimately, everything you do when you analyze a stock boils down to what you'll find in this report: **specific investment decisions**. The **Recommendations Table** tells you exactly what professional securities analysts who cover the company have decided to do regarding its stock.

*Analyst recommendations and revisions*

|  | As of 22/04/1999 | As of 4 weeks ago | As of 8 weeks ago | As of 12 weeks ago |
|---|---|---|---|---|
| 1 Strong buy | 6 | 5 | NA | NA |
| 2 Buy | 8 | 7 | NA | NA |
| 3 Hold | 7 | 7 | NA | NA |
| 4 Underperform | 0 | 0 | NA | NA |
| 5 Sell | 0 | 0 | NA | NA |
| Mean rating | 2.0 | 2.1 | NA | NA |

The table contains five possible investment recommendations: strong buy, buy, hold, underperform and sell. They are based on the five recommendation categories used by most investment advisory organizations. The terminology may vary from one firm to another (for example, some might label the third recommendation 'neutral' instead of 'hold'). But whatever set of labels you see, you can *assume that the investment advisors are ranking stocks in a five-step, best-to-worst sequence.*

Critics of Wall Street research point out that brokerage firm analysts are quick to recommend purchases of stock, but almost never advise customers to sell. You can evaluate this by examining Market Guide recommendation tables for a large number of stocks. If you do that, you are very likely to find that *'underperform' and 'sell' recommendations are extremely rare; 'neutral' ratings aren't quite so scarce, but they do appear far less frequently than do 'strong buy' and 'buy' recommendations.* Fortunately for you, I/B/E/S compiles, and Market Guide presents, additional information that enables you to derive worthwhile real-world Wall Street recommendations despite the fact that analyst ratings tend to cluster towards the top of the scale.

The last row of the table presents the *mean rating*. This is a weighted average of all the individual ratings. The best possible score would be 1.0 (to achieve that, every analyst would have to rate the stock a 'strong buy') and the worst possible score would be 5.0. Realistically, given the aforementioned top-of-the-rating-scale bias, you should expect most mean ratings to fall in the 1.00–3.00 range. But within that context, you still can, and should, *compare a stock's mean rating to those of others you are considering and favour those with better (i.e. lower number) scores.*

Also, *look at the columns showing the recommendations four, eight and twelve weeks ago.* If you are a momentum investor, you will want to favour stocks for which there are a gradually increasing number of top recommendations or improving mean rating scores. Those who prefer out-of-favour stocks may take a different approach. Such investors would prefer stocks for which the mean rating has been deteriorating. A mean rating that is stable (or modestly better) from the four-week-ago period to the present after having deteriorated from the twelve- to eight- to four-week-ago intervals might be especially interesting. This trend could be signalling the early stages of a turnaround. A gradual increase in the number of recommendations over the past twelve weeks would indicate that Wall Street is turning its eye toward a company that had previously been ignored or undiscovered.

## Performance

Excellent sites like Market Guide provide data allowing you to compare price performance of stocks relative to major indices and the industry they are in. You can also get a feel for this from sites with graphing facilities. These are mainly viewed in two ways by most people.

*Value investors* may look for underperformers on the basis that these stocks will eventually 'catch up' with the rest of the index, even if in the short term they will underperform and drag down a whole portfolio. *Growth investors* may well look for those that lead the market in terms of performance.

For instance, the Market Guide **Price Performance Table** shows you the stock's percentage price movements over each of five measurement periods: 4 weeks, 13 weeks, 26 weeks, 52 weeks, and year to date (YTD). Large percentage changes, as shown in the second (actual %) column, will obviously catch your eye. But the other three columns are the ones that can add important depth to your understanding of the stock's recent performance.

*Price performance*

| Period | Actual (%) | V. S&P 500 (%) | Rank in industry | Industry rank |
|---|---|---|---|---|
| 4-week | 5.2 | −1.1 | 71 | 64 |
| 13-week | 21.3 | 8.7 | 78 | 78 |
| 26-week | 54.9 | 19.9 | 86 | 83 |
| 52-week | 69.4 | 40.2 | 95 | 89 |
| YTD | 13.6 | 6.1 | 74 | 83 |

**Note:** Rank is a percentile that ranges from 0 to 99, with 99 = best

Column three compares the stock's price activity with that of the benchmark S&P 500 Index. It shows the percentage point differential between your stock and the index. Column four shows you how the stock performed relative to the average for the industry in which the company operates. This is a 'percentile' rank. Looking at this sample, we see that the four-week tally is 71. This means that the stock performed better than those of 71 per cent of the companies in its industry. Now look at the fifth column, which contains an *industry rank*. It shows a percentile score of 64. This tells us that the industry performed better than did 64 per cent of the industries in the Market Guide universe (viewed from a different perspective, 36 per cent of the industries in the Market Guide universe performed better).

## Institutional ownership

| | |
|---|---|
| % shares owned | 69.77 |
| # of institutions | 1,556 |
| Total shares held (Mil.) | 944.064 |
| 3 Mo. net purchases (Mil.) | 118.945 |
| 3 Mo. shares purchased (Mil.) | 192.377 |
| 3 Mo. shares sold (Mil.) | 73.432 |

*Institutional ownership*

**Institutional Ownership Tables** show the extent to which institutional investors (pension funds, mutual funds, insurance companies, etc.) own a stock.

Traders take account of institutional ownership for several reasons, one of which is that if the major institutions are buying, with all their high-flying analysts backing a stock and their millions of dollars vested in these companies, then perhaps we should be more assured in our own decisions.

There is also another way institutional ownership can back or provide trading ideas. If institutions that own a position in the company is small that would indicate that the company has been noticed a little by institutions with potential for greater recognition. But the stock may rise as it gets better known and more institutions decide to buy in. Many believe it is best to own a company that is between 5 and 20 per cent owned by institutions. Such a level would suggest that there is some institutional interest and some knowledge of the company, and that there's also ample room for more institutional interest in the future.

## Insider trading

| | |
|---|---|
| Net insider trades | −6 |
| # Buy transactions | 0 |
| # Sell transactions | 6 |
| Net shares purchased (Mil.) | −0.405 |
| # Shares purchased (Mil.) | 0.000 |
| # Shares sold (Mil.) | 0.405 |

*Insider trading (previous 6 months)*

Who knows a company even better than institutions? Maybe the company's executives and senior officers do. These are the insiders. If they are buying then perhaps we should be too, or at least be reassured. But not just their buying, but their level of holding can be an important sign too.

However, when insiders own a very large and controlling percentage of the company, they may not feel responsible to outside shareholders. This is particularly visible in companies with multiple classes of stock, with insiders/management retaining voting control over the company.

Insider selling can, and often does, reflect little more than a desire on the part of key employees to convert part of their compensation (e.g. stock options) to cash for other uses. So it need not automatically be bearish. However, this is what makes insider trading a difficult gauge of a good or bad stock.

But buying by insiders could be a different story. Here, people are putting new money into the stock of their corporations, and possibly reducing the diversification of their personal assets. It's highly unlikely that any insider would do this unless he/she had a favourable assessment of the company's prospects. But of course insiders could be buying after a big fall in the stock price in an effort to show faith in the company – and that may be a desperate attempt to encourage outsiders to invest, who, if they do not, could mean the stock keeps falling. Also, insiders could simply be wrong in their assessment about the future prospects of the company. Nevertheless it is a useful indicator to take note of.

## The sites

## Thomson Research ***

www.thomsonresearch.com

### How to use this site and what for

Although costly this site is for the seriously serious online trader. The quality of information is second only to something from Goldman Sachs.

## Hoover's ***

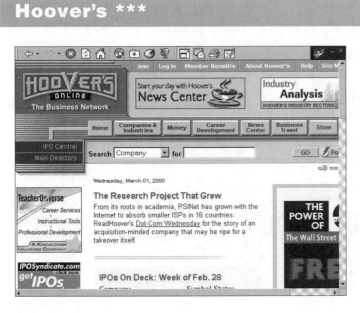

www.hoovers.com

### How to use this site and what for

This one also covers, mainly for subscriptions, the types of information we have looked at in this chapter. It has proprietary company profiles which are syndicated to some other financial portals.

## Market Guide ***

www.marketguide.com

### How to use this site and what for

See Fundamentals on page 96.

## Multex Investor Network ***

`www.multexinvestor.com`

### How to use this site and what for

This site has a multitude of broker research reports ranging from the free to the very expensive. I tend to focus on the free ones since I am an active trader. Those who are longer-term investors may want to invest in a report to back up their trading decisions.

# Insider Trader **

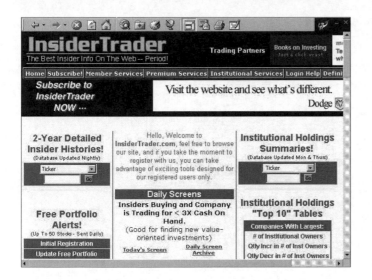

www.insidertrader.com

## How to use the site and what for

If you liked the ideas discussed above about insider trading then this is the one for you. The site collates in one useful place the key insider buying and selling of corporate executives.

## Stockpoint **

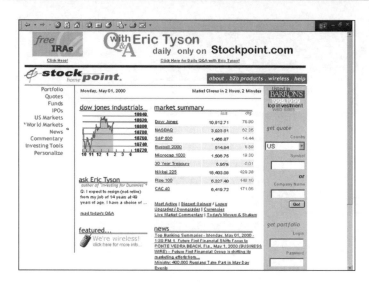

www.stockpoint.co.uk

### How to use the site and what for

This UK site is a good source for the types of data we have discussed in this chapter, although the data can be sketchy at times.

## Summary

This has been one of the key chapters of the book. It reveals in essence what many professional investors look for and lays the foundations for understanding why stock prices move and to what end businesses are run. It also tells us that when companies are not focusing on these ends then we should be worried. Remember always, fundamental analysis is a tool used mainly by longer-term investors since the fundamentals take time to be reflected in the prices in many cases.

# 6

# Fundamentals: earnings

## In this chapter

Earnings get undue prominence from online traders as a way of generating trading ideas. Novices ask if a company is making a profit. That is too simple a question to ask when judging likely future company performance. This chapter reveals how to find the most relevant pieces of information.

## Objective

■ **Using earnings information as a source of trading ideas.**

## Earnings estimates

At the end of this chapter we examine some of the best web sites to find earnings-related information. You may have gathered from the previous chapter that the one I like best is the excellent *www.marketguide.com*.

Below is a sample of a complete I/B/E/S *earnings estimates report* on McDonald's. You will find reference to this in the discussion of the various components of the report below.

Updated: 22/04/1999

| Expected earnings announcements | Release date |
|---|---|
| Quarter ending 06/99 | 17/07/1999 |
| Quarter ending 09/99 | 18/10/1999 |

**Earnings per share estimates**
**Diluted EPS**

| | # of ests. | Mean est. | High est. | Low est. | Std. dev. | Proj. p/e |
|---|---|---|---|---|---|---|
| **Quarter ending 06/99** | **12** | **0.38** | **0.38** | **0.37** | **0.01** | – |
| Quarter ending 09/99 | 12 | 0.38 | 0.40 | 0.37 | 0.01 | – |
| **Year ending 12/99** | **23** | **1.41** | **1.45** | **1.39** | **0.02** | **31.60** |
| Year ending 12/00 | 16 | 1.58 | 1.61 | 1.52 | 0.02 | 28.32 |
| LT growth rate | 18 | 13.58 | 22.70 | 10.00 | 2.98 | – |

**Analyst recommendations and revisions**

| | As of 22/04/1999 | As of 4 weeks ago | As of 8 weeks ago | As of 12 weeks ago |
|---|---|---|---|---|
| 1 Strong buy | 6 | 5 | NA | NA |
| 2 Buy | 8 | 7 | NA | NA |
| 3 Hold | 7 | 7 | NA | NA |
| 4 Underperform | 0 | 0 | NA | NA |
| 5 Sell | 0 | 0 | NA | NA |
| Mean rating | 2.0 | 2.1 | NA | NA |

**Quarterly earnings surprises**
**Estimated vs. actual EPS**
**Diluted EPS**

| | Estimate | Actual | Difference | % Surprise |
|---|---|---|---|---|
| March 1999 | 0.29 | 0.29 | 0.00 | 0.00 |
| December 1998 | 0.32 | 0.32 | 0.00 | 0.00 |
| September 1998 | 0.34 | 0.35 | 0.01 | 2.94 |
| June 1998 | 0.33 | 0.33 | 0.00 | 0.00 |
| March 1998 | 0.26 | 0.26 | 0.00 | 0.00 |

**Historical mean EPS estimates trend**
**Diluted EPS**

|  | As of 22/04/99 | As of 4 weeks ago | As of 3 months ago |
|---|---|---|---|
| Quarter ending 06/99 | 0.38 | 0.37 | 0.37 |
| Quarter ending 09/99 | 0.38 | 0.38 | NA |
| Year ending 12/99 | 1.41 | 1.41 | 1.41 |
| Year ending 12/00 | 1.58 | 1.58 | 1.57 |

**Earnings estimates revision summary**

|  | Last week | | Last 4 weeks | |
|---|---|---|---|---|
|  | Revised up | Revised down | Revised up | Revised down |
| Quarter ending 06/99 | 1 | 0 | 1 | 0 |
| Quarter ending 09/99 | 0 | 0 | 0 | 0 |
| Year ending 12/99 | 1 | 0 | 2 | 0 |
| Year ending 12/00 | 0 | 0 | 1 | 1 |

**Note:** All EPS values are reported on a diluted basis by I/B/E/S

## Expected earnings announcements

Earnings release dates are very important. The run up to the announcement can be an active time for the stock. Following the announcement the stock can often move sharply too, of course. If earnings meet expectations or even exceed them, there can be a sell-off in accordance with the market saying 'buy the rumour and sell the fact.' A few days later the uptrend can resume as the earnings are digested by the outside community and possible positive statements flow. If the earnings estimate fails to meet expectations, we would expect the stock price to fall. However, as we note later – all is not that simple.

Conference calls follow announcements (where the company discusses results with the analysts from brokerage houses that follow the company). These too can lead to institutions' shifts in view of the stocks and announcements by them and can affect the stock price.

As important as release day is, the month or so before the release can be even more crucial. During this period, you should be alert for 'pre-announcements' that can impact stocks even more dramatically than the actual earnings reports. As corporate executives get closer to finalizing the upcoming financial reports, they compare their own data with analysts' projections. If there is a significant discrepancy, many will issue a written announcement (often followed by a conference call) telling the financial community that results are likely to differ significantly from consensus expectations.

The last few days before the release date are important even if there are no corporate pre-announcements, as analysts fine-tune their estimates. Increasingly large share-price movements during this period, especially if accompanied by above-average trading volume, can signal changing expectations even before those changes are formally issued by the analysts. This is why your closest stock monitoring should occur in the week before release date.

## Earnings per share estimates

This is where you'll find a summary of brokerage house earnings estimates for the company.

The *number of estimates, high estimate, low estimate* and *standard deviation*: as you look at these remember this – a wider range of estimates means greater disagreement among analysts; greater disagreement reflects increased uncertainty; and Wall Street tends to dislike uncertainty and there may be greater stock volatility.

On the one hand, you may choose companies for which analyst estimates are close to one another. But if such a company reports weaker-than-expected results, it will be taken by Wall Street as a harsher surprise and the stock might suffer more dramatically than would be the case if uncertainty (as indicated by a wide range of estimates) had been prevalent beforehand. There is no completely foolproof way to resolve this dilemma.

Remember: a diversified portfolio will reduce the risk of the inevitable earnings shock that results in a quick, sharp fall in the price of your holdings.

When studying the range of estimates, keep these points in mind:

■ Note the number of analysts. A large number of analysts can add a measure of confidence to the estimates. But a smaller number of analysts can raise the possibility of a stock being a diamond in the rough; a relatively undiscovered company whose stock could perform especially well as more investors learn the story.

■ Finally, you can compare these forward-looking p/e ratios to the consensus growth rate. Dividing the p/e by the growth rate will result in a PEG ratio. Many interpret PEG ratios above 1.00 (p/e ratios that are above the growth rate) as signifying stock overvaluation, but you can still use it to compare relatively 'overvalued' stocks versus each other.

# Earnings surprises

You will have seen comments such as these:

*XYZ Inc. shares (XYZ – 30) lost 15 points, or one-third of their value, after the company reported first quarter earnings per share of $0.26. The result was well ahead of last year's $0.20-per-share first quarter performance, but shy of analysts' $0.29-per-share consensus estimate.*

Earnings surprises often generate rapid and large share-price movements.

Look at the earnings surprise component in our table and see what has happened over time. Years ago, when companies didn't do much to guide analysts, earnings surprises meant that the analyst was wrong. But nowadays, earnings surprises have increasingly come to mean that corporate management is wrong. And in the financial markets, few things are as bearish as a belief, among investors, that top management does not have a firm grasp on its own business.

Fair or unfair, earnings surprises today are perceived as company errors, not analyst errors. And the simultaneous receipt of and reaction to the bad news by a large number of institutional investors sets off the selling waves that drive share prices sharply lower as soon as the news is disseminated.

In theory, the same set of reactions should occur when surprises are favourable. If one expected $0.50, couldn't one be equally leery of management's comprehension if the company reports $0.54 a share? Shouldn't the stock likewise fall in response to the favourable earnings surprise? But in fact, this doesn't happen.

When the surprise is favourable, euphoric reaction to the traditional perception that good news will persist indefinitely wins out over concerns about company error. This is not a logical balance.

## What is to be done?

The easy answer is to say you should be bullish on companies that tend to report positive surprises, and bearish on companies that fall short of consensus estimates. And indeed, for many investors on many occasions, that is the correct answer. However, consider the following:

■ A lot will depend on the size of the shortfall and the range indicated by the company. If the company indicated $.1–.11 range and the result came in 1c shy, that may not be as bad as falling 1c short if the range was a lot more precise and the 1c fall was a larger percentage of it.

■ The vigour with which management offers its guidance will be another factor. So, check price charts and make sure the surprises that occurred in the past were actually perceived as significant by the market.

■ If a stock is pummelled to deeply depressed levels by a surprise that does not truly signal recurring trouble or management problems then that can be an opportunity to buy in. Apple computers faced this when it failed to meet demand due to stock shortage resulting from a lack of semiconductors after the Taiwan earthquake in mid-September 1999 (Diagram 6.1). The stock fell some 25 per cent and presented an excellent buying opportunity (a 100 per cent return in six months from that point). Conversely, a soaring stock price following a string of significantly favourable earnings surprises might signal unreasonably optimistic expectations that the company may be hard pressed to continue meeting. The Unisys chart (Diagram 6.2) reveals that – the sharp drop came after a surprise earnings warning.

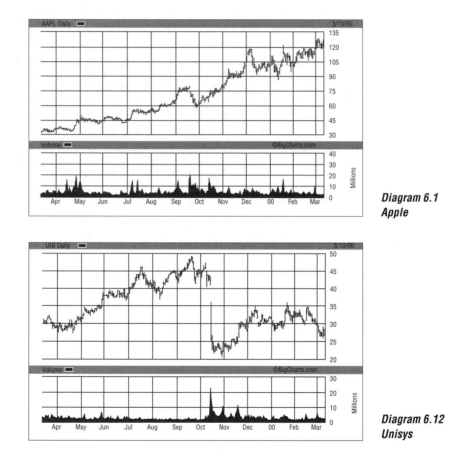

**Diagram 6.1**
**Apple**

**Diagram 6.12**
**Unisys**

## Estimates trend

The tables available from Market Guide and their explanation of their uses can hardly be bettered:

Before discussing how the *estimates trend table* can help you reach an investment decision, let's look at the reasons why estimates are revised.

- Changing expectations about the economic environment: As economists raise their expectations about the performance of the economy, analysts are likely to raise their estimates of corporate EPS. The more cyclical a company's business is, the greater the likely extent of any upward EPS estimate revision. The reverse, lower estimates, would occur if economists forecast a slowing in economic activity. Similarly, changes in expectations for different aspects of the economy could affect estimates pertaining to some companies. For example, changing interest rate forecasts would have an impact on estimates for companies in the financial sector, and other interest-sensitive businesses (such as housing); revised expectations for commodity prices would affect EPS estimates for food processing companies and restaurants.

- Changing expectations about a company's markets: In the late 1970s, analysts covering broadcasters devoted considerable attention to factors that were likely to influence demand for commercial advertising. That was the primary determinant of revenues (along with whatever impact inflation had on ad. rates). Today, even if analysts could be equally certain of their ability to estimate the dollar amount that would be spent on such advertising, they'd have other vital market-oriented issues to assess. How much of the television advertising pie would go to broadcasters and how much would go to cable networks? How valuable is any television program as an advertising vehicle considering that audiences have so many more options (i.e. can a successful network program in 1999 hope to capture the same number of 'eyeballs' as a comparably successful telecast in 1979)? To what extent is the internet siphoning away eyeballs and ad. dollars that might once have gone to network television? Etc.

As you can see, even with no changes whatsoever in economic expectations, changing markets have given analysts covering broadcast stocks many new things about which they must think and worry. Note, too, that changing markets isn't just an internet phenomenon. The political climate surrounding health care needs to be factored into estimates for those stocks. Increased energy efficiency has played a major role in revised earnings expectations in that sector. Politics surrounding nuclear energy and deregulation compete with weather conditions for prominence on utility analysts' checklists of concerns. Etc. The examples here show issues that have come about gradually. But changing markets can also affect quarter-to-quarter analyst expectations. Case in point: it's reasonable to assume that retail analysts today are carefully assessing e-commerce as threats to and opportunities for traditional retailers. Indeed, at the May 1999 Berkshire Hathaway annual meeting, Warren Buffett made it clear that he's doing this.

- Changes that are unique to individual companies: Corporate strategies change. So, too, does the extent to which management succeeds in executing business plans. New information along these lines requires analysts to modify earnings estimates.

- Changes in how analysts assess the information available to them: As important as the three aforementioned factors are, perhaps the single most frequent source of estimate revisions is the corporate earnings announcement (or anticipatory pre-announcement) itself. However skilled and diligent members of the financial community may be, analysts can never be sure their estimates are on target. And the corporate executives who 'guide' analysts toward their estimates are plagued by many of the same uncertainties that affect Wall Street. (How many banking executives truly know *exactly* where interest rates will go in the next quarter or year? How many retailers can say, in June, *exactly* how strong the upcoming holiday selling season will be?) Interim earnings reports and pre-announcements are important sources of feedback that help corporate executives and investment analysts fine tune their assessments of how the economy and various markets are performing and how much money companies will make under those conditions.

By now, it should be apparent that *estimate revisions* are a fact of life. You cannot reasonably expect to construct an equity portfolio that is immune to corporate earnings surprises. Instead, you should try to identify and own shares of companies that are most likely to have favorable surprises, or at least avoid those that seem vulnerable to major negative surprises.

The estimates trend table helps you do this. If the table shows that estimates have been increasing over time, that means that analysts have been surprised for the better. Sometimes, the surprise surfaces in a formal manner, through an official corporate earnings release or through a pre-announcement in which analysts are guided to revise their estimates. At other times, the surprise surfaces in an informal way; i.e. when an analyst gets information – whether from management or another source – showing him/her that estimates need to be changed. Either way, upward trending estimates show a recent history of favorable surprises. Conversely, downward trending estimates show a recent history of negative surprises (formal and/or informal).

Bear in mind that the information presented here took place in the past. One can never be certain that the future will always continue along the same lines. So there is risk/reward balancing that needs to be done. The longer a particular trend is in place, the more aggressive the stock is likely to react should that trend ever reverse. For example, a negative earnings surprise is likely to have a more dramatic effect on a company with a long history of favorable surprises, especially if the surprises are big, than would be the case if analysts had previously become accustomed to receiving occasional bad news.

## The sites

## Earnings Whispers **

www.earningswhispers.com

### How to use this site and what for

We have discussed companies meeting, exceeding or falling below earnings expectations, and some argue that it is not the published expected earnings that matter but 'whisper numbers' or the real figures Wall Street insiders are examining. They would argue that that is why stock prices sometimes fall on apparently better than expected earnings – because the figure did not meet Street expectations. Use this site to get a handle on what the whisper numbers are and also why they are important.

## Market Guide ***

www.marketguide.com

### How to use this site and what for
I have already complimented this site's excellent earnings and other fundamental data. Use the earnings table you will find from the home page for any company you are investing in.

## First Call **

www.firstcall.com

### How to use this site and what for
See the consensus change link for the most useful part of the site for private investors. Beyond that I prefer other sites for other earnings information. Most things are premium so really this is for the 'heavy duty' earnings player.

## Zacks Investment Research ***

www.zacks.com

### How to use this site and what for
There are few more respected companies on the web. Use the free services for earnings data. There are subscription services too for much more such as e-mail portfolio earnings updates. Use the one-month free trial. The site is particularly useful if you are looking for free earnings surprise information.

## Hemmington Scott ***

www.hemmscott.co.uk

**How to use this site and what for**

The company syndicates its content to most UK online sites providing financial information and so you may want to go straight to the source. Its earnings and dividends link is the key one in relation to our discussion above, but the site has a wealth of other corporate information.

## Yahoo! Finance UK **

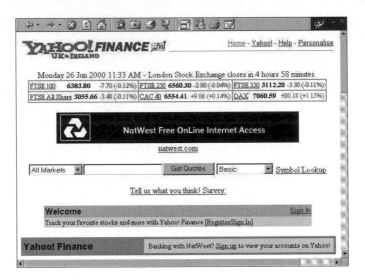

finance.uk.yahoo.com

**How to use this site and what for**

The site improves monthly and should be used as a one-stop shop for financial information including the type of information discussed in this chapter.

## Summary

Earnings, contrary to popular belief, are not the be all and end all for explaining share price movements – but they are the end to which all other data, such as a chairman's comments, are analysed. Earnings themselves can be a false barometer of future growth since much depends on how they were calculated and exceptional items in the accounts. For these and other reasons an understanding of earnings is both essential and difficult. This chapter should have steered you through the path of least resistance.

# 7

# Global investing and American depository receipts

## In this chapter

How about foreign stocks? Why simply invest in companies in your own country? Now we take a look at *why* you may want to invest in foreign stocks and *how* to get ideas about what to invest in.

## Objectives

- Decide whether you should be investing abroad.
- Find out what the technicalities are.
- Learn where to get trading ideas.
- See how to invest in, say, internet companies or telecoms companies worldwide but only in one currency.

## Trade the world online

As the internet allows us a window on global finance through the browser, I find I want to own more foreign stocks. I already own some Nokia, Ericsson, Telefonos de Mexico, Satyam and Infosys stock. Between them those five companies have produced a 65 per cent return since the start of the year. None of these companies is British or American, indeed the last two are Indian IT companies and they have had the best returns – more than double. So how do we trade them?

And why should we miss out on owning some world-beating stocks producing exceptional returns just because we do not have the often tens of thousands of pounds needed for a private client account with a major investment bank that would allow us to access global markets? Online trading allows us to trade foreign stocks cheaply, efficiently, quickly and easily through American depository receipts (ADRs).

ADRs are dollar-denominated US securities backed by and related to the underlying company stock – which may for instance be UK-listed shares. The price of the ADR and the underlying stock will generally move in tandem. A complete list of ADRs is available on the excellent *www.global-investor.com*.

Of course in place of trading ADRs we could always open multiple foreign online trading accounts with different brokers, holding them in different currencies – facing conversion costs and of course learning the language of each country since their e-broking sites are often not in English. Try E*Trade Korea – *www.etrade.co.kr* – for a taster of the difficulties. We can also face the problems of double taxation on our gains in those companies. Or perhaps, for instance, the Korean government has rules about how much currency you can convert from Sterling to local currency and how long you have to keep it in the country. In any event, do you know of a cheap online broker through which you can buy Telecomunicacoes Brasileiras 100 per cent in the past 18 weeks? The efficient solution then becomes ADRs, which avoid all of these difficulties.

## Good reasons for doing it

The reasons for trading in foreign stocks are compelling. Firstly, other global regions may be experiencing superior growth rates to our own economy. Trading their stocks could significantly improve our performance. When the recession comes we may be able to avoid a downturn in our own performance by tapping into the economic cycle of a country or region going through a growth phase of its economic cycle. As one Salomon Smith Barney analyst commented about Latin America for instance, 'The region enjoys unique characteristics that could turn it into the hottest internet market in the world.' Now, through ADRs I can act and profit from that analysis.

Secondly, I can have a more diversified portfolio exposed to a whole industry group I may find exciting but which is global rather than local. For instance, a favourite of mine and of many traders is the telecoms sector, and in particular the telecoms equipment and wireless telephony industries. ADRs allow me to take advantage of spectacular growth affecting the whole industry by not being restricted to only US companies in the field.

The third reason I find ADRs a compelling proposition is that the choice provides me with a wider selection of companies from which to choose the very best. The wider the choice, the greater the chance I will pick winners assuming my research remains diligent.

A further advantage of trading ADRs is that they are traded like any other US security. You are only holding dollars, not numerous other currencies. You do not have stamp duty costs and you pay US online trading commissions which can be far lower than, say, for UK stocks.

These advantages can be equally applicable for trading the ADRs of UK-listed companies like Colt Telecom or Vodafone for instance. If you had bought £10,000 of

Vodafone stock through, say, DLJ Direct (*www.dljdirect.co.uk*) it would have cost £87.50 in commissions and stamp duty. Buy the same value in dollars through Ameritrade and it costs $8 (around £5). Do two of those trades a month per year and you are paying around £2000 extra per annum for the self-same stock by buying it in its non-ADR form!

Of course with the ADR you have the currency risk of holding dollars and the conversion costs involved. But if you intend to put away for several months a pool of money for trading in dollar stocks and don't intend to convert back and forth, those costs and risks can be minimized.

## Simple

The practicalities of trading ADRs are straightforward. It is just like trading any US security. You would use a US e-broking account as you would for trading in, say, Microsoft or Intel. Which online broker should you use for trading ADRs? The same one you use for your US stock trading, and if you don't have one yet then I usually recommend Ameritrade (*www.ameritrade.com*) or Datek (*www.datek.com*) because of positive personal experience and good feedback about them from others.

UK-based brokers also offer US stock trading. Popular ones include Schwab (*www.schwab-europe.com*) whose frustratingly long telephone response times may have improved now that they have a new call centre in Milton Keynes. DLJ Direct (*www.dljdirect.co.uk*) also offers ADR and other US stock trading. For a list of UK-based brokers offering US stock trading visit the quaint but useful and informative GoShare site (*www.goshare.fsnet.co.uk*).

Sites for the ADR investor include Global Investor (*www.global-investor.com*), the content-rich Worldly Investor (*www.worldlyinvestor.com*) and the professional *www.adr.com* by JP Morgan as well as the Yahoo!Finance sites for each region, although not always in English (*www.yahoo.com*).

## The sites

## Worldly Investor ***

www.worldlyinvestor.com

### How to use this site and what for

A gob-smacking site. Use the excellent columns to get the best ideas for the various regions you are interested in. Use the ADR stock screener to generate ideas of ADRs, although it is a bit basic. Sign up for the various free e-mail newsletters according to sector and region, e.g. Internet Europe.

## Global Investor ***

www.global-investor.com

### How to use this site and what for

This is a site oozing the passion of its designers and content providers. Use it for resources and facts about foreign markets rather than columns offering stock ideas. See the table on market performance for an idea of top-performing markets:

*United States (dollar) investor Oct 98 to Oct 99*

| Market | Value Oct 98 | Value Oct 99 | Change % | Change % ($) |
|---|---|---|---|---|
| Straits Times [Singapore] | 1204.62 | 2047.15 | 69.9 | 66.3 |
| Nikkei-225 [Japan] | 13564.50 | 17942 | 32.3 | 47.7 |
| MSCI World [] | 1026.28 | 1469.75 | 43.2 | 43.2 |
| Hang-Seng [Hong Kong] | 10154.94 | 13256.949 | 30.5 | 30.2 |
| SP500 [United States] | 1098.67 | 1362.93 | 24.1 | 24.1 |
| CAC40 [France] | 3522.92 | 4888.62 | 38.8 | 23.6 |
| 300-Composite [Canada] | 6208.60 | 7256.2 | 16.9 | 22.9 |
| MSCI-EAFE | 1275.10 | 1532 | 20.1 | 20.1 |
| AEX [Netherlands] | 450.68 | 571.82 | 26.9 | 13.0 |
| FTSE-100 [United Kingdom] | 5438.40 | 6256 | 15.0 | 12.7 |
| All-Ordinaries [Australia] | 2647.30 | 2885.1 | 9.0 | 11.6 |
| DAX [Germany] | 4671.12 | 5525.4 | 18.3 | 5.3 |
| Gold | 294.00 | 299.3 | 1.8 | 1.8 |
| ML Tot Ret Bd Idx – Global Govt Bond | 359.74 | 356.67 | −0.9 | −0.9 |
| Commodity Research Bureau CRB | 203.28 | 201.52 | −0.9 | −0.9 |
| ML Tot Ret Bd Idx – Treasury Master | 707.68 | 697.47 | −1.4 | −1.4 |

## ADR ***

www.adr.com

### How to use the site and what for

This site is run by JP Morgan. It is very well designed, easy to use and professional. Use it to research specific issues as well as by region and sector. The search facility then allows you to list all the stocks, say in a particular sector, by return or other criteria.

For example which sector of ADRs has the greatest return for the year to date at the time of writing?

**Sort by:**

| Industry | # of companies | Today's return | 6 mo. return | 12 mo. return | YTD return |
|---|---|---|---|---|---|
| **Go to:** | | | | | |
| Biotechnology | 1 Companies | −0.41% | +285.71% | +205.65% | +211.54% |
| Internet | 2 Companies | +7.19% | +273.62% | | +96.89% |
| Broadcasting | 1 Companies | +2.53% | +210.34% | +238.03% | +94.07% |
| Computer Soft/Hardware/Svcs. | 8 Companies | +3.55% | +319.10% | +281.24% | +80.24% |
| Media/Entertainment | 11 Companies | +2.09% | +64.76% | +75.98% | +36.99% |
| Electrical Equip./Semiconductors | 8 Companies | +2.17% | +133.64% | +280.00% | +25.05% |
| Publishing | 5 Companies | +0.73% | +54.92% | +51.12% | +23.98% |
| Telecommunications | 74 Companies | +1.74% | +90.72% | +115.75% | +23.21% |

And which are those 'internet' and 'biotech' ADRs? Ebookers.com, China.com and Biacore (Sweden). And which of those telecoms companies has the best return year to date?

| | | | |
|---|---|---|---|
| Telemig Celular [TMB] | Brazil | +3.05% | +104.72% |
| Jazztel [JAZZ] | United Kingdom | +7.38% | +84.26% |
| Tele Centro Oeste [TRO] | Brazil | +2.75% | +79.81% |
| Olivetti [OLVXY] | Italy | +13.33% | +77.38% |
| Tele Celular [TSU] | Brazil | −6.01% | +66.34% |
| Ericsson [ERICY] | Sweden | +0.50% | +53.00% |
| China Telecom [CHL] | Hong Kong | −1.86% | +51.65% |
| Telefonica Argentina [TAR] | Argentina | +0.13% | +51.21% |
| Telefonica del Peru [TDP] | Peru | +0.94% | +50.93% |
| Tele Sudeste Celular [TSD] | Brazil | +0.65% | +49.92% |

| | | | |
|---|---|---|---|
| APT Satellite [ATS] | Hong Kong | +0.00% | +48.65% |
| CANTV [VNT] | Venezuela | +0.69% | +48.48% |
| Tele Nordeste Celular [TND] | Brazil | −0.08% | +47.03% |
| Iusacell [CEL] | Mexico | +2.99% | +45.76% |
| Olivetti [OLVTY] | Italy | +3.12% | +43.13% |
| Portugal Telecom [PT] | Portugal | +0.40% | +43.10% |
| Ericsson [ERICZ] | Sweden | −2.01% | +41.61% |
| France Telecom [FTE] | France | +3.00% | +41.53% |
| Telesp [TSP] | Brazil | +4.64% | +41.43% |
| KPN [KPN] | Netherlands | +4.25% | +40.62% |
| Cable & Wireless [CWP] | United Kingdom | +1.56% | +38.13% |
| Hong Kong Telecom [HKT] | Hong Kong | −0.97% | +37.94% |
| TelMex [TFONY] | Mexico | +2.56% | +36.36% |
| Telecom Italia [TIA] | Italy | +0.61% | +35.54% |
| MATAV [MTA] | Hungary | +2.65% | +34.72% |
| TelMex [TMX] | Mexico | −0.74% | +34.67% |
| Telesp Celular [TCP] | Brazil | −0.55% | +33.78% |
| Cable & Wireless [CWZ] | United Kingdom | +1.50% | +33.04% |
| Deutsche Telekom [DT] | Germany | +0.88% | +31.07% |
| Telecom Italia [TI] | Italy | +2.48% | +31.07% |
| Rostel [ROS] | Russian Fed | +5.39% | +29.41% |
| Vodafone [VOD] | United Kingdom | +1.61% | +27.40% |
| OTE [OTE] | Greece | −0.82% | +27.35% |
| AsiaSat [SAT] | Hong Kong | +6.10% | +24.29% |
| HOLDRS [TBH] | Brazil | +1.17% | +23.74% |
| Tele Danmark [TLD] | Denmark | +0.13% | +23.01% |
| SK Telecom [SKM] | Korea | −0.40% | +22.80% |
| Telebras Basket ADR [RTB] | Brazil | +0.00% | +21.77% |
| Energis [ENGSY] | United Kingdom | +5.46% | +20.84% |
| Nizhegorodsvyazinfo [NZGIY] | Russian Fed | −9.03% | +20.40% |
| STET Hellas [STHLY] | Greece | +4.66% | +19.67% |
| Tele Leste Celular [TBE] | Brazil | +0.50% | +19.41% |
| CTC [CTC] | Chile | −4.95% | +18.49% |
| Nortel [NTL] | Argentina | +1.71% | +14.84% |
| Telefonica [TEF] | Spain | +0.71% | +13.08% |
| Nokia [NOK] | Finland | +1.45% | +12.23% |
| Tele Norte Celular [TCN] | Brazil | +2.41% | +11.50% |
| Telecom Argentina [TEO] | Argentina | −2.11% | +9.85% |

| Alcatel [ALA] | France | +3.97% | +9.03% |
| Embratel [EMT] | Brazil | +5.44% | +6.65% |
| Swisscom [SCM] | Switzerland | +4.56% | +6.17% |
| Tele Norte Leste [TNE] | Brazil | +0.00% | +4.17% |
| Shin Corporations [SHNZY] | Thailand | +2.94% | +4.05% |
| Equant [ENT] | Netherlands | +7.85% | +2.79% |
| VimpelCom [VIP] | Russian Fed | +3.11% | +2.24% |

The site also has an excellent charting tool which allows you to compare the performance of the ADR with that of the underlying security and the major US indices and the underlying security's country's major indices – hours of fun online:

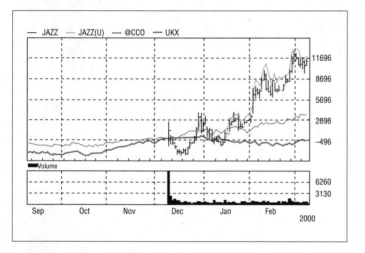

## Exchanges

If you are looking to invest in foreign stocks then you may find the list of exchanges in Appendix 8 a useful resource.

## Brokers

As well as the chapter on online brokers the following table may be of use in choosing global brokers. Remember that commission rates change very regularly and books do not! So the commissions shown are indicative only.

*Online brokers worldwide*

| Country | Broker / URL | Commissions | Notes |
|---|---|---|---|
| Australia | **Green Line**<br>*www.pont.com.au* | A$29: trade value < 10,000<br>A$39: 10,000 < trade value < $20,000<br>A$49: 20,000 < trade value < $75,000<br>0.065%: 75,000 < trade value | |
| Australia | **Macquarie Equities**<br>*www.macquarie.com.au* | 0.50%: per trade A$10,000 – A$50,000<br>The maximum value for an individual<br>internet transaction is $50,000 | |
| Australia | **E*TRADE Australia**<br>*www.etrade.com.au* | A$49.50: per trade A$75,000 | For residents of Australia<br>and New Zealand |
| Canada | **E*TRADE Canada**<br>*www.canada.etrade.com* | $27.00: per trade<br>$0.0005 per share: stock price <<br>1.00; trade > 5,400 shares<br>$0.002 per share: 1.01 < stock price<br>< 3.00; trade > 1,400 shares<br>$0.003 per share: 3.01 < stock price;<br>> trade > 1,000 shares | For residents of Canada |
| France | **CPR-E*TRADE**<br>*www.cpretrade.com* | 0.79%: 1–100,000 euros<br>0.54%: 100,000–300,000 euros<br>0.30%: >300,000 euros<br>10 euros: minimum | For residents of France |
| France | **Self Trade**<br>www.selftrade.fr | 14.95 euros HT: per trade, 0 to<br>10,000 euros 0.15%: > 10,000 euros | |
| Germany | **FIMATEX**<br>*fimatex.de* | | |

| Country | Broker / URL | Commissions | Notes |
|---|---|---|---|
| Germany | **comdirect**<br>www.comdirect.de | 0.49%: trade value < 15.000<br>0.40%: 15,000 < trade value < 30,000<br>0.30%: 30,000 < trade value < 50,000<br>0.24%: 50,000 < trade value < 150,000<br>0.10%: 150,000 < trade value | |
| Germany | **Bank24**<br>www.bank24.de | | |
| Germany | **ConSors**<br>www.consors.de | | |
| Hong Kong | **Boom Securities**<br>www.boom.com | 0.25%: per trade HK$88: minimum | |
| Sweden | **E\*TRADE Sverige**<br>www.etrade.se | | For residents of Sweden, Denmark, Finland, Iceland and Norway |
| United Kingdom | **Xest**<br>www.xest.com | £20 – XEST registration including CREST membership – for the initial period | Subsidiary of Charles Stanley |
| | | £45 – annual service charge – due 1st April each year<br>£20 – trading fee per eligible transaction | |
| United Kingdom | **Barclays**<br>www.barclays-stockbrokers.co.uk | 1.5% – first £5,000<br>0.85% – for the next £10,000<br>0.5% – balance over £10,000<br>£17.50min | |

| Country | Broker / URL | Commissions | Notes |
|---|---|---|---|
| United Kingdom | **Charles Schwab** <br> *www.schwab-worldwide.com* | 0.9% – first £2,500 <br> 0.75% – for the next £2,500 <br> 0.1% – balance over £5,000 <br> £15min, £75max <br> [£19.50 – Frequent Traders Club] | |
| United Kingdom | **DLJ direct UK** <br> *www.dljdirect.co.uk* | 1.0% – first £2,500 <br> 0.5% – for the next £2,500 <br> 0.1% – balance over £5,000 <br> £15.00min | |
| United Kingdom | **StockTrade** <br> *www.stocktrade.co.uk* | £25 – annual Crest Sponsored Membership service charge <br> £25 – up to £12,500 <br> 0.2% – over £12,500 | Subsidiary of Brewin Dolphin |
| United Kingdom | **E*TRADE UK** <br> *www.etrade.co.uk* | £14.95: any trade £1,500 or below <br> £24.95: trade > £1,500 [first 10 trades] <br> £19.95: trade > £1,500 [next 15 trades] <br> £24.95: trade > £1,500 [over 25 trades] | For residents of the United Kingdom |
| United States | **Charles Schwab** <br> *www.eschwab.com* | $29.95 per stock up to 1,000 shares <br> $.03 per share for over 1,000 shares | |
| United States | **Datek Online** <br> *www.datek.com* | $9.99: Any executed stock trade placed online for up to 5,000 shares <br> Free: Marketable orders not executed within 60 seconds | |

| Country | Broker / URL | Commissions | Notes |
|---|---|---|---|
| United States | **E*TRADE** <br> *www.etrade.com* | $14.95: Market orders for listed securities <br> $19.95: All OTC stock orders, both market and limit, regardless of size <br> $19.95: Listed securities placed as a limit or stop order <br> $0.01: For listed securities orders over 5,000 shares, per share for the entire order | |
| United States | **Waterhouse Securities** <br> *www.waterhouse.com* | $12: per trade, up to 5,000 shares <br> $0.01: Trades over 5,000 shares will incur a 1 cent per share charge for the entire order | |
| United States | **Suretrade.com** <br> *www.suretrade.com* | $7.95: Market Order $9.95: limit orders | |
| United States | **InvestIN Securities** <br> *www.invest.com* | $9.95: Up to 1,000 shares (including market, limit and stop orders) $0.01: Trades over 1,000 shares incur a 1 cent per share charge for shares over 1,000 | |
| United States | **Ameritrade** <br> *www.ameritrade.com* | $8: per trade $13: limit, stop and stop limit orders | |

## Summary

ADRs are an exciting, simple way to trade global markets. As the internet and global communications and travel make companies into multi-nationals and open up new opportunities the demand for investing through ADRs will increase.

I use them extensively, not least because by having exposure to foreign markets in dollars provides me with diversification and lower risk. The Nobel committee need to start offering a few prizes to their creators.

# Sites and using them profitably

# 8

# The trade planned

**❝** *You can't just go out there and
wildly speculate* **❞**

**Bill Lipschutz** Former Global Head of Foreign Exchange, Salomon Brothers

## In this chapter

A trading plan is probably the most important part of any trade. It is also the most neglected. We examine your trading strategy in brief and what planning a trade ought to involve. Then you will be able to use this in an actual trade and produce an actual trading tactic. To avoid the many pitfalls of trading we also examine keeping a journal, diversification and the types of traders that fail.

## Objectives

- **Learn to produce and use a trading strategy and trading tactics as part of a trading plan.**
- **See how to keep a journal as part of profitable trading.**
- **Examine the types of traders that fail.**
- **Look at the phenomenon of day-trading.**
- **Understand proper diversification.**

## What works? Building a trading strategy

So, having examined both fundamental and technical analysis in broad outline together with some common things followers of those techniques use, you may well be tempted to ask what works. Does looking for analysts' upgrades of stock performances work? Does an examination of stock momentum work?

The unfortunate answer is that nothing works and everything works. Nothing works, because if it did it would be consistently profitable and the puzzle of the markets would be solved. Everything works in that all the individual techniques are successful part of the time – that is why they are followed.

## A guide to a DIY trading strategy

So where do we go from here? The best advice to give you is, first, read a lot more about fundamental and technical analysis from the recommended reading.

Second, develop a trading strategy. A trading strategy is a set of rules which must be met before you enter a trade, as opposed to trading tactics, which are the actual specific plans for what to do once you enter a trade (discussed below).

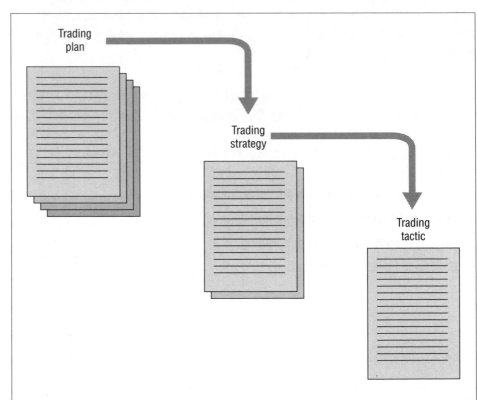

*Illustration 8.1
The plan, the strategy,
the tactic*

# Steps to building a trading strategy

## Select some indicators

Having examined what fundamental and technical analysts commonly look for, and having done some reading about those subjects, choose some indicators you think may be potentially indicative of a rising market.

## Hypothesize!

Choose some rules you consider worth testing, bearing in mind the period of time you want to be in and out of the market for each trade. Choose a target price for exit, a stop loss figure and other circumstances for exit.

### Example

A fundamental analyst of company stocks may choose to buy a stock only if the following rules are met:

- p/e ratio less than 7
- analyst recommendations all being buy or higher
- profit margin of 12 per cent or higher
- dividend yield of 12 per cent or higher
- target price: rise of 15 per cent
- stop loss: drop of 10 per cent
- exit if one of these fundamental factors changes adversely.

A technical analyst may choose stock purchase rules based on:

- MACD crossover
- stochastic crossover
- rising parabolic SAR
- a bounce off a trendline
- target price: rise of 15 per cent
- stop loss: drop of 10 per cent
- exit if one of the above technical factors changes adversely (Diagram 8.1).

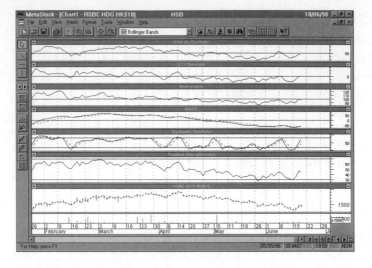

**Diagram 8.1**
**A technical approach**

**Overfitting** *There is a tendency when testing trading rules to 'overfit' the rules (i.e. amend them) to the data at hand so the results are good for those data only. To avoid this, do some 'out-of-sample testing', i.e. test the same rules on a completely different set of data. But beware: it may be that your trading rules do genuinely only work with that one company, both historically and in the future, and you may be throwing away a good system by out-of-sample testing. To avoid this, do some paper trades on the same stock as well.*

## Test

Now test the rules. Select some stocks and obtain their historical price charts (see skeleton plans for sites). Next see what would have happened had you used your trading strategy. What would a notional $10,000 have been at the end of one year, after dealing costs? Is the return better than bank rates of return? Did you beat the Dow or a typical mutual fund?

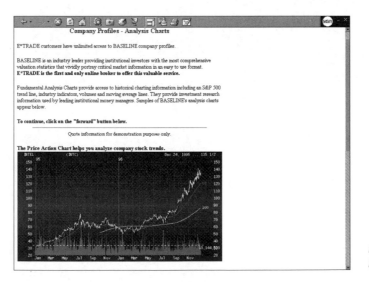

**Diagram 8.2**
**Looking to buy**

## The preponderance of evidence rule

When testing and developing look for a balance of probability. Examine many different indicators, e.g. news stories on your product, analysts' views, market momentum. When there is a preponderance of evidence suggesting price movement, make a paper trade. Keep doing this until you are comfortable that what you are doing works. If it does not, find out what aspects do not work, e.g. the technical indicators are always wrong, and either amend or ditch that particular indicator.

Always paper trade with different methods of selecting trades. For instance, you may try to combine stock filters with technical indicators and plot the results together with other systems, and go for what appears to make sense and is profitable.

When you find a trading strategy you are fairly happy with you are then ready to trade.

### Action plan

1 Decide if you need or want to find out more about fundamental and technical analysis.

2 Surf sites which provide analysis for your product choice.

3 Choose site(s) which you like the best for fundamental and/or technical analysis.

4 Develop a trading strategy using the guidelines provided in this chapter, then test it to satisfaction (if need be, return to Step 2 in this programme of action).

### Hot tip

**How to back test well**

*1* I tend to test one indicator at a time and add more and more and see how that affects results.

*2* Look at a chart and identify areas in which your indicators should produce signals and then find indicators that tend to.

*3* Are the results very volatile, e.g. large losses and profits (even though overall profitable)? Can you handle such losses along the way?

*4* Do not just test bull markets, test bear and sideways or find a different set of indicators for each type of market (Diagram 8.2).

**Risk–reward** *As a rule of thumb your upside target should be a greater percentage than your stop loss.*

## Creating a trading tactic

1   Using your trading rules contained in your trading strategy go through the relevant stocks, etc.

2   Select the best possibilities for price moves. Remember the preponderance of evidence rule.

3   For each possibility list the pros and cons (see Table 8.1). Select the best of the best to trade.

4   Set an upside target. What do you expect the price to reach and in what time frame? You may want to attach a rough probability of this occurring.

5   Set a stop loss – a point at which you will exit the trade: either a specific price level or a percentage.

6   Set a point at which you will sell irrespective of 4 and 5 in this list, i.e. you may get negative news on the company and decide to sell even though the stop loss has not been reached.

### Hot tip

**The mind of a trader**
*Stick to your plan. Do not start hoping for price moves, or denying losses. Try to keep objective. Do not get attached to a position: each day is a clean slate. To learn more about trading plans and trading like a professional you might consider reading* The Mind of a Trader *(FT Pitman Publishing, 1997).*

**Table 8.1  Part of a simple trading tactic**

| Pros | Cons |
| --- | --- |
| MACD crossover occurred | Sector undergone long bull run |
| Stochastic crossover | |
| SAR upward | |
| Trendline bounce | |
| All analysts buy or strong buy | |
| Sector strong | |

## Journal keeping

I am regularly asked by traders what they can do to improve their trading. One of the easiest and simplest steps that can be undertaken is to keep a journal. Imagine all that information and experience you collect as you trade. Without a journal you are throwing so much of it away. Without a journal you are in serious danger of repeating your mistakes. In this regard, keeping a journal is a money and risk management technique. By identifying possible trading problems, you can start to resolve them. So, make journal keeping a goal.

# What to record

**1** You will want to have a copy of your goals, and note your progress in achieving them.

**2** The anatomy of every trade. Write down, from the moment you started analyzing a stock to the moment after you sold it, how you felt at each key moment about every activity you undertook. You may want to compare that with what you know about how you should have reacted, in light of what you have read in this book. For example, how did you feel as you approached your stop loss?

**3** Write down what feels good and what feels uncomfortable about what you are doing.

Remember to keep your notes clear and well presented. You will have to return to them at a later date.

# Trading types

There are many types of trader. An awareness of the varieties when looking at your trading plan allows you to avoid the pitfalls.

## Disciplined

This is the ideal type of trader. You take losses and profits with ease. You focus on your system and follow it with discipline. Trading is usually a relaxed activity. You appreciate that a loss does not make for a loser.

## Doubter

You find it difficult to execute at signals. You doubt your own abilities. You need to develop self-confidence. Perhaps you should paper trade.

## Blamer

All losses are someone else's fault. You blame bad fills, your broker for picking the phone up too slowly, your system for not being perfect. You need to regain your objectivity and self-responsibility.

## Victim

Here you blame yourself. You feel the market is out to get you. You start becoming superstitious in your trading.

## Optimist

You start thinking, 'It's only money, I'll make it back later.' You think all losses will bounce back to a profit, or that you will start trading properly tomorrow.

### Gambler

You are in it for the thrill. Money is a side issue. Risk and reward analysis hardly figures in your trades; you want to be a player: you want the buzz and excitement.

### Timid

You enter a trade, but panic at the sight of a profit and take it far too soon. Fear rules your trading.

## Day-trading in Britain: no thanks

I have recently noticed an abundance of adverts in UK financial magazines offering 'courses in day-trading'. The arguments against day-trading are legion yet traders remain fascinated, while those wiser around them know it is overwhelmingly detrimental to their financial health. These are reasons why I don't day-trade, and why neither should you, and why Howard Davies, chairman of the FSA, need not worry about it becoming popular in the UK.

### The activity

Firstly, what is day-trading? When I buy shares, like most people I usually pay the offer price to buy them and the bid price to sell. The spread, that is, the difference between the bid and offer prices, is pocketed by the market-maker – the institutional individual on the other end of the deal.

A day-trader tries to put himself in the position of the market-maker by trying to buy stock at the (lower) bid price and sell it at the (higher) offer price through direct access to the market without using a broker but using special software and hardware from home or a trading booth at a day-trading firm. The day-trader makes his money from this spread, although sometimes from any share price move as well.

### The problems

The main problem of day-trading is that you are trying to make a profit from small price differences. Take day-trading Barclays stock standing at 1725 bid and 1728 ask. With £10,000 the day-trader would buy 579 shares at 1725. Selling those at 1728 would merely realize £17.37 profit before costs.

Capital and time are required by day-traders in abundance to make the activity worthwhile. Firstly, a lot of capital is needed to plough into the trade so that, multiplied by the small price, it results in an acceptable profit. Secondly, they need to trade a lot so those small profits become something respectable, and that takes a lot of time.

Few people have the inclination to sit in front of a trading screen each day. What about the day job? If you leave the screen for a few seconds the price could quickly move against you and since you are relying on small price moves from which to profit, could easily result in a very large loss.

Commissions are another excellent reason why I do not day-trade and why it will not be popular in the UK. A single £10,000 day-trade (buying and selling) using, say, Barclays Stockbrokers internet service (*www.barclays-stockbrokers.co.uk*) would cost £79.98 in commission. In the above example even trading £40,000 worth of Barclays stock would not overcome the commission, let alone produce enough money to live on or to compensate you for the time spent on the activity, and you would be buying at offer and selling at bid in any event, because online brokers do not provide direct market access.

Relatively high commissions in the UK compared to the US where the above trade could cost $8 with Ameritrade (*www.ameritrade.com*) make the activity a good way to pay the wages of brokers and little else. Add 0.5 per cent stamp duty and that makes day-trading in the UK even more unattractive. It is also another reason why the FSA's concerns were premature.

The availability of inexpensive technology makes day-trading for private individuals in the UK unfeasible compared to in the US. Day-traders need 'level II' quotes to trade effectively. Such quotes not only display the bid and the ask (level I) but also which firms have other orders at various prices. Whilst such quotes are readily available in the US, either through software for your home PC or via specialist day-trading firms, it is very rare to find either in the UK available for the private investor. Reuters (*www.reuters.com*), Bloomberg (*www.bloomberg.com*) and Topic 3 (*www.primark.com*) screens are designed for and marketed to market professionals not private traders; their lease costs run at over £10,000 per annum.

Why not day-trade US stocks if technology and commissions for day-trading UK stocks are prohibitive? Even then costs are high. A UK site, InvestIN (*www.investin.co.uk*) offers US day-trading at US commission levels, but in common with many US trading firms its software costs $300 a month.

## Even the internet is a problem

The internet is too slow for day-trading. A dedicated high-speed line (ISDN is too slow) is recommended by most advocates of the activity since day-trading requires speed of reflex to capture small price moves and the ability to exit quickly when larger price moves occur, magnifying losses. Such technology in the home does not come cheap and specialist day-trading firms providing it to private clients do not yet exist in the UK.

The skills required to be a day-trader are yet another reason why I dislike the activity. Looking for those small price moves, and knowing where and when to find them, while all the time the well-trained boys and girls from institutional banks like Lehman Brothers are also chasing them with state-of-the art technology, places the odds definitely against the untrained individual amateur.

## Losers galore

Most day-traders lose money: another reason why it will not become popular in the UK, to the FSA's relief. The North American Securities Association undertook a seven-month study and found that the high number of trades involved meant on average you needed to produce a 56 per cent annual return just to break even. The same study found that 70 per cent of day-traders lose money. The SEC in the US found that in one firm 67 out of 68 day-traders were losing money. These are definitely not my kinds of odds. The SEC also estimates there are in any event only 5,000 day-traders at most in the USA. A lot of hoopla by a few over very little in my view.

If you are still curious and want to find out more then visit the FSA site at *www.fsa.gov.uk* Daypicks (*www.daypicks.com*), the Trading Tactics website (*www.tradingtactics.com*), Elite Trader (*www.elitetrader.com*) for online chat about day-trading, and Active Traders Network (*www.activetraders.net*) for more educational materials. For a UK perspective try *www.daytrader.co.uk*.

Finally, the *good* thing about day-trading is that, rather like poor gamblers at the roulette wheel, day-traders remove themselves from the market anyway.

## Diversification

Remember the four rules of diversification:

1  **Too much** can be as bad as too little (on the basis that you will be spread too widely to monitor your positions properly).

2  **Correlation.** There is no point buying ten different stocks, say, if all are in the same sector because they will be highly correlated.

3  **Size of positions.** It is not diversification to have $100 in nine positions and $10,000 in the tenth.

4  **Risk.** There needs to be similarity of risk between your positions for diversification to be effective. Futures and stocks hardly count as diversifying each other.

## Summary

The professional trader examines a combination of technical and fundamental analysis as part of a trading plan. It is possible to make a list of factors commonly examined by fundamental and technical analysts and then test these historically against price data as part of a trading plan. The key thing to remember is to enter a position when the evidence is overwhelming in favour of a price move – otherwise stay out.

- A good trading tactic results in the selection of the best prospects presented by the trading strategy.
- Upside and downside targets should be set as well as exiting after passage of time.
- Journal keeping and an awareness of the types of failing traders are two additional ways to reduce potential losses.
- Abide by the four rules of diversification.

# 9

# Mutual funds, investment trusts and unit trusts

**❝ The market has intelligence beyond what our minds can comprehend ❞**

**Pat Arbor**  Former Chairman, Chicago Board of Trade

# In this chapter

This chapter has a selection of the best sites for mutual funds and investment trusts/unit trusts (the UK equivalent of mutual funds).

*Table 9.1 Comparison of mutual fund sites*

|  | Ranking | Quotes | News | Filters | Fundamental analysis |
|---|---|---|---|---|---|
| Mutual Fund Investor's Center www.mfea.com | ** | ✓ | ✓ | ✓ | ✗ |
| Interactive Investor www.iii.co.uk | ** | ✓ | ✓ | ✓ | ✓ |
| Morning Star www.morningstar.net | *** | ✓ | ✓ | ✗ | ✓ |
| Mutual Funds Online www.mfmag.com | *** | ✓ | ✓ | ✓ | ✓ |
| Net Worth networth.galt.com | ** | ✓ | ✓ | ✓ | ✓ |
| Moneyworld www.moneyworld.co.uk | * | ✓ | ✗ | ✗ | ✓ |
| Trustnet www.trustnet.co.uk | * | ✓ | ✗ | ✗ | ✓ |
| Brill www.brill.com | *** | ✓ | ✓ | ✗ | ✓ |
| Fabian www.fabian.com | *** | ✗ | ✓ | ✓ | ✓ |
| Find a Fund www.findafund.com | ** | ✓ | ✓ | ✓ | ✓ |
| Micropal www.micropal.com | *** | ✓ | ✓ | ✓ | ✓ |

*** A very good, model site that is easy to navigate and has a large selection of high-quality information.

** A good site with much information of use provided in a readily accessible manner.

* Some useful bits of information and worth a visit. Could come in useful.

Any site below * is not listed as it is simply not recommended or the sites already listed cover the same material better.

## The sites

## Mutual Fund Investor's Center **

www.mfea.com    US

### How to use this site and what for

This site is produced with the mutual fund investor in mind and is an excellent resource. The Mutual Fund Education Alliance has produced it and the principal aim is to provide high-quality information for the individual mutual fund investor. Use this for its portfolio tool as well as sound mutual fund commentary and use the performance ratings to get a quick handle on some of the top funds.

## Interactive Investor **

www.iii.co.uk   UK

### How to use this site and what for

Micropal is a definitive source of quality information relating to investment trusts and unit trusts. This site also has links to some leading trusts such as GAM, M&G and Fidelity; iii is loaded with investment trust and other personal finance information. Use this part of the site to get details on investment trust performance and to find out about things like quotes, areas of specialization and strategies, e.g. income, growth etc.

## Morningstar ***

www.morningstar.net    US

### How to use this site and what for

Morningstar is one of the most respected providers of mutual fund data and analysis and its research reports are some of the most thorough available. This site is perfect for the serious mutual funder. It has excellent message boards and probably has more mutual fund discussions than just about any other site. Also use this one for detailed mutual fund information as well as performance information of course.

## Mutual Funds Online ***

### Mutual Funds Online

### Quick Registration Desk - It's Free!

Welcome to our Quick Registration Desk. Registration is fast, free, and without obligation. It's the only way assure continuing access to Mutual Funds Online. Just use the form below, or call 800-442-9000 or [Place a Call] and one of our representatives will call you back within 5 minutes.

You receive these benefits when you register now:

- Weekly e-mail newsletter (optional; see below)
- Wondering what funds to buy now? You'll receive a free copy of one of *Mutual Funds Magazine's* sister advisory publications: *Mutual Fund Forecaster, Mutual Fund Buyer's Guide, Fund Watch,* or *Income Fund Outlook.* (Postal address required )
- Unlimited access to current and all back issues of *Mutual Funds Magazine*
- Fund Performance Calculator ("Screens, Reports, Tools")
- Load Performance Calculator ("Screens, Reports, Tools")
- Top Performing Fund of the Day ("Screens, Reports, Tools")

To enjoy all these benefits, fill out this short form. Click the "Done" button when you're finished.

Asterisks [*] indicate required answers

Email Address......... [_____] * (xyz@mycompany.com)
Name (First/M/Last) .. [_____] * [_] [_____] *
Company

www.mfmag.com   US

### How to use this site and what for

I like this clear and easily navigable site. There is ample information and while some of it overlaps with other sites a lot of it complements the information on other mutual fund sites. Use this site for the screening facility, which allows you to search for a mutual fund based on criteria you enter.

## Net Worth **

networth.galt.com    US

### How to use this site and what for

One of the earlier and most reputable sites to have an internet presence. It covers all the major categories of information we would look for in a mutual fund site. Again, use this site for its screening tool. Other information, such as mutual fund profiles, news and commentary, mirrors that available elsewhere.

## Moneyworld *

www.moneyworld.co.uk **UK**

### How to use this site and what for

It does its job, without bells or whistles. This is more a personal finance site and has some excellent educational material – well worth an examination. Use the site for investment trust background information – like why they are good to own – as well as for specific information about particular investment trusts.

## Trustnet *

www.trustnet.co.uk    **UK**

### How to use this site and what for

Since you are starved of choice in the UK for investment trust information, this is as good as it gets. There is little wrong with the site, but by mutual fund site standards it is impoverished. Use this just to check there isn't investment trust information here that is not elsewhere.

## Brill's Mutual Funds Interactive ***

www.brill.com

### How to use this site and what for

This is a well-designed site and one of the best. Use it for the excellent commentary on mutual fund and industry issues. Use the message boards as a source of quality information too.

## Fabian Investment Resources ***

www.fabian.com

### How to use this site and what for

Use this site for its buy and sell recommendations. It also has a 'lemon list' of the worst mutual funds. The editor's picks and market overview are good too.

## Find a Fund **

www.findafund.com

### How to use this site and what for

Use the 'Top Performers' pages to find funds that beat common industry-wide benchmarks that week and see the 'Category Spotlight' for funds which specialize in particular industries. Use also for its excellent educational materials.

## Micropal ***

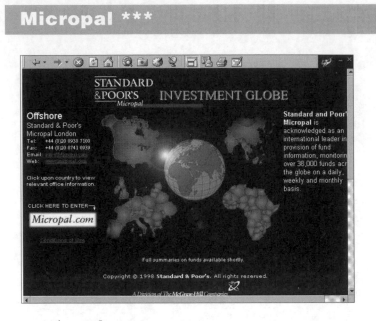

www.micropal.com

### How to use this site and what for

Use this one as a complete global mutual fund resource. The performance talks are useful in that they compare funds within each sector.

## Summary

With so much money invested with fund managers, there is an incredible amount of information on the internet about such funds, much of the information being free. Even if your money is fully invested, the internet can be a good way of keeping an eye on things.

# 10

# The future and its options: futures and options sites

*" Fewer and fewer traders trade by the seat of their pants and the traders that do tend to be futures traders "*

**Jon Najarian**  Chairman and CEO, Mercury Trading

## In this chapter

In this chapter the most helpful sites for futures and options traders are listed and described. Of course, futures and options exist in relation to underlying products and these sites deal not only with the futures and options but with the many underlying products, e.g. equities and commodities. However, their emphasis tends to be on the nature of futures and options. Here I want to explain how to use the best sites.

## The mark of quality: good futures and options sites

### Quotes

Given the vast number of futures and options contracts available on just one underlying asset, quotes and 'chains' can be very useful. Real-time would be most helpful since we're talking leverage and want to keep a close eye on prices.

### Market commentary

The more frequent the better. A good site will be quite detailed and produced by a competent trader.

### Charts

Again, preferably intra-day.

## Education

A peculiarity of futures and options sites is the wealth of educational material. This is where the internet comes into its own: free education, 24 hours a day. A good site will have well-designed and easy to understand articles and essays.

## Discussion groups

Always useful for bouncing ideas around.

*Table 10.1  Comparison of futures and options sites*

| Name and web address | Ranking | Quotes | Market commentary | Charts | Education | Discussion forum |
|---|---|---|---|---|---|---|
| 1010 Wall Street www.1010wallstreet.com | *** | ✗ | ✓ | ✗ | ✓ | ✗ |
| Commodity Futures Trading Commission www.cftc.com | * | ✗ | ✓ | ✗ | ✓ | ✗ |
| Futures Net www.futures.net | *** | ✓ | ✓ | ✓ | ✓ | ✓ |
| Futures Online www.futuresmag.com | *** | ✓ | ✓ | ✓ | ✓ | ✓ |
| FutureSource www.futuresource.com | *** | ✓ | ✓ | ✗ | ✓ | ✓ |
| INO Global www.inoglobal.com | *** | ✓ | ✓ | ✓ | ✓ | ✓ |
| MarketPlex www.cbot.com/mplex | *** | ✓ | ✓ | ✓ | ✓ | ✗ |
| Options Direct www.options-direct.co.uk | * | ✗ | ✓ | ✓ | ✓ | ✗ |

*** A very good, model site that is easy to navigate and has a large selection of high-quality information.
** A good site with much information of use provided in a readily accessible manner.
* Some useful bits of information and worth a visit. Could come in useful.
   Any site below * is not listed as it is simply not recommended or the sites already listed cover the same material better.

## The sites

## 1010 Wall Street ***

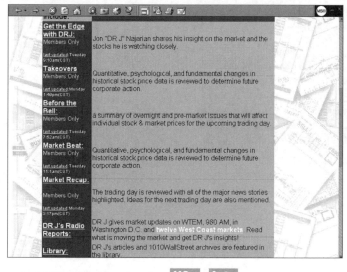

www.1010wallstreet.com  US  Int

### How to use this site and what for

Jon Najarian, who founded this site and was profiled in *The Mind of a Trader*, is a director of the Chicago Board Options Exchange and a leading options trader as well as chairman of Mercury Trading. The commentary here is excellent because it is provided by him and not only is he phenomenally successful at what he does, he is experienced and actually trades: he doesn't just stand on the sidelines. The downside is that all the commentary is by subscription only. But would you really expect it for free when it's that good?

Use this site to get a blow-by-blow detailed insight into how an experienced, successful trader thinks about his positions. It is similar to James Cramer (*www.thestreet.com*) or Alpesh Patel (*www.ukinvest.com*)!

## Commodity Futures Trading Commission *

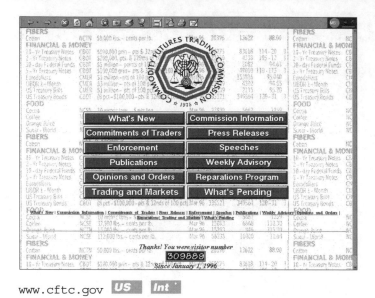

www.cftc.gov  US    Int'

### How to use this site and what for

This regulatory body's site should be used for industry news and legal matters concerning futures. Your aim in visiting it is mainly to keep half an eye on the future of futures, and for general background to your trading rather than actual trading tips, ideas or news.

## Futures Net ***

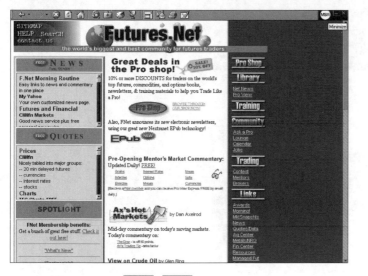

www.futures.net  US  Int

### How to use this site and what for

The main attraction of this site, which claims to be 'the world's biggest and best community for futures traders', is its discussion group. While it will not be useful for all futures traders, it is a dedicated and focused area. Use it for seeing what others are talking about, which may provide useful trading ideas, or use it to post your own queries. Whilst it has lots of other features, the discussion frame is the best.

## Futures Online ***

www.futuresmag.com  **US**  **Int**

### How to use this site and what for

This online version of the offline magazine has useful and professionally written market commentary and full articles from the magazine. Use the site for trading pieces about improving trading performance as well as for broader futures issues.

## FutureSource ***

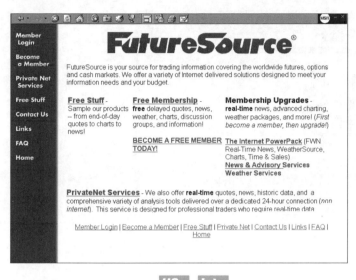

www.futuresource.com  US  Int

### How to use this site and what for

Future's World News provides the news and market commentary for this site which is its key feature. Worth a visit if you are looking for market commentary to see how it ties in with your needs compared to the other sites. It also has futures quotes and you can use it for the customizable portfolio as well as for charting. Again, the discussion boards can be useful and are of a good standard.

## INO Global ***

www.ino.com  **US**  **Int**

### How to use this site and what for

'Global' is correct: this is an umbrella site with ample links and its own content, which, taken together, provide comprehensive coverage of futures- and options-related materials.

Use eXtreme Futures for a useful list of the biggest winners and losers of the futures contracts. You can set these to get alerts too. Also, use the message boards to get a feel for what devoted amateur and professional traders are concerned about.

## Market Plex ★★★

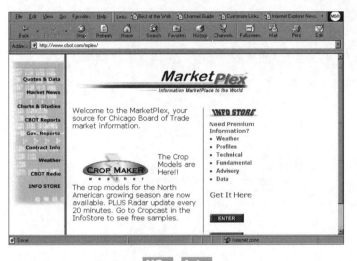

`www.cbot.com/mplex` US Int

### How to use this site and what for

This site is part of the Chicago Board of Trade's excellent web site. MarketPlex is another umbrella site and an excellent source of information for the futures and options trader. It is actually geared for professional traders and so is more than adequate for the non-professional. The focus is on all the ancillary information a trader might need, e.g. weather information for, say, FCOJ traders.

## Options Direct*

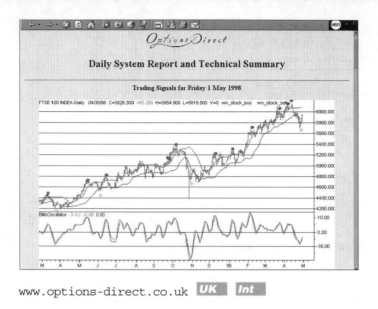

www.options-direct.co.uk   **UK**   **Int**

### How to use this site and what for

Options Direct is actually a brokerage firm but provides useful information and analysis for the UK options trader. While anaemic compared to US sites, if you're trading LIFFE products this site is actually one of the best!

## Summary

Futures and options sites cover a wide range of underlying products because there is a wide range of products on which futures and options are available. The choice and coverage of markets are diverse for the trader and the individual considering derivatives. Because most derivatives traders tend to be more experienced than stock traders, sites tend to be more professional. There is certainly no shortage of quality information.

# 11

# Options analysis software

*❝ Sudden money is going from zero to two hundred dollars a week. The rest doesn't count ❞*

**Neil Simon**

## In this chapter

Whether they use fundamental analysis or technical analysis or a combination of both, and whether they trade stocks, futures, indices or currency options, many options traders also use special options analysis software which helps them in making their trading decisions. Such software relates specifically to the technicalities of options. The details of the sites explain what the software does. This will, of course, make most sense to you if you have an understanding of options, for which see the appendix on understanding options basics and the educational sites.

Although it is often possible to trade successfully without such software, the calculations should be undertaken by options traders whether they use the software or not. Consequently such software is most useful if:

- You plan to undertake more complex strategies, e.g. butterflies, rather than simple call and put purchases.

- You are not confident (despite reading the options basics appendix and following the options educational sites) with the mathematical calculations.

- You require to do the calculations speedily.

- You would prefer a graphical representation of likely option scenarios.

- You are concerned you may be missing out on greater profits by using different strategies.

Here we list sites of the best options analysis software vendors.

## What to look for

Options analysis software needs to be able to do certain things in order to be more than a mere unnecessary add-on.

### Option pricing model

The software will calculate a fair value for the option based on industry standard option pricing models. This can be a useful benchmark guide for comparing prices with the market price. The idea of course is to find overvalued options for sale or undervalued ones for purchase.

### Auto-position search

Good software should be able to search which options strategies are the most suitable, based on the user's trading objectives. The search should be based not only on common strategies, such as call and put purchases, but also on less common ones such as butterflies and strangles.

Usually the user can enter assumptions about target price, volatility and expiry. The software will then apply each strategy to the assets available, given the user's assumptions. A list should then be produced ranking each strategy by corresponding likely profit (and sometimes maximum profit and risk). The more ranges the user can input the better. For example, instead of having to input a target price, the user might input a range or a date and then, based on the asset's underlying historical volatility, the software will use the most likely price at that date.

### Option breakdown

Any software in this category should be able to analyse totally any given option, providing information such as volatility, 'Greek' risk measurements (delta, gamma, vega, theta, rho, lambda), time and intrinsic value, and open interest. Of course, you would have to be familiar with how to use this. See the reading list if you are new to options.

### Position charts

These can be a helpful visual aid graphically showing how the position's profit/loss profile will look as time passes. Software should display 'what if' scenarios based on the user's own assumptions, so best, worst and most likely case scenarios can be built up. These charts help you to understand risk better.

### Probability calculator

This calculates the probability of the underlying or option price being at a certain level by a certain time (input by the user). The purpose behind this is to calculate the chances of your making money on a particular trade.

---

### Hot tip 👍

*Check it out   Although many of the top options analysis software providers deliver the same services, there are, after all, only so many ways to calculate an option's theoretical fair value. It is the way they display the information and how user-friendly the software screens are that make the major difference. So, make sure you take the time, and have the patience, to try their demos first.*

## Major quote vendors supported

We obviously want a software package that supports data downloads from the major quote vendors. That reduces additional costs. It also means that we are not tied to the software provider's own data.

## Other features

These can be a useful but non-essential bonus. Two common ones are pager alerts, i.e. you are paged when certain price targets are met, and the portfolio tracker, to track your option positions.

Table 11.1 contains a breakdown of various options analysis vendors and their products (see also Diagram 11.1).

*Table 11.1 Summary of options analysis vendors and products*

| Name and web address | Option pricing model | Auto-position search | Option breakdown | Position charts | Probability calculator | Products* | Major quote vendors | Other features |
|---|---|---|---|---|---|---|---|---|
| OptionStation (Omega Research) www.omegaresearch.com | ✓ | ✓ | ✓ | ✓ | ✓ | csifb | ✓ | Alert |
| OptionVue (Option Vue) www.optionvue.com | ✓ | ✓ | ✓ | ✓ | ✓ | csifb | ✓ | Portfolio tracker |
| Optionscope (Equis) www.equis.com | ✓ | ✗ | ✓ | ✓ | ✗ | csifb | ✓ | |
| Option Pro (Essex Trading Co) www.essextrading.com | ✓ | ✓ | ✓ | ✓ | ✓ | sf | ✓ | Portfolio tracker |
| Options Lab (Mantic Software) www.manticsoft.com | ✓ | ✗ | ✓ | ✓ | ✗ | csifb | | |
| OptionTrader (AustinSoft) www.austin-soft.com | ✓ | ✓ | ✓ | ✓ | ✗ | csifb | ✓ | Portfolio tracker |

* c = currency options; s = stock options; i = index options; f = futures options; b = bond options

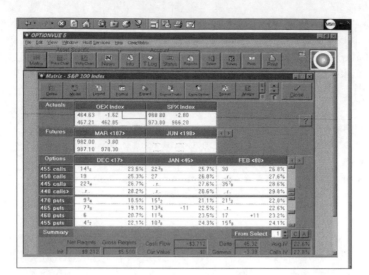

*Diagram 11.1*
*OptionVue*

# Summary

The internet sites of options analysis software provide detailed online brochures and often downloadable demos. The chances of making a bad decision should be negligible. The key thing to remember is to take your time in making your decision because the chances are you will be using the software for a long time.

# 12

# Exchanges

> **❝** *Nobody ever achieved greatness by doing nothing.*
> *You have got to step out and do something*
> *and take a chance and get your teeth kicked in* **❞**

**Pat Arbor**  Former Chairman, Chicago Board of Trade

## In this chapter

This chapter contains all the internet sites operated by the exchanges. The best thing about them is that they are **all free.**

## Top exchange sites

Exchanges can be a good source of free or heavily subsidized educational and background material. A good exchange site should have the following character-istics, so look for them and use them – it's what they are there for.

### Exchange history/working

Such a section in the site tells you more about how the exchange came into being and why, and also how it works today, how orders are routed, the main products it deals in, etc.

### Publications list

A good site should have a list of recommended reading for both beginners and more advanced traders. It should also provide a wide variety of free educational materials including videos and printed matter which can be ordered from the site. Where possible I have ordered a selection of free publications to gauge their value.

### Data download/quotes

Skeleton plans will rarely refer to an exchange as a source of data. Exchanges are, of course, the source for all commercial data providers and sometimes – if the exchange is on a sufficiently commercial and experienced footing – the exchange itself can be a good and efficient source of historical and daily price quotes.

*Hot tip*

*Remember, the product you are interested in may be traded on several different exchanges, so if you want to know more about it, check for free information available from each of the exchanges – that way if there is something you do not understand from one of the exchange's free publications, you may understand it from another.*

## Market reports

Although these tend to be a little bland on exchange sites, often only reporting volume and describing chronological price changes, they can be a good way to get a better feel of what actually happened that day. Exchanges rarely attempt to place a journalistic spin on a day's market activities, leaving you to make your own mind up.

## Rules

Some exchanges list their membership rules – for most readers this will be of curiosity value only.

## Other

Some exchanges are beginning to realize that there is nothing stopping them developing internet sites similar to those provided by commercial financial sites and so are now including charts, fundamental research, news, listing of the most active products, etc.

Table 12.1 shows a ranking of major US exchanges (see also Diagrams 12.1, 12.2, 12.3). Table 12.2 covers the major global exchanges (and see Diagrams 12.4–12.7).

*Diagram 12.1
Chicago Board of
Trade*

*Table 12.1  Comparison of major US exchanges*

| Name and web address | Rating | Products | Exchange history/ workings | Publications | Data download/ quotes | Market reports | Additional comments |
|---|---|---|---|---|---|---|---|
| American Stock Exchange www.amex.com | ** | Stocks and derivatives | ✓ | ✓ | ✓ | ✗ | |
| Arizona Stock Exchange www.azx.com | * | Stocks | ✓ | ✗ | ✓ | ✗ | |
| Chicago Board of Trade www.cbot.com | *** | Bonds, financial futures and options, commodities | ✓ | ✓ | ✓ | ✓ | The world's largest futures and options exchange |
| Chicago Board Options Exchange www.cboe.com | *** | Options on stocks and all futures | ✓ | ✓ | ✓ | ✓ | |
| Chicago Mercantile Exchange www.cme.com | *** | Futures and options on financial products and commodities | ✓ | ✓ | ✓ | ✓ | The world's third-largest futures and options exchange |
| Chicago Stock Exchange www.chicagostockex.com | ** | Stocks, warrants, notes, bonds | ✓ | ✗ | ✓ | ✗ | The second-largest stock exchange in the US. A good source of free stock research information |
| Coffee, Sugar, & Cocoa Exchange www.csce.com | ** | Futures and options on milk and coffee, sugar, cocoa | ✓ | ✓ | ✓ | ✗ | |
| Kansas City Board of Trade www.kcbt.com | ** | Futures and options on wheat, gas, value line stock indices | ✓ | ✓ | ✓ | ✓ | |
| Mid-America Exchange www.midam.com | ** | Liquid futures contracts | ✓ | ✓ | ✓ | ✗ | |
| Minneapolis Grain Exchange www.mgex.com | * | Grain and fish futures and options | ✓ | ✓ | ✓ | ✗ | |
| Nasdaq Exchange www.nasdaq.com | ** | Mainly technology stocks | ✓ | ✓ | ✓ | ✓ | Good basics for stock investors |
| New York Cotton Exchange www.nyce.com | ** | Futures and options on cotton, oranges, potatoes, financials | ✗ | ✗ | ✓ | ✓ | |
| New York Mercantile Exchange www.nymex.com | *** | Futures and options on energy, Eurotop, metals | ✓ | ✓ | ✓ | ✓ | |
| New York Stock Exchange www.nyse.com | ** | Over 2,500 stocks | ✓ | ✓ | ✓ | ✓ | The largest stock exchange in the US |
| Pacific Exchange www.pacificex.com | ** | Stocks and options | ✓ | ✗ | ✓ | ✗ | |
| Philadelphia Stock Exchange www.liffe.com | *** | Stocks and options on sectors, stocks, currencies | ✓ | ✓ | ✓ | ✓ | A good site for educational materials |

*** A very informative site with ample free educational material, easy to navigate and a model exchange site.

** A very good site with some free material. Should be informative.

* Worth a visit and most traders should end up learning something about the exchange or the products it trades.

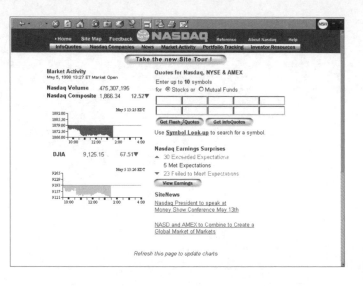

*Diagram 12.2*
*Nasdaq*

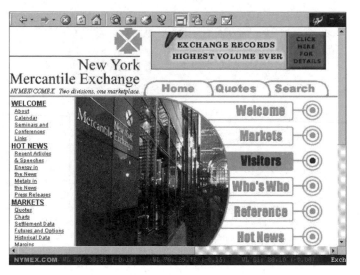

*Diagram 12.3*
*Nymex*

*Table 12.2 Comparison of major global exchanges*

| Name and web address | Rating | Products | Exchange history/ workings | Publications | Data download/ quotes | Market reports | Additional comments |
|---|---|---|---|---|---|---|---|
| Australian Stock Exchange www.asx.com.au | ** | Stocks and bonds | ✓ | ✓ | ✓ | ✓ | |
| Bombay Stock Exchange www.bseindia.com | ** | Stocks | ✗ | ✗ | ✓ | ✓ | Portfolio manager |
| Deutsche Terminboerse www.exchange.de | ** | Futures and options | ✓ | ✓ | ✓ | ✗ | |
| Hong Kong Futures Exchange www.hkfe.com | ** | Futures and options on financial products | ✓ | ✓ | ✓ | ✓ | |
| Italian Stock Exchange www.robot1.textnet.it/finanza | * | Stocks | ✗ | ✗ | ✓ | ✗ | |
| Kuala Lumpur Options & Financial Futures Exchange www.kloffe.com.my | * | Financial futures and options | ✓ | ✓ | ✓ | ✗ | One of the world's newest exchanges |
| Kuala Lumpur Stock Exchange www.klse.com.my | ** | Stocks | ✓ | ✓ | ✓ | ✓ | |
| Lisbon Stock Exchange www.bvl.pt | * | Stocks | ✗ | ✗ | ✓ | ✗ | |
| London International Financial Futures Options and Commodities Exchange www.liffe.com | *** | Futures and options on most products | ✓ | ✓ | ✓ | ✓ | The world's second-largest futures exchange |
| London Metal Exchange www.lme.co.uk | ** | Metal futures and options | ✓ | ✗ | ✓ | ✗ | |
| London Stock Exchange www.stockex.co.uk | * | Stocks | ✓ | ✓ | ✗ | ✗ | |
| Madrid Stock Exchange www.bolsamadrid.es | ** | Futures and options | ✓ | ✓ | ✓ | ✓ | |
| MATIF www.matif.fr | ** | Financial futures and options | ✓ | ✓ | ✓ | ✗ | Based in Paris |
| MEFF www.meff.es | ** | Fixed income futures and options | ✓ | ✓ | ✓ | ✗ | Based in Barcelona. Some excellent internships |
| Montreal Exchange www.me.org | ** | Stocks, options and futures | ✓ | ✓ | ✓ | ✗ | |
| OM Stockholm www.omgroup.com | ** | Futures and options | ✓ | ✓ | ✓ | ✗ | Some information in Swedish only |
| Paris Stock Exchange www.bourse-de-paris.fr | ** | Stocks | ✓ | ✓ | ✓ | ✗ | |
| Santiago Stock Exchange www.bolsantiago.cl/ingles | ** | Stocks, futures and options | ✓ | ✓ | ✓ | ✗ | |
| Singapore International Monetary Exchange www.simex.com.sg | *** | Futures and options | ✓ | ✓ | ✓ | ✓ | |
| South African Futures Exchange www.safex.co.za | ** | Futures and options | ✓ | ✓ | ✓ | ✗ | |
| Sydney Futures Exchange www.sfe.com.au | * | Futures and options | ✓ | ✓ | ✓ | ✗ | |

continued overleaf

*Table 12.2 continued*

| Name and web address | Rating | Products | Exchange history/ workings | Publications | Data download/ quotes | Market reports | Additional comments |
|---|---|---|---|---|---|---|---|
| TIFFE www.tiffe.or.jp | ** | Futures and options | ✓ | ✓ | ✓ | ✗ | |
| Tokyo Grain Exchange www.tge.or.jp | ** | Commodity futures and options | ✓ | ✓ | ✓ | ✓ | |
| Tokyo Stock Exchange www.tse.or.jp | ** | Stocks, options and futures | ✓ | ✗ | ✓ | ✗ | |
| Vancouver Stock Exchange www.vse.com | * | Stocks | ✓ | ✓ | ✓ | ✓ | |
| Warsaw Stock Exchange yogi.ippt.gov.pl/gielda/gielda | * | Stocks | ✗ | ✗ | ✓ | ✗ | |

***    A very informative site with ample free educational material, easy to navigate and a model exchange site.

**    A very good site with some free material. Should be informative.

*    Worth a visit and most traders should end up learning something about the exchange or the products it trades.

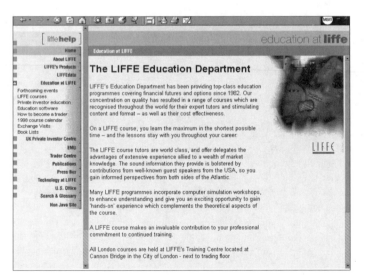

*Diagram 12.4*
*LIFFE*

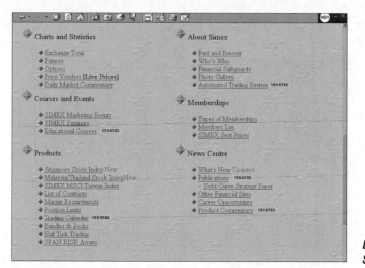

**Diagram 12.5**
**SIMEX**

**Diagram 12.6**
**Sydney Futures Exchange**

Diagram 12.7
SAFEX

## IPO or no?

Fancy doubling your money in one day? Well, in February 1999 an amazing 70 per cent of all US internet initial public pfferings (IPOs) – when a company sells its shares to the public – doubled on day one. It is because of the success of these types of stocks that IPO prospectors continue on the quest for the next Yahoo! With an increasing number of UK internet IPOs, such as the most recent, QXL.com and the prospective Scottish Telecom and Lastminute.com, how does an online trader get on the apparently gilded bandwagon? It is not as obvious as one might think and if you get it wrong, you can watch in agony as the value of your investment sinks and sinks.

Virtually every twenty-something internet entrepreneur with a smell for money and a taste for Lear Jets knows the theoretical route to becoming a self-made billionaire. You take an idea for a UK web site from one already up and running in the US. Next, stick the idea into something resembling what your MBA teacher told you was a business plan, give it a name ending in '.co.uk' or '.com' and tout it to a few venture capital funds who will gladly give you £20 million to get it started. After that, and this is the key element to making serious money, IPO it and raise £500 million from the share-buying public. All this before you turn 30.

## IPO jumpers

Shares in the UK's largest internet company, Freeserve, catapulted to a premium of 43 per cent above their offer price of 150p within minutes of their first day of trading. The US Drugstore.com was trading at a 200 per cent premium to its offer price on its first day of trading. A survey by Worldfinancenet.com found that the average gain from offer price to end-of-day one close for US internet IPOs in the first half of 1999 ranged from just under 150 per cent in February to around 45 per cent in June.

The large premium is largely due to too much money chasing too few shares. But in some cases it may also be due to underpricing by the investment banks who are bringing the issues to the market. They have an incentive to underprice to ensure the flotation is not a flop and a lot of positive, valuable publicity is created.

However, you would be wrong to think buying at the offer price is a 'sure-thing' strategy. The problem of buying at the offer price is that so many institutions have pre-allocated shares so you and I are unlikely ever to get as much stock as we would like. Moreover, you often will not know your allocation, and so will be unable to trade it until some time after day one.

## More problems

The other problem of buying at the offer price is that that is the key moment when the least is known about the company in terms of its worth, for the simple reason that its share price performance and the cumulative judgement of the market are not available. Yet that is the moment at which the most hype surrounds the stock from overanxious PR agencies and investment bankers. That makes it a dangerous strategy to buy at the offer price. Rather like the parents of a newborn child, you do not know what you have on your hands until many moons afterwards: star or flop?

A far worse strategy than buying at the offer price is to hold on to the stock until after the first day, or worse still, *buying* on the first day the stock hits the market. Worldfinancenet.com found that those who bought new net issues in the first six months of 1999 at day-one inflated prices lost an average of 9 per cent as of 25 June. Some were very much worse than the average of course – Autobytel.com, the car auction site, was down 60 per cent and Topjobs.net, a job-search site, was down 63 per cent. Exchange Holdings, the UK's second-largest internet company, fell below the issue price on the third day of trading.

Even buying several days or weeks after the flotation can be very risky – just ask the holders of Freeserve shares. That stock has fallen well below its offer price. The US IPOs often fare little better. Three of 1999's most hyped IPOs were Fashionmall.com, Comps.com, and NetObject. They currently lie 44 per cent, 60 per cent and 40 per cent respectively off their offer prices.

## Lessons

So what can we learn from all this? I have certain rules when it comes to IPOs. Firstly, if I do get stock at the offer price, I sell before the close of day one if the stock rises, and especially if it does not. If I do not know my allocation until some time after day one, then I sell at that point – I should usually still have some profit above the offer price.

Secondly, I do not buy on the first trading day of the stock. Thirdly, if this is a stock I would be interested in for the medium to long term then I monitor the price and wait for it to break its first day's highs or fall below its offer price and then rise back above it before I even consider buying it, and even then only after ample research into the stock.

If you want to find out more about IPOs and what is in the pipeline, visit *www.ukinvest.com/freeserve* and click on the IPO link, or visit *www.ipo.com*. Excuse me while I cross the 't's and dot the dot coms on my business plan …

*Diagram 12.8*
*ipo.com*

## The hidden costs of online trading

One of the key attractions of online trading is the low commission costs. Indeed, some brokers like to offer commission-free trades for limited periods.

But often overlooked by many online traders are the substantial hidden costs that gnaw away in small measures at your returns every time you trade. It is these that can kill a good trade. For the brokers too they are a concern because it is their reputations being savaged on online bulletin boards by private traders who have faced the realities of online trading costs. Reducing these hidden costs can be relatively straightforward and can save a small fortune for the online trader and indeed protect the reputation of a broker.

The greatest hidden cost to online trading is quickly becoming the inability to access your online account and therefore the inability to trade at the price you want and having to return to the market when the price has moved against you. This could be where you want to buy a stock, or sell it.

## Outages

The reasons for such broker 'outages' where you simply cannot connect to the broker's web site or log in to access your account often comes down to the fact that many online brokers can be swamped by demand for their services. In the UK market this will be a growing problem as the number of online accounts grows exponentially in the early months of the UK industry. According to JP Morgan UK online trading accounts will total two million by 2002, compared with the current level of well under 250,000. The massive potential growth is illustrated by the US experience: there the number of online trading accounts by 2002 will equal the metropolitan populations of Seattle, Chicago, Atlanta, Miami, Denver, Dallas, Boston and San Francisco combined, according to the Securities and Exchange Committee (SEC).

Schwab and DLJ Direct are just two to suffer recently from outages. The market falls after a prolonged rally, or rises sharply after a few relatively quiet days, and a legion of online traders, often short-term traders, rush to their terminals, consuming the brokers' entire electronic infrastructure: a traffic jam on the electronic super-highway. I can't get through and have to resort to swearing in five different languages; in cyberspace no broker can hear you scream.

## UK too

Halifax's (*www.halifax-online.co.uk*) recent online trading 'outage' was novel in that, rather than the cause being excess demand, their site had to be shut down due to a potential security problem. However, the reason you can't place a trade makes little difference when you see those potential profits sliding away.

Imagine that your trade size is $5,000 and you tend to do two trades a week. Now imagine you wanted to sell some Microsoft shares. As I write, today they have moved 10 per cent. So it is not inconceivable that a site outage could lead to a 5 per cent move being missed in a particular share. I have had worse, and the price rarely moves in my favour after an outage. That means a potential hidden cost of $250. If that happens once a month on average, by the end of the year you have under-performed by $3,000. I accept that this is just a hypothetical example and there are many 'if's and 'but's. However, it indicates how quickly small opportunity costs can mount up.

## Help

So, what are the practical steps you can take to reduce some of these hidden costs from not being able to place a trade? Firstly, if you are looking to sell some of your holdings, make a note of the time and the best bid. If you can't get through to the broker, this could be used as a basis for the calculation of hidden costs and complaints against a broker.

Secondly, make sure you know the telephone backup number of the broker in case internet access is down. Often it is more expensive to trade using the broker's phone service than internet service, so explain to the broker you expect only to pay the internet commission charges as their site was down and you had to use their phone service.

It is advisable to have a backup brokerage account up and funded with a different broker in case you cannot access your main broker's account.

If you feel you have suffered a loss and want to take things further then contact the broker and ask to speak to a trading desk manager or compliance officer. Follow this up with a letter detailing times and best bid prices and the eventual price at which you traded. If you get no joy then pay the SEC site a visit or in the UK the SFA site through *www.sfa.org.uk* and follow their complaints procedure and recommendations.

## Guardians

Consumer complaints to regulatory bodies seem to work in the US. The New York attorney general commenced an investigation earlier this year (2000) into online brokers following complaints stemming from site outages. The SEC, the US regulatory body charged with regulating online brokers, is also investigating outages. Even the Congressional Committee on Commerce has taken evidence on the matter. Maybe there aren't enough votes in it in the UK.

With such high-profile credibility-damaging outages you might think that technology is the greatest cost for online brokers. It's not. Maybe human resources to man all those backup phone lines and call centres? No. The major cost for online brokers is marketing to increase numbers of accounts the brokers can hardly serve. Perhaps a realignment of resources is needed to shift the current balance between customer service and customer acquisition.

In an effort to make my trading more efficient I have been thinking ever more about hidden costs recently. To make money trading online is about more than replacing a full service broker with an execution-only one, or replacing a telephone call with an internet call.

## More costs

When you place an order with an online broker, if internet traffic is busy, you may lose a few seconds before the order is executed. This often means a trader sees one price on the screen but finds that the order has executed or 'filled' at a far worse price. In my experience the 'fill' is rarely if ever at a better price than on the screen. This 'slippage' can represent a significant hidden cost to the online trader. Recently, I seem to have been particularly prone to this type of cost.

Imagine, you want to buy $5,000 of XYZ stock and the current real-time quote from your online broker is 121½ to buy. So you decide to buy 4,115 shares and place the order, expecting to pay 121½ to buy. If you are filled at 122, only a mere ½c out, then you have paid $20.58 more than you had expected.

If you have that sort of slippage on half your trades, when you are looking both to buy and to sell, and if you place two trades a week, over a year you are facing over $1,000 less in profits. And that is just one of the many hidden costs I am highlighting.

## More slippage

Another cause of slippage, in addition to heavy traffic on the internet, is insufficient broker capacity to deal with the volume of demand that can occur from time to time. The problem is so acute in America that there are dedicated sites devoted to monitoring the speed of online brokers' order execution. One such site is Keynote (*www.keynote.com/measures/brokers*).

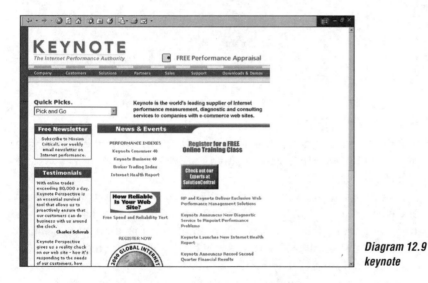

**Diagram 12.9**
**keynote**

All this is not to say you should use a traditional phone-based broker; their lines can be engaged, and that can be the case even with the world's largest brokers – I speak from infuriating experience.

## Price improvers

Some online brokers, aware of the problem of slippage, display a price 'fixed' for, say, 20 seconds, in which you can trade at that price. DLJ Direct (*www.dljdirect.co.uk*) is one such online broker providing that, although market conditions dictate whether such a 'fixed' price can be provided. Schwab (*www.schwab-europe.com*) has a similar concept. Others, like Barclays Stockbrokers (*www.barclays-stockbrokers.com*), offer 'price improvers' that try to improve on the best bid and best offer in the market – which raises the question: what were they doing before they offered that service?

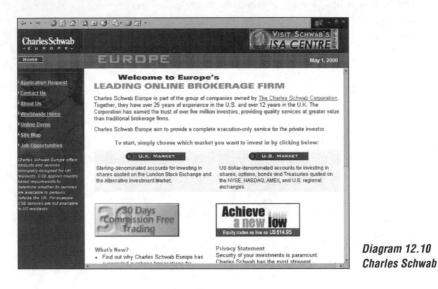

*Diagram 12.10*
*Charles Schwab*

## Reducing slippage

What can an online trader do to reduce slippage? There are several easy ways to reduce it; unfortunately each can have a negative consequence which you have to be aware of and handle with care.

Firstly you can use the limit order. A market order is an order to buy or sell as soon as possible at the best price available. A limit order, offered by most online brokers, is to buy or sell at a set price or better. In the above example you may have placed a limit on the purchase of 121¾. The downside to this is that limit orders are usually charged at a higher commission rate, and if they cannot be filled because the price has moved away from your order then you could end up with no stock as the price runs away. So those are risks to weigh up. I recently used the limit order to buy Nasdaq traded Satyam, only to find that the price kept moving away from me, and a market order may have been a cheaper option. I tend to place limit orders on very volatile stocks when I know I do not want to buy the stock above a certain price – which is close to the current price.

Another way of reducing bad fills is to be aware of how the market behaves at different times of the day. The widest spreads, the difference between the bid and the ask price, are almost always near the market open and often for half an hour afterwards, as brokers tentatively, and sometimes not so tentatively, enter orders on to order books. It is at this time you may end up paying ridiculously high prices for stock or receiving incredibly small amounts on sales.

You may have realized from the above that one of the worst things you can do is to place a market order after market close to be executed the next day.

Finally, you could just trade less! The less often you trade and the longer you hold the purchases, the less often you lose a bite out of your profits to slippage. But where's the fun in buy and hold?

## Manic markets

You know a market is getting manic when even your cleaner is putting her savings into shares with the comment, 'If I waste my time researching I will miss the price rises.' Time for me to get out maybe? The exponential growth in online trading and the irrational exuberance (or crazy hype) provide even more reason to make sure we are making as much money as we think we are from the markets.

One significant hidden cost of online trading rarely accounted for by most online traders is phone charges. Most online traders do undertake some form of research about their investments and would do so online. Typical research may involve examining price charts, news about the company and markets, and company accounts online. Most online traders would also tend to keep their portfolios online and monitor them regularly. Incidentally, the best single site I have found which provides all these services for free and to the highest level of sophistication in the UK is UK-iNvest (*www.ukinvest.com*).

## Time not on my side

A truly hidden cost probably neglected by every online trader is the cost of your time spent trading. Imagine you are one of those attracted by the seemingly great returns available by trading online. You may well reason that you want to spend six hours a week researching and monitoring your positions; then you will be spending just over 300 hours per year on trading. Assuming that the monetary gain is the only benefit you receive from online trading, based on the previous example where after taxes (but before other costs) you are left with $8,000, you are being 'paid' $27 per hour for your time.

The irony is that in order to generate larger profitable returns you need more capital, and you are likely to have more capital if you already earn far more than $27 per hour. Those working at McDonald's or near the minimum wage may find $27 per hour of their time attractive but are unlikely to have a trading lump sum necessary in the first place to trade with and generate hourly profits of that level. And of course more hours spent online do not mean more earnings; they could just mean lower profits per hour.

Account and administration charges are the final hidden costs of online trading worth mentioning. I tend to ignore these when selecting an online broker, and instead focus on service (can I get through to place an order?) and commission rates. Nevertheless, they are an out-of-pocket expense and most relevant if you have relatively little, for instance $1,000, in trading capital. Online brokers vary widely in the charges they levy, and many are quite coy about displaying these openly on their web sites. An excellent site for easy comparison of e-broker levies is MoneyWorld (*www.moneyworld.co.uk/trading/onlinetrading.html*).

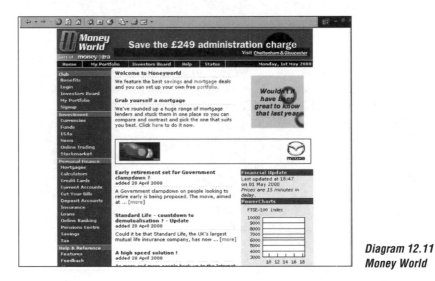

**Diagram 12.11**
**Money World**

## Earnings problems

Imagine you own a stock that month on month over several years produces a consistently rising share price. In the space of two and a half years you have a 900 per cent return. You see the price double in a year, but on one particular day, the stock has dropped 40 per cent compared to the previous day. A full year's worth of gains erased in a few hours. What does an online trader do?

The culprit under scrutiny is Unisys – a company with a market capitalization at one point recently of over $10 billion. It provides software and hardware solutions for companies. Clients include Dell, BT, UBS, and Alliance & Leicester. Not exactly a fly-by-night, high-risk, penny-share company.

However, the sharp share-price fall could have been in any company, and most people will have experienced this difficult situation I was recently faced with. Only now do I feel able to talk about it – after much psychotherapy. The cause of the fall, as is often the case with such events, was an earnings announcement.

# Choices

An online trader in this situation has three choices. You can buy more stock, do nothing, or sell out. The argument for buying more stock could be that it is now 'cheaper', that such an unusually large drop may have been a market overreaction and represent a buying opportunity.

I do not consider buying more to be a good idea after such a traumatic event to the stock price. If I have bought the stock based on certain criteria, such as expectations about growth, earnings and profits, then I would now be buying this stock right after an announcement telling me that I was wrong. In any event, a buy decision on any stock should also be based on a comparison to opportunities elsewhere. A company having made a negatively interpreted earnings announcement is rarely going to be one of the best buy opportunities around.

The second option is to do nothing. This may well be attractive if I had bought the stock to buy and hold until retirement. However, while I have some long-term holdings – stocks like Vodafone, Cisco, Oracle, Lucent and Sun Microsystems, I generally trade short-term. You see I feel life is too short to buy and hold until the day before I die, and spend the money on my death bed.

The danger of doing nothing in this situation is that we are choosing to ignore a very important piece of market information. Buy and hold is one thing; buy and hope is quite different.

Option three is to sell some or all of the holdings. This is a difficult choice for most traders because, as Pat Arbor, the former Chairman of the Chicago Board of Trade, explains in *The Mind of a Trader*, 'a loss is not just a loss of money but a blow to the ego'. Needless to say I do not suffer from such ego problems!

# Handling losses

A loss is also difficult to face because many traders feel that they need to win on every trade. The important thing is not the number of winners you have, but how much money you make and the two are not always directly linked. I know many traders who win nine trades in a row only to lose on the tenth all the previous nine gains.

But how does one know whether the stock has fallen to the point where it should be sold? There are many reasons why one may wish to sell a stock, but there is one overriding rule that should be used in order to limit downside risk. The rule, taken this time from Bill Lipschutz, former Global Head of Forex at Salomon Brothers, presented in *The Mind of a Trader*, is to risk only about 2 per cent of your total trading capital on any single trade.

For instance, if you have £20,000 to trade with, and divide that into 20 portions of £1,000 in order to reduce risk through diversification, then you should not suffer a loss greater than £200 on any single £1,000 trade. That is because £200 is 2 per cent of your total trading capital of £20,000. With the downside protected, you could go through prolonged losing streaks without the fear that you will exhaust your capital. Again, a buy and holder may well just hold on.

Equally important to learning to love your small losses so you can redeploy the capital into a more fruitful trading opportunity is to learn something from those losses – after all, if I have paid the market something, I sure want to get some value out of the expense.

## Lessons learnt

So what did I learn from the Unisys case? Perhaps more analysis? Well, the company had revenue growth that doubled the previous year, decreasing expenses year on year, increasing operating income, reduced debt and interest expenditure and therefore increased earnings per share each year resulting in strong share-price growth.

An important lesson I was reminded of was that expectations drive prices, even for very profitable companies. If earnings miss expectations then even if they and revenue, assets etc. grow, the price can drop. But that is trading for beginners: there was a more important lesson.

The price jumped because what occurred was unexpected. The unexpected by definition is very difficult to, well, expect. It is unforeseeable, and that is why once it occurred the price jumped downwards. The ultimate lesson from this was that 'sh*t happens', so deal with it. Follow the 2 per cent rule to limit risk. Of course, you are free to try to sell well before facing a 2 per cent loss; the rule is just an absolute bottom line to protect trading capital.

If you wish to plot the price chart of Unisys, or for that matter any UK or US stock (or Canadian or Italian stock!), I recommend *www.ukinvest.com* for charting. Newswires provide a quick and easy way to discover what corporate earnings expectations are. AFX is available through brokers like DLJ Direct (*www.dljdirect.co.uk,*) and other such news companies include FT.com (*www.ft.com*) and Bloomberg (*www.bloomberg.co.uk*).

*Diagram 12.12*
*Bloomberg.co.uk*

# Just for non-Americans: the hows and whys of trading US stocks online

I am even more convinced that UK online traders should have a large number of US stocks in their portfolios. I think the major reason UK investors persist with UK stocks is a lack of information about the sound reasons and practicalities involved in trading US stocks. It is far easier in my experience to trade US stocks than UK ones. Before I explain why, I recap the three key attractions of the US market: commissions, stamp duty and performance.

## Commissions, stamp duty and performance

Commissions tend to be significantly lower trading US stocks through a US discount broker, such as the excellent and highly reliable Ameritrade (*www.ameritrade.com*) or the popular Datek (*www.datek.com*), than trading UK stocks through a UK online broker. For instance, Ameritrade charges $8 commission flat rate on any size of trade.

Additionally, there is no stamp duty on the purchase of US stocks, thereby reducing cost of purchase even further. Visit *www.stampoutstampduty.co.uk*, the online campaign to abolish that tax, for more details. UK stamp duty is a disservice to great UK companies because it encourages traders such as me to invest instead in foreign stocks.

US market outperformance continues to support my decision to have a significant number of US positions. All major US indices, including the Nasdaq 100, S&P 500 and Dow Jones Industrial, have significantly outperformed the FTSE 100 over the past ten years although, admittedly, the TechMark index has outperformed all major US indices since its inception.

## Service

Commissions, stamp duty and performance aside, the level of e-broker service is a key attraction to trading US stocks. I have never had a 'denial of service' problem, where the site is down due to heavy traffic, with my US broker. My experience with UK e-brokers (including US ones with a UK base) is that I would feel privileged and extremely lucky to be able to access their web sites during busy market periods.

The excellent site *www.actualit.com/keynote/uk_onlinetrading* measures the site access times of e-brokers and other UK financial sites. The new TD Waterhouse (*www.tdwaterhouse.co.uk*), MyBroker (*www.mybroker.co.uk*), DLJ Direct (*www.dljdirect.co.uk*) and Stocktrade (*www.stocktrade.co.uk*) are four of the best performers, while Schwab (*www.schwab-europe.com*) and E*Trade (*www.etrade.co.uk*) are two of the worst performers for site access times. Keynote in the US (*www.keynote.com*) does the same for US e-brokers.

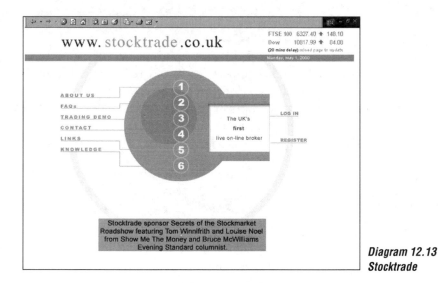

**Diagram 12.13**
**Stocktrade**

Regarding the level of service, the quantity and quality of free research available on US e-broker sites, (such as stock screening based on fundamental criteria) beyond the basic quotes, company profiles and graphs are far superior to those of their UK cousins, making stock-picking ideas and decisions a lot easier. Compare for instance the quantity of information on the Ameritrade site (*www.ameritrade.com*) with that on Barclays Stockbrokers (*www.barclays-stockbrokers.co.uk*) – the latter is anorexic by comparison, yet both are discount brokers.

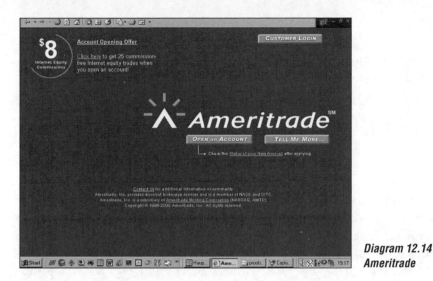

Diagram 12.14
Ameritrade

This will change with the growth of sites such as the new and promising The Street (*www.thestreet.co.uk*) and the insightful and focused CityWire (*www.citywire.co.uk*). UK-iNvest offers stock screening and Digital Look will do so imminently. For a start, UK e-brokers need to begin making alliances with these types of sites and those such as Bloomberg and FT.com to find a way of offering some of their content on e-broker sites. It makes sense for broker, customer and content provider. Yet e-broker management seem slow in knowing which deals to strike and with whom.

Diagram 12.15
Citywire

## Choices

Choice of stocks is an added advantage of trading the US markets. For instance one of my favourite sub-industry groups is the telecoms equipment service companies. In the US I have around 300 stocks to choose from in this group, including Corsair, Anadigics and Westell Technologies, each of which has currently increased over 200 per cent since the start of 2000. In the UK, there are not even that many stocks in the whole of the TechMark.

Choice of stocks is further enhanced by the availability of ADRs and ADSs (American depository receipts and stocks) which can essentially be thought of as the listings of non-US company shares in dollars traded on US exchanges. So I can diversify my holdings to include non-UK and non-US companies without worrying about opening accounts in different currencies and countries. Consequently some of my key ADS holdings include the two Indian giants, Infosys and Satyam, and Telecom Italia, France Telecom, Deutsche Telecom, Ericsson, Nokia and Telefonos de Mexico.

But what are some of the key practical difficulties to trading US stocks? Opening a US brokerage account is as easy as opening a UK one; simply go to the relevant web site and download the online application form. Transferring funds is equally straightforward; the application form will provide instructions on wiring funds from your UK bank account to the US brokerage account.

Of course you will be converting into dollars, but the cost of that and the currency risk appear minimal at present – after all the mighty dollar is the world reserve currency.

## Taxes

Taxes should not prevent you from trading US stocks. If you pay capital gains tax on your UK trading, you would also do so on your US trading (gains being converted from dollars to sterling). Most Britons would not be taxed in the US, and the e-broker will usually provide you with a 'W-8 form' exempting you from US taxes.

You would receive annual reports, dividends and trade confirmations in the same way you do with a UK e-broker. But what about the UK brokers offering US share dealing, such as Schwab and DLJ Direct? I prefer going to the US brokers directly as opposed to through the UK conduit. There are more US brokers to choose from (a list of the highest ranked can be found at *www.gomez.com*) than UK brokers offering US trading.

And what about investor protection? The UK has the FSA as its e-broker regulatory body; the US has the SEC, which has far more resources, albeit more firms to regulate, and a far more vocal, proactive and prominent chairman acting on the behalf of private investors. Your investments would of course be covered by regulatory financial safeguards.

So, clearly, US stock trading is *Yankee Doodle Dandy*!

# Trade Europe online

I want to buy European stocks online. Not that I am tired of UK and US companies: it's just that there are a lot more out there and it is easier to trade than ever. From my workstation I can reach further and faster and own more thanks to online trading. It is becoming cheap and easy, albeit with cautions.

## Choices, choices

So do you fancy being able to own a bit of Telecom Italia, France Telecom, Deutsche Telecom, Canal+, Mannesmann (I know some executives at Vodafone might be interested in this one). For those not technology-inclined, how about some Nestlé washed down with some Heineken before you leave in your BMW, or Fiat if you prefer? In any event, having the choice would be nice.

The reasons for trading European stocks are compelling. Firstly, Europe leads the US on mobile telephony and wireless applications. We are the home of the leading exciting mobile communications companies – Vodafone, Ericsson, Nokia and Orange to name just four. It is European research and development that is at the forefront of most wireless web access.

Secondly, internet growth and adoption are behind those in the US, but catching up as companies learn from US experiences. This has led to a wave of US money and corporations flooding this way. We are the emerging market now, the New World for the internet. The land grab is here. This makes European companies even more valuable assets for takeover mergers, allies, or just plain organic growth.

Thirdly, the choice of European picks provides me with a wider selection of companies from which to choose the very best. The wider the choice, the greater the chance I will pick winners, assuming my research remains diligent. Moreover, I am diversified across economies, which should reduce risk. Of course with global companies you can do that anyway.

But choice brings difficulties. I suggest that for private investors it is going to be a problem to monitor more than 30 stocks closely at a time. Even that is a high number if you are trading short-term and have a day job. I try to keep 20 in my portfolio, although it can sometimes reach more, and have another ten or so on a watch-list ready to replace any ill-performers in my holdings. Most of my holdings are US and UK – presently.

## No guarantees

Just because you can buy European stocks does not mean you are guaranteed success but it *can* increase your chances of success for the above reasons. However, you still have to conduct the same detailed research you might do for UK stocks and monitor markets just as closely. Indeed, it can be more difficult since you would now need a feel for European markets and countries, which is going to be harder when not based in those countries. There are always European investment trusts to rely on if it all gets too much.

## Practicalities

So what are the practicalities? Ideally, I want a site which offers me a single place from which to get the quotes (real-time and for free, of course), price charts (detailed analysis and Java-based please), company news and research, and market news – up to the minute. I want to be able to buy Dutch stocks as easily as German ones using the same account, everything instantly updated and added to my online portfolio on which I can monitor real-time in different currencies the value of my holdings.

The site will have to be easy to navigate; the brokers need to be big, reputable and experienced at traditional and online trading. I want an execution-only, low-cost commission with no annual fee or hidden costs. Efficiency and speed are taken for granted, as is phone backup that is not forever engaged. I want ready access to my cash through a cheque book and debit card and the ability to transfer funds by phone. If the site is down because of high volume then I want to have the authority to fire the managing director and the technical guys for incompetence.

This is some wish-list and the logistics are near impossible, not to say incredibly expensive for the companies. But who comes closest? Well there are nearly 700 companies offering e-broking in nine European countries according to BlueSky. Little wonder that European online traders will reach eight million users by 2002 from a mere 100,000 in 1998, according to JP Morgan. Sweden already has 53 per cent of the population owning shares directly, compared to 25 per cent in the UK. Must be those cold, dark nights.

## Sites

For placing trades the best site I have come across is e-cortal (*www.e-cortal.com*) and I am in the process of opening an account. The site covers online trading for the US, Germany, Holland, the UK, Italy, France, Switzerland and Spain. I note they have a 'trade commission-free for a month' offer at present. But for a one-stop site for European company and market information I really like European Investor (*www.europeaninvestor.com*).

There are country-specific sites, of course. The major one in English is ConSors (*www.consors.com*), which gave my browser a lot of trouble. Unfortunately there are numerous others that are in local languages (e.g. *www.comdirect.de*, *www.selftrade.com*, *www.boursedirect.com*) not offering a translated version of the site. If they did, they could increase business, but that would be too easy.

**Diagram 12.16**
**European Investor**

# Buying shares: shooting-stars or dogs?

## A problematic dilemma

All things being equal, should an online trader buy a stock that has doubled over the past year, or halved in value over that time frame? I was recently asked this at a lecture, and it became clear that the answer is not as obvious to some as it is to me. Of course, all things are seldom equal, but it is a common dilemma among traders whether to focus on the shooting-star stocks that just keep going up, or the dogs that just keep on drowning. It annoys me how many get the answer wrong; equally interesting is what it reveals about them as traders and people.

The dilemma often starts like this: our first trader, let us call him Richard Traderman, is always on the lookout for stocks which are at their lows. At present, he would be salivating over stocks like Somerfield and Storehouse.

## Fallacies

His reasoning for buying into such stocks can be explained by three fallacies. The first fallacy is the 'if you burn it, they will come' fallacy. It goes like this 'The stock cannot keep falling forever; the sellers are likely to sell too much and their overreaction will see buyers flood in and the price rise.'

The second fallacy is the 'white knight' fallacy and the reasoning is thus: 'If the stock price does keep falling and the company gets cheaper, then someone is bound to come in and take the company over or institutional investors and shareholders will force a management restructuring which will see the company share price rocket.'

The final fallacy of Richard Traderman and his ill-thinking ilk is the 'human infallibility' fallacy, which runs like this: 'I have an insight into the management and prospects of this company that the rest of the market has yet to see. Soon, clouds of ignorance will be removed from before the eyes of market makers and traders and they too will see the light and the promised value this company surely deserves – according to me.'

Our second trader, Alec Smart, always examines the share-price trend first before even considering a stock purchase. He wants to see it rise smoothly upward, with the stock becoming progressively more expensive in absolute terms each month. He for instance may currently be looking at stocks like Orange and Vodafone. The latter has risen from 240p to 1,400p in two and a half years, but Traderman would have found it 'too expensive', 'overvalued' or 'ripe for a fall' every step of the way.

Both Richard Traderman and Alec Smart want the same thing from their trading: they want to make money. Who is more likely to be successful? You may have guessed whose side I am on.

## Who wins?

In my view, it will almost always be Alec who will be the more successful. Firstly, while occasionally management overhauls occur and white knights appear, the timing is unpredictable. A stock can languish at depressingly low values for months if not years, and companies do go bust. A tax write-off is not a legitimate investment strategy.

Secondly, you would sensibly want to diversify your holdings so that you are looking at maybe 10, possibly even 15, stocks to invest in. Any more than 15 stocks to monitor and it is unlikely you would have the time to keep an eye on them. Out of all the stocks in the investment universe can it be that those performing worst are the ones you have to rely on? What does it say about the state of the British corporate economy if you are left to rely on basket-case companies to produce an investment return?

Another reason Traderman's strategy will fail him is that he is ignoring the most important piece of information the market has about a stock: its price. And remember: the market is never wrong. To Richard Traderman, if the stock was worth buying at 100p and it halves to 50p it is all the cheaper and more attractive. If it should halve again, he will buy some more at 25p; after all, now his average cost of purchase and therefore his break-even point are even lower.

What Traderman does not realize is that if the price is falling then stock holders are having to sell the stock at lower prices to find buyers. People are just not willing to pay any more. That should tell you something about what others think about the company.

On the other hand, if the price of a stock is rising consistently then it indicates that people are willing to pay more for it. There is likely to be market confidence in the company, and it is a good place to start further research into the stock, and its earnings, news flow, cash-flow, market and sector.

## But ...

Of course overvaluations occur (ask anyone who bought US internet stocks in April 1999), but among other things, a good 'trailing stop' should limit that. So for instance you may have a rule that if the stock falls 20 per cent from its current level you will exit.

Richard Traderman is not real, but you will find his spirit in online chat rooms throughout the web. The poor souls are in share purgatory. To me it seems as if they may even get some perverse joy about worrying over their stock performance. Maybe they are punishing themselves. Or maybe they are congenital optimists.

To these poor, helpless souls I can give the advice of businessman Elbert Hubbard: 'The safest way to double your money is to fold it over once and put it in your pocket.'

Since I consider the price trend the first thing for any medium- to long-term investor to examine, which are some of the best UK sites for seeing what the price trend looks like for a stock? It is surprising how few online brokers offer decent online stock charting facilities to their clients – revealing an ignorance of how people buy stocks maybe? Probably the best charting site for UK stocks is at *www.etrade.co.uk*; try also *www.dljdirect.co.uk*, which has a functional charting site, without bells and whistles.

*Diagram 12.14*
*E\*trade*

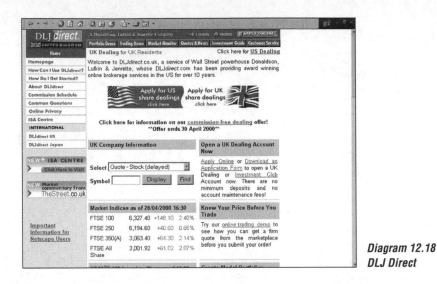

*Diagram 12.18*
*DLJ Direct*

## Summary

In many respects the world's exchanges are an often forgotten source of top-notch information. They are improving all the time and beginning to recognize their unique positions and roles on the financial internet. Unlike commercial sites these sites are funded with the non-profit motive of encouraging trading. I feel added comfort when using these sites.

# 13

# Finding a good broker: what you need to ask

**"** *Place the trade and walk away* **"**

**Phil Flynn**  Vice-President, Alaron Trading

## In this chapter

What are all the issues we should be concerned about and aware of when choosing an online broker? In this chapter we look at some of the key and lesser-known issues concerning broker selection, and also at some sites that monitor brokers.

## Objectives

- **What are the things I should look for in a broker?**
- **How do I choose a broker suitable for me?**
- **Who are the best brokers?**

## Benefits of an online broker

- **Cost.** Internet services tend to cost less than comparable offline services with the lower costs being passed on, in part, to the consumer, in the form of lower commissions and margin rates and competitive rates of interest on credit balances.
- **Convenience.** You can enter an order at any time, night or day, and so suit your own timetable. Useful if like me you do your analysis late at night.
- **Quick confirmation.** Your trade is usually confirmed electronically, saving you the time to hang around on the phone, or call back busy brokers.
- **Total account keeping and monitoring.** Because everything is done electronically, most online brokers have a facility to permit users to access their accounts and positions on the net. This again is another minor convenience.

# So who are the best?

There are sites that rank brokers according to different criteria. For instance on *www.gomez.com*, at the time of writing, the ranking for overall score was:

## Firm

| | | | | | |
|---|---|---|---|---|---|
| 1 | E*Trade | 9 | DLJ Direct | 15 | Discover Brokerage |
| 2 | NDB | 10 | Wang | 16 | Ameritrade |
| 3 | AB Watley | 11 | Firstrade | 17 | My Discount Broker |
| 4 | TD Waterhouse | 12 | Suretrade | 18 | AFTrader |
| 5 | Datek | 13 | Fidelity Investments | 19 | Bidwell |
| 6 | Web Street | 14 | Trading Direct | 20 | Brown |
| 7 | Charles Schwab | | | | |
| 8 | ScoTTrade | | | | |

Smart Money (*www.smartmoney.com*) produced the ranking shown in Table 13.1, just to prove no two broker-watch sites are the same.

Some sites offer a comparison of other brokers. Table 13.2 is from ScoTTrade.

*Table 13.1  Smart Money's complete rankings*

| Rank | Firm | Toll-free no. | Trading costs | Breadth of products | Mutual funds | Online trading | Extra services | Staying out of trouble | Responsive-ness | Web reliability |
|---|---|---|---|---|---|---|---|---|---|---|
| 1 | Muriel Siebert | 800-872-0711 | 14 | 8 | 8 | 4 | 5 | 7 | 1 | 1 |
| 2 | Waterhouse Securities | 800-934-4410 | 11 | 1 | 3 | 3 | 1 | 14 | 14 | 12 |
| 3 | Quick & Reilly | 800-262-2688 | 16 | 5 | 11 | 2 | 3 | 7 | 19 | 14 |
| 4 | Bidwell | 800-547-6337 | 4 | 12 | 5 | 15 | 8 | 14 | 4 | 8 |
| 5 | Charles Schwab | 800-435-4000 | 21 | 3 | 16 | 1 | 4 | 7 | 15 | 6 |
| 6 | National Discount Brokers | 800-417-7423 | 3 | 5 | 6 | 8 | 13 | 19 | 5 | 5 |
| 7 | Accutrade | 800-882-4887 | 13 | 14 | 2 | 13 | 13 | 1 | 3 | 15 |
| | T. Rowe Price | 800-225-5132 | 20 | 8 | 15 | 17 | 11 | 1 | 1 | 3 |
| 9 | Ameritrade | 800-454-9272 | 2 | 16 | 1 | 14 | 17 | 7 | 13 | 9 |
| 10 | Jack White | 800-233-3411 | 9 | 1 | 6 | 10 | 2 | 14 | 20 | 12 |
| 11 | Vanguard | 800-992-8327 | 15 | 13 | 14 | 18 | 9 | 1 | 10 | 7 |
| 12 | DLJ Direct | 800-825-5723 | 6 | 10 | 4 | 8 | 12 | 1 | 15 | 17 |
| 13 | Discover | 800-584-6837 | 5 | 14 | 12 | 7 | 6 | 7 | 11 | 19 |
| 14 | American Express | 800-297-8800 | 17 | 3 | 19 | 6 | 19 | 1 | 7 | 9 |
| 15 | USAA | 800-531-8343 | 17 | 16 | 10 | 21 | 10 | 1 | 17 | 4 |
| 16 | Fidelity | 800-544-8888 | 19 | 5 | 9 | 11 | 7 | 7 | 9 | 18 |
| 17 | E*Trade | 800-387-2331 | 8 | 11 | 13 | 5 | 15 | 14 | 21 | 20 |
| 18 | Brown & Co. | 800-822-2021 | 1 | 18 | 20 | 20 | 18 | 14 | 11 | 1 |
| 19 | Sottsdale | 800-619-7283 | 6 | 19 | 20 | 15 | 16 | 7 | 6 | 16 |
| 20 | Dreyfus | 800-896-8284 | 12 | 20 | 18 | 19 | 20 | 21 | 17 | 11 |
| 21 | Datek | 888-463-2835 | 10 | 21 | 17 | 12 | 21 | 19 | 8 | 21 |

*Table 13.2 ScoTTrade's broker comparison chart*

| | ScoTTrade® | E*Trade | Ameritrade | DLJ Direct | Schwab |
|---|---|---|---|---|---|
| Personal broker | Yes | No | No | No | Yes |
| Branch offices nationwide NASDAQ | 101 | 0 | 0 | 0 | 300 |
| Market orders NYSE and AMEX | $7 | $19.95 | $8 | $20.00 + $0.02/share over 1,000 | $29.95 up to 1,000 or $0.03/share for orders over1,000 shares |
| Market orders NYSE, AMEX, and NASDAQ | $7 | $14.95 | $8 | $20.00 + $0.02/share over 1,000 | $29.95 up to 1,000 or $0.03/share for orders over 1,000 shares |
| Limit orders | $12 | $19.95 | $13 | $20.00 + $0.02/share over 1,000 | $29.95 up to 1,000 or $0.03/share for orders over 1,000 shares |
| Margin interest rate with $7,500 debit balance | 7.50% | 9.25% | 9.00% | 8.50% | 9.25% |
| Credit interest | 4% | 2.00% | 2.50% over $1,000 0% under $1,000 | 3.50% | 4.70% $100 min. Money Mkt. |
| Real-time account | Yes | No | No | No | Yes |

# Pssst . . . Security: how safe is the process?

## The site

All the major online brokers assure their clients that they have unbreachable security in terms of someone placing rogue trades or transferring money out of their account. Security is usually assured through several procedures:

- The broker will have audit trails of all trades and cancellations which are available for you to inspect.

- In addition to this, all firms listed in this book have some form of insurance protection (usually SIPC, Securities Investor Protection Corporation) ensuring client funds are either segregated or protected, should the firm have financial difficulties. However, as E*Trade points out in its small print 'Protection does not cover the market risks associated with investing.' Pity!

■ Use of firewalls. These are like, well, walls of fire, that prevent access from the outside through links, etc.

■ Use of account numbers, user names and passwords.

## The browser

If you are using Internet Explorer 4 or 5 or Netscape Navigator 4 or higher then you are using a secure browser. Data passing through your browser to and from your broker will be encrypted. You can tell you are in a secure site because:

1 The URL changes from http: to https:.

2 A pop-up window informs you that you are about to enter a secure site.

3 In Internet Explorer, a lock icon appears in the bottom left-hand corner.

4 In Netscape Navigator, an unbroken key icon appears in the bottom left-hand corner of the browser.

## You

The most important thing you can do to help yourself is guard your personal identification number, account number, and username. The PIN is the most important of these.

## What to look for

### At a glance

■ Competitive commissions:
– Check for what size trade the advertised 'low' commission applies.
– Any maintenance or handling charges (i.e. hidden costs)?
– Commissions sometimes vary on the price of the stock, e.g. extra charges for a stock trading less than 50c.

■ Account details:
– Minimum initial deposit.
– Minimum account balance.
– Interest rates for idle funds.
– Good brokers ought to sweep excess funds automatically to a high-interest account.
– Margin and chequing accounts:

　　i　A margin account will allow you to borrow – what are the rates?

　　ii　It will be convenient to be able to write cheques.

　　iii　Is there a cost for wiring funds from the account?

　– Availability of account data online.

　– How often is the account updated? Intra-daily may be important for the day-trader.

■ Established on the net, not new – with potential teething problems.

■ Price quotes.

■ Methods of confirming orders (an online screen, and an e-mail at least).

■ Emergency back-up.

■ Types of orders accepted (see appendix on orders).

■ Portfolio monitoring:
　– How often is your portfolio updated?
　– Is a tax summary available?
　– Is an automatic performance measure calculated?
　– Is a transaction summary available?

■ News.

■ Research available:
　– What is available, is it free, is it online or posted?

■ Customer support:
　– Phone, fax, e-mail is ideal.

## E-brokers of choice: how a UK online trader should choose a UK online broker

Another week, another online broker opens up virtual-shop in the UK. Recently, we have seen Freeserve and DLJ Direct (*www.dljdirect.co.uk*) offering online trading, as well as newcomer E*Trade UK (*www.etrade.co.uk*) and old hand Charles Schwab Europe (*www.schwab-europe.com*), among others, feasting at the table of internet share trading. The indigenous tribes include Barclays Stockbrokers (*www.barclays-stockbrokers.co.uk*), Stocktrade (*www.stocktrade.co.uk*) and Killik (*www.killik.co.uk*). In online trading, the natives remain pygmies; the invaders have been at it for years on their own shores before setting sail to this land of cyber-milk and cyber-honey.

So, since it almost feels like there are as many online brokers as online traders in the UK, how does a wily online trader decide which broker to open an account with? The factors to consider often only enter the equation after bitter experience. These are my conclusions.

## Price

Of course price is of primary concern. Online trading is popular partly because it offers discount commissions for investors who do not want to pay a full-fee broker for advice they could have discovered themselves on the internet, or for trades where they do not want advice. But even among online brokers the commissions can vary greatly and comparison is near impossible with each calculating commissions on different bases – some using the value of your trade, others the number of shares bought, and others the frequency with which you trade.

Take the purchase of £10,000 of shares as your first online trade with three of the largest US online brokers with UK presence: Schwab, DLJ and E*Trade. The commission for the trade would be £46.25, £42.50 and £24.95 respectively. The best advice is to calculate what size of trades you expect to make normally and then visit the web sites to work out who would offer you the cheapest commission.

## More than money

But there is more to online broker selection than price; if there wasn't, then Schwab in the US, which is one of the most expensive online brokers, would not have the largest market share. The most important factor in selecting an online broker was customer service according to a recent study by JD Power and Associates. The same study, based only on US brokers and traders, found that Schwab topped the list for offering greatest customer satisfaction.

## Reliability

Reliability in service is an essential prerequisite for any online trader. There is no point saving £20 in commission on buying a stock, only to find you can't sell it because your online broker has broken down. Such 'downtime' by online brokers is becoming increasingly frequent in the US, even the mighty Schwab had one full hour where trades could not be placed. In a survey by The Street, again a survey of US brokers by US clients, DLJ Direct came top in the category of reliability.

## Execution

Poor execution too can override price as a concern for an online trader. The price at which your trade is 'executed' should be as close as possible to the real-time price quote you see on the screen before you trade. Poor execution can often end up swamping any commission savings. In The Street's survey, Schwab came above DLJ Direct, which in turn narrowly beat E*Trade on the issue of execution prices.

While these surveys are conducted on US brokers, I still look at them with interest, on the basis that the UK apple will not drop too far from the US tree. If you like such almost-scientific surveys of online brokers then see *www.gomez.com*. Their internet broker 'overall score' rankings placed E*Trade in pole position, followed by DLJ Direct and Schwab in third and fourth places respectively. There is also the new *www.gomez.co.uk*

## Design

Site design is an important consideration for me. There is nothing worse when you are trying to find a quote, do some research or quickly place a trade than to find navigation around the site as difficult as up the Amazon (the river, not the site). I want my online broker easy to use and intuitive. There is only one way to see what suits you and that is to visit the sites themselves. I am sorry to report I find the purely UK online brokers, unlike US brokers with UK sites, too often competing for the titles of Most Offputting Site and Most Turned-Away Potential Customers – that is, when they are not racing to see who can be the most expensive. Did these site designers speak to a single online trader?

## Free research

Online trading is about more than placing a trade through an online broker instead of phoning a traditional broker. Trading online profitably still requires research to arrive at stock picks, and the internet is an excellent resource to offer this. I always check to see what research the online brokers offer. Do they provide free portfolio monitoring, charting, news from major wires, research from renowned institutions and commentary, or are they just a web site appended to a traditional brokerage?

All in all I much prefer the big US brokers' UK sites to the sites of purely UK brokers because of site design, commission and research available. As between the US brokers themselves, I prefer the biggest players like the ones mentioned above, because it is they, with their leverage and clout, who can offer quality research, and I have the security of knowing they have the money to spend on resources.

Maybe new American entrants will put some of the smaller UK 'wannabes' out of their misery by buying them out as part of a market-entry strategy.

# Broker watch

In this section we take a run through sites which rate and rank brokers according to different criteria such as performance, speed, commissions, etc.

## Gomez ***

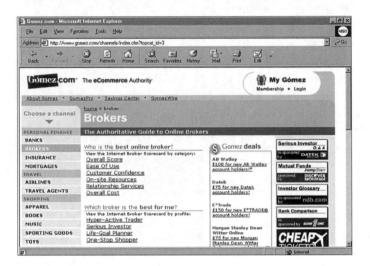

www.gomez.com

### How to use this site and what for

Use this excellent site to see how online brokers rank based on different criteria such as cost, customer service, resources and 'overall'.

## Internet Investing **

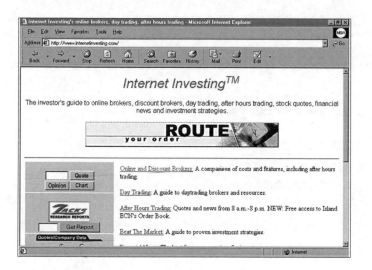

www.internetinvesting.com

### How to use this site and what for

Use this one for more specific details on the commission rates and minimum account sizes plus account information about main e-brokers. A bit textual rather than tabular and slightly semi-professional in look.

## Keynote Web Brokerage Index **

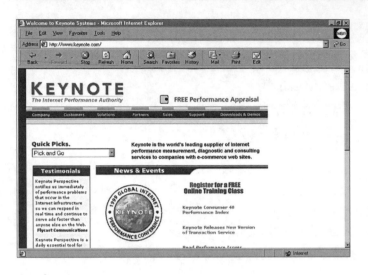

www.keynote.com

### How to use this site and what for

Use this for an intriguing look at which e-brokers' sites are the fastest for access; useful when time is of the essence for short-term active traders.

## Smart Money Broker Ratings ***

www.smartmoney.com

### How to use this site and what for

An excellent site and magazine. Use this site for things like the seductive broker speedometer. The site has brokers ranked by lots of criteria. It is a great lesson in how to present information too.

## Brokers

To help you gauge the sites, I have provided a rough-and-ready rating for them, based on general impressions of the services from inspecting their sites and the charges they inflict.

## E*Trade UK ***

### Key

*** *Good value for money: appear on the ball and client-orientated*
** *Worth investigating: good rates and fair information on the site*
* *A little expensive but potentially a good service provider*

www.etrade.co.uk

### How to use this site and what for

The UK version of the US site is among the very best of all the sites open to UK investors. The charting section is especially good. Offers portfolios, message boards (which could be better-organized but are among the most active in the UK for stock chat), news and research. Well-designed and organized. Did I mention that the commissions are among the UK's cheapest?

# E\*Trade \*\*\*

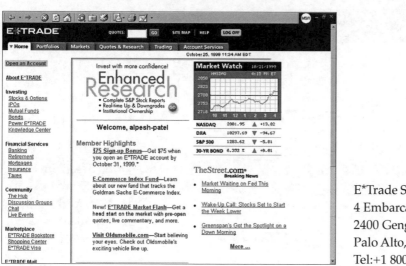

E\*Trade Securities
4 Embarcadero Pl.
2400 Geng Road
Palo Alto, CA 94303
Tel:+1 800 786 2575

www.etrade.com

## How to use this site and what for

A site with a lot of features, some free before you register, others for account holders. The site is easy to navigate and the information is very easy to find. On the Gomez rankings they have been the Number 1 overall broker for some time. As brokers, they have a lot of awards and positive reviews making them a must-consider broker.

Message boards and financial services are also available from the site.

## Datek ***

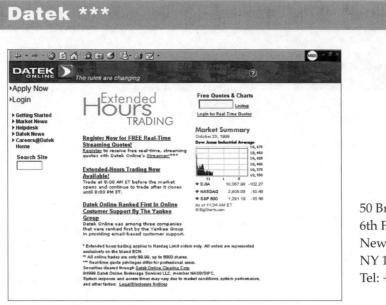

www.datek.com

### How to use this site and what for

50 Broad Street,
6th Floor
New York,
NY 10004
Tel: +1 212 514 7531

Not only is Datek cheap, but I do keep on hearing good things about it from chat boards, e-mails and press comment. Either it has a very good CIA-like undercover publicity machine, or it is, in fact, very good. The site also has a reassuring number of positive press reviews. I always find that comforting when considering a site marketing itself on the basis of having a very low cost base.

## Charles Schwab ***

Charles Schwab
101 Montgomery
Street
San Francisco,
CA 94104
Tel: +1 415 627 7000
     +1 800 435 4000

www.eschwab.com

### How to use this site and what for

Charles Schwab is not the cheapest broker, and it doesn't care because it is the largest. Very experienced at what it does, and has an enormous number of positive press comments. If you are a little concerned about trading on the net then a broker such as Schwab provides some added security in that you are dealing with an old hand in internet broking. I wish they would use their size to do even more strategic alliances and offer their clients even more free stuff.

## Ameritrade ***

Ameritrade
PO Box 2209
Omaha,
NE 68103 2209
Tel: +1 1 800 454 9272

www.ameritrade.com

### How to use this site and what for

A very good site. The home page is a lesson in simplicity coupled with professionalism. The site is quick; research is not as good as others but then again the broker is one of the cheapest around. Very easy to navigate, and designed very well and less cluttered than other sites.

## ScoTTrade **

www.scottrade.com

### How to use this site and what for

The site seems to be extremely slow. It is supposed to be cheap however, and I liked the design and layout of the site.

## Charles Schwab Europe ***

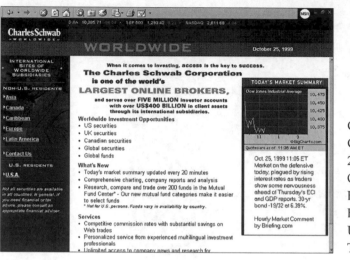

Charles Schwab
Cannon House
24 The Priory
Queensway
Birmingham
B4 6BS
UK
Tel: +44 121 200 7788

www.schwab-worldwide.com/worldwide/europe
www.sharelink.com

### How to use this site and what for

An increasingly impressive site, with free research, easy navigability and good design. There is also a phone brokerage service for those not quite ready to jump on to the cybertrain. Also offers UK investors the opportunity to buy US securities.

## Xest **

www.xest.com

### How to use this site and what for

A much improved site, but still needs some improvement to assist download speeds. Some of the graphics did not seem to download, and knowing where to start or open an account was not as easy as on some other sites. Seems to have been designed by IT specialists without consultation with an online trader.

## Redmayne Bentley **

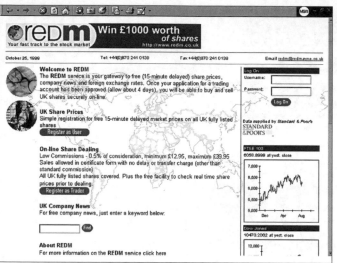

Tel: + 44 1870 241 0138

www.redm.co.uk

### How to use this site and what for

Now a pretty good home page showing some free price charts and news. Easy to see how you would open an account, but someone forgot to tell us why we would *want* to open an account; whatever happened to explaining what you get by way of research and about portfolios, and what about showing some demos?

## Discover **

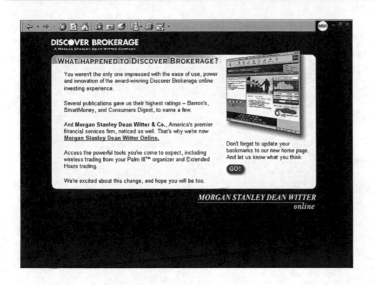

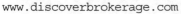
www.discoverbrokerage.com

### How to use this site and what for

Owned by Morgan Stanley, but the site does not come in as having the cheapest commission, or the best design, or the most research. It sort of does a bit of everything without excelling at any one, or indeed all. However, given who owns it, it provides the security you may want in an online broker.

## DLJ Direct UK ***

UK Dealing for UK Residents                    Click here for US Dealing

Welcome to DLJ*direct*.co.uk, a service of Wall Street powerhouse Donaldson, Lufkin & Jenrette, whose DLJ*direct*.com has been providing award winning online brokerage services in the US for over 10 years.

*** Available now... 

---and---

US and UK Dealing -- FREE in the UK into the MILLENNIUM!

**UK Company Information**

Select [Quote, Chart & News    ▼]

Symbol [        ] [Display] [Find]

**Open a Sterling Account Now**

Download an application form. Follow the simple guidelines and within days you could be trading UK securities from the comfort of your own PC.

**Market Indices as of 25/10/1999 16:29**

| | | | |
|---|---|---|---|
| FTSE 100 | 6,009.00 | -49.90 | -0.82% |
| FTSE 250 | 5,535.50 | +8.70 | 0.16% |
| FTSE 350(A) | 2,880.50 | -19.70 | -0.68% |
| FTSE All Share | 2,804.07 | -17.94 | -0.64% |

**Know Your Price Before You Trade**

Try our online trading demo to see how you can get a firm quote from the marketplace before you submit your order!

**FTSE™ 100 Intraday Chart as of 16:30**

6125
6095

**Create Model Portfolios**

Create a model portfolio without committing any funds. Model portfolios let you track your own

www.dljdirect.co.uk

### How to use this site and what for

A relatively new entrant to the UK market, and the site is well-constructed with good research available. It is fast and slick. Liked it.

## DLJ Direct ***

www.dljdirect.com

### How to use this site and what for

The US site is very nice and well-organized. It gives you reasons to open an account, and makes it easy to find commission rates. DLJ realizes it has to offer added value through research and does so. The only thing is that it is not the very cheapest.

# Trying to profit from the growth in online trading

If online trading is supposed to be taking off worldwide, especially in Europe, then how come e-broker stocks have been sinking faster than the *Titanic*? What is an online trader to do who wants to profit from the revolution of which he is a part?

Each week a new survey reveals the strong growth of online trading in Europe. Online share trades in the UK advanced 73 per cent in 1999/2000, according to the Association of Private Client Investment Managers and Stockbrokers; in Europe as a whole there are around 900,000 online account holders and JP Morgan predict over 8 million by 2002. That represents a greater growth rate than in the US.

Trading online specifically and the internet in general are 'frontier' activities. So the frontier culture of the US has meant it is US companies over here that are seemingly reaping the rewards. For instance, Schwab has an 83 per cent share of the UK online trading market.

## Buy e-brokers?

So, should we all buy some internet broker stocks, perhaps the likes of Schwab, E*Trade and DLJ Direct, who are the three largest US online brokers to have entered the European market? If making money were that easy, then I would not be cursing the poor price performance of these stocks.

Since April 1999, $10,000 invested equally in each of those three companies would by the end of 1999 have been worth approximately $7,700 before currency fluctuations. During the same period the Dow Jones Industrial rose 12 per cent.

The unfortunate story for those of us wanting to take advantage of these virginal European online trading shores by buying the shares of US online brokers in this market is that their share prices have hardly reacted to their European forays for numerous reasons.

### Competition

Firstly, no sooner does one online broker set up camp in Europe than another plane seems to arrive with another US broker competing for the same cyber-gold. To confound it all, even the natives are getting in on the act, with Freeserve, NatWest Stockbrokers and Killik among others announcing they will offer online trading. Entering a crowded market place, even a growing one, where margins are low to begin with, has not provided a boost to US brokers' stock prices.

### Overvalued stocks

Another reason why the growth of European online trading has not fed back into the stock prices of these US brokers is that their stocks were already overvalued and are now falling fast. It may be that news of European growth has slowed the decline, but a downward trend remains in place.

### Culture

Although European online trading is growing, it is small compared to US online trading which still makes up the bulk of profits for these US online brokers. Schwab for instance has a mere 26,000 online accounts in Europe compared to 6.2 million in the US, which is largely a reflection of the fledgling nature of the UK market as well as of cultural investment and population differences.

So should we then buy into European internet companies offering online trading for whom online trading activities may have a more direct effect on their share prices? After 17 August 1999 when Freeserve announced it would be offering online share trading, its price dropped about 10 per cent, partly because as soon as it made its announcement most commentators realized that the US brokers will be stiff competition and discounted the announcement, despite the company's being the UK's largest ISP and therefore potentially a big online trading fish this side of the pond.

If that is what happens to the largest ISP in one of Europe's most important on-line-trading growth markets, what point is there hunting native minnows in other European ponds? So much for buying into European companies undertaking online trading.

## How to take advantage?

There appears a dilemma here. You can't take advantage of the growth in online share trading in Europe through buying US online brokers' stock because they are in a downward decline with little sign of changing course, and there seems little point buying into European companies offering online trading because they would be facing so much competition from the more experienced, well-entrenched and wealthier US companies.

## Strategy

My own strategy is cautiously to buy into only the biggest US brokers who are showing a willingness to travel abroad aggressively (and so find new sources of profit as the US market matures), innovate new products to encourage increased online trading and diversify into financial service not directly related to online trading, but which their online trading audience would be very interested in buying. Diversification offers profit away from low-margin discount online broking.

Good examples of stocks in this category remain Schwab and E*Trade. Schwab is the world's largest online broker, and E*Trade is not far behind. Both are expanding their empires abroad, a little like the Spaniards and Portuguese of centuries past when the Pope decreed the world outside Europe could be divided between them for their feasting.

Both companies are diversifying into financial services with Schwab providing mutual funds and even annuities and life insurance and E*Trade providing visa cards, mortgages and insurance among other financial services. Maybe they will merge and challenge Citibank.

Schwab remains ahead of the game in innovation, with an announcement recently of its funding of hardware development to permit 'mobile trading' through hand-held devices which allow trades to be placed away from the PC. And as if to prove me wrong, Salomon Smith Barney produced a report this past week rating E*Trade a 'buy'; the kiss of death indeed for my analysis as soon as any institutional analyst agrees. Salomon were neutral on both DLJ Direct and Ameritrade.

Volatile share prices dictate that these have to be long-term purchases and in small chunks; *caveat emptor* indeed.

# How online traders can exploit full-service brokers

'If your broker's so great, how come he still has to work?' asks an advert for E*Trade over a picture of a dishevelled old man in a wrinkled overcoat on an underground train; one presumes a full-service broker catching the last train home.

Too often online traders neglect the service offered by full-service brokers. As the assault on full-service brokers or full-fee brokers (those that charge a relatively high fee for offering advice and research, plus other benefits that discount brokers do not provide) by online discount brokers increases, how can the online trader benefit from the defensive metamorphosis of the traditional full-fee broker like Merrill Lynch?

I do not use a full-service broker, although I did in my early teens, but now that I am a big boy capable of making my own decisions I have stopped using them for advice – for which I would have to pay. Instead recent freebies on their web sites have attracted me to them. There is simply more award-winning, in-depth, insightful and original equity and market research from top-notch investment bank web sites for free that no serious online trader should miss, compared to research done by the fifty-year-old wannabe highflyer in my high street broker's office whose musings are eminently forgettable.

## The preserve of the few?

Previously these high-quality services were only available to a select few willing to pay commissions of between $100 and $1,000 but are now available to the great unwashed masses – if only they knew where to look.

Remember too that online discount brokers cannot offer advice, because by law they are restricted to being execution-only. Whilst they may offer news feeds, which can include broker recommendations, for truly detailed analysis and the highest-quality investment ideas nothing can beat the analysis of 'the best on the street', as long as you can get it for free.

In response to the growth in discount online brokers, Merrill Lynch has been the highest-profile traditional full-fee broker to offer online trading and to open its gates to its highly prized research which is still currently available for free from *http://askmerrill.com/international*.

Barclays Capital (*www.barclayscapital*) too used to offer excellent research free online prepared for their traders; indeed I used to await each morning's market report from them religiously. Unfortunately they have now password-protected everything, restricting it to clients only. Not even a bribe of a copy of *Trading Online* would get them to e-mail a password my way.

## Competition

Another full-service broker forced by the competition from online brokers to offer its research to the public is Paine Webber, who has an excellent service at *www.painewebber.com* offering equity, market, industry and thematic research.

The mighty Salomon Smith Barney at *www.salomonsmithbarney.com* too offer worldwide research from macroeconomic to individual-equity level, plus my favourite, special reports on internet and technology stocks generally. None of these are second-rate findings from an intern that they deem worthy of being given away free just before binning them – it is good-quality stuff I would gladly scour the bins outside their offices for.

Lehman Brothers list their ten 'uncommon value' stock picks. In 1999 those stocks produced over a 50 per cent return. The ten for 2000 are at *www.lehman.com*. I was pleased to see Microsoft up there given that I am a stock holder.

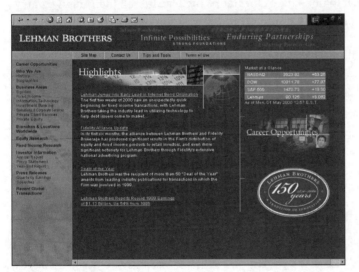

*Diagram 13.1*
*Lehman Brothers*

## More top research

When it comes to top-quality internet and technology stock research available for free on the web, no one beats Morgan Stanley Dean Witter in my opinion. You can find their excellent and hefty reports at *www.ms.com*. The downside is that the download will take forever and a good few trees as there are hundreds of pages in each report; try saving them to hard disk and save the forests.

Of course, there are many people who do not want to do their own research or trade through a discount online broker and prefer relying on a full-service broker for advice and not just free research; so much so that Merrill's web account attracts about $3 billion in new assets each quarter, whereas the execution-only broker, Charles Schwab (*www.eschwab.com*) attracts $30 billion per quarter, according to industry sources.

If you are tempted to consider the service of a top full-service broker such as Merrill, it charges most of its retail customers more than $50 per trade, and sometimes as much as $200 – far higher than the $5–30 charged by discount online brokers. Merrill combines broker advice and online trading in an account charging $1,500 minimum per annum. For that you get not only research but advice.

John Steffens, head of Merrill's retail business, estimates that average customers have between $350 and $450,000 in their new full-service web trading accounts, whereas a survey by The Street reveals that most online discount broker account holders trade with less than $5,000. It may be that wily traders make the big decisions with the advice of the big brokers, and rely on their own judgements with small amounts.

Full-service brokers have been late to recognize the threat of online trading to their businesses; at the start of 1999 none offered online trading. As they do, more will offer their research to non-clients for free, which is after all their main competitive advantage over online discount brokers. Keep a regular watch on the sites of the full-service brokers mentioned above. Use the free research they provide to place trades 'on the cheap' through execution brokers.

## Broker rankings for Europeans

The excellent BlueSky rankings to be found on the European Investor site (*www.europeaninvestor.com*) help both European and US residents to choose the best brokers for trading European stocks. Here are some findings at the time of writing from a site that has to be essential visiting. BlueSky ranked the sites from over 700 brokers in Europe. Visit European Investor for the latest rankings.

### Germany: Top rated broker sites

| Broker name | Residency nationality requirement | Mutual fund offer | Offers options, warrants | Offers IPOs | No. of markets traded | Special offers | Overall BlueSky rating |
|---|---|---|---|---|---|---|---|
| Consors | Non-German residents accepted | yes/buy online | buy online warrants and options | yes/online | 11 | Guaranteed order routing within 1 minute | 309 |
| Brokerage24 | German residents only | yes/buy online | buy online warrants, no options | yes/online | 32 | Client magazine | 308 |
| Comdirect | Non-German residents accepted | yes/buy online | buy online warrants, no options | yes online for Comdirect IPOs | 8 German, others by phone | free account first 6 months | 262 |

## UK & IE: Top rated broker sites

| Broker name | Residency nationality requirement | Mutual fund offer | Offers options, warrants | Offers IPOs | No. of markets traded | Special offers | Overall BlueSky rating |
|---|---|---|---|---|---|---|---|
| E*Trade UK | UK residents only | unit trusts and investment trusts | no | no | 1 | 3 free trades when signing up | 250 |
| TD Waterhouse | UK residents only | no | no | no | 1 | free membership | 244 |
| Sharepeople | UK residents only | offer unit trusts | buy online warrants (UK warrants only), no options | no | 4 | no | 233 |

## US: Broker sites who accept European clients

| Broker name | Residency nationality requirement | Mutual fund offer | Offers options, warrants | Offers IPOs | No. of markets traded | Special offers | Overall BlueSky rating |
|---|---|---|---|---|---|---|---|
| E*Trade | Excluded are residents of UK, Canada, Korea, Cuba, Libya and Australia | yes/buy online (only for US residents) | buy online options, no warrants | yes/online (only for US residents) | NYSE Nasdaq AMEX foreign stocks only by phone | E*Trade stock game | 315 |
| Schwab | Non-US residents accepted | yes/buy online | buy online options, no warrants | yes/online (only for US residents | NYSE Nasdaq AMEX Pacific Stock Exchange | no | 306 |
| Quick & Reilly | Non-US residents accepted | yes/buy online | buy online options, no warrants | research but no trading | NYSE Nasdaq AMEX | Get rewards through Platinum Visa Card | 286 |

### Switzerland: Top rated broker sites

| Broker name | Residency nationality requirement | Mutual fund offer | Offers options, warrants | Offers IPOs | No. of markets traded | Special offers | Overall BlueSky rating |
|---|---|---|---|---|---|---|---|
| UBS | Potential customers should consult their local laws and rules | yes/buy online | buy online warrants, no options | no | 7 | Quicken software | 277 |
| Credit Suisse | Potential customers should consult their local laws and rules | no online order | buy online warrants and options | no | 18 | no | 245 |
| Youtrade | Potential customers should consult their local laws and rules | no | buy online warrants, no options | no | 4 | no | 237 |

### Netherlands: Top rated broker sites

| Broker name | Residency nationality requirement | Mutual fund offer | Offers options, warrants | Offers IPOs | No. of markets traded | Special offers | Overall BlueSky rating |
|---|---|---|---|---|---|---|---|
| SNS Bank | Applicants must have or open Dutch bank account | yes/buy online | buy options only by phone, no warrants | no | 1 | First three trades are free | 264 |
| Robeco Advies | Applicants must have or open Dutch bank account | yes/buy online | no | no | 1 | no | 245 |
| Sem van Berkel | Non-Dutch residents accepted | yes/buy online | buy online options, no warrants | no | 1 | no | 218 |

*Belgium: Top rated broker sites*

| Broker name | Residency nationality requirement | Mutual fund offer | Offers options, warrants | Offers IPOs | No. of markets traded | Special offers | Overall BlueSky rating |
|---|---|---|---|---|---|---|---|
| *E banking* | Only for European citizens | yes/buy online | no | yes | 22 | Free software offer | 306 |
| *One Two Trade* | Only for residents in Belgium | no | no | no | 4 | no | 269 |
| *Keytrade* | Non-Belgian residents accepted | no | warrants | no | 12 | no | 247 |

*France: Top rated broker sites*

| Broker name | Residency nationality requirement | Mutual fund offer | Offers options, warrants | Offers IPOs | No. of markets traded | Special offers | Overall BlueSky rating |
|---|---|---|---|---|---|---|---|
| *Consors* | Foreign applications accepted | yes/buy online | options/warrant | yes | 19 | no | 301 |
| *CPR E*Trade* | Foreign applications accepted | yes/buy online | warrant | yes | 2 | no | 271 |
| *SelfTrade* | Foreign applications accepted | yes/buy online | warrant | yes | 5 | no | 267 |

# 14

# Eyes and ears open: monitoring

**ff** *It takes a lot of patience and energy and motivation* **JJ**

**Bernard Oppetit** Global Head of Equity Derivatives,
Banque Paribas, discussing trade

## In this chapter

Having executed your position after analyzing numerous possibilities, monitoring your open positions and positions you may open is a key part of any trader's time. In this chapter we examine what you monitor, when and why, and how it fits into the overall trading approach.

## Objectives

- Understand the importance of portfolio monitoring.
- Examine how the internet can assist in the task.
- Further add to a professional approach.

## Monitoring what?

Traders monitor:

1 What they own in anticipation of the time when they will want to sell according to their trading plan.

2 Possible other products they may buy but for which as yet all the factors they look for are not quite aligned, e.g. the price may not be too high or too low as yet.

3 The price of the product.

4 In the case of an open position, all the fundamental and technical factors which led to the decision to buy and are contained in the trading tactic.

**5**   In the case of a potential position, all the fundamental and technical factors the trader usually examines as part of the trading strategy before entering a position.

In other words, monitoring involves a constant reanalysis and revaluation of a position to see what has changed (Diagram 14.1).

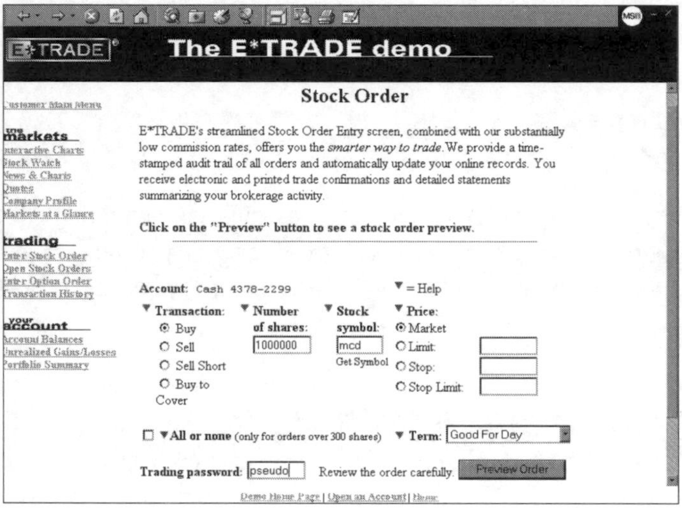

Diagram 14.1
To have or not to have
a Big Mac

Having examined fundamentals state what they are. And then if looking to exit in one month, say, monitor every two days.

## Monitoring when?

How often you monitor depends mainly upon two things:

**1**   Your trading-strategy time frame: are you looking to enter and exit in a short, medium or long period of time? Table 14.1 should help.

**2**   How close is the position to your stop or target? The closer it is the more regularly you need to monitor.

***Table 14.1 Suggested monitoring time frame***

| Period expecting to enter and exit | Monitor |
|---|---|
| 24–96 hours | Constantly – hourly |
| 1–2 weeks | Twice during day monitor price; end of day monitor everything else |
| 1 month | End of day monitor price; every 2 days monitor everything else |
| 3–9 months | 3–4 days monitor price; every week monitor everything else |
| 9 months + | Monitor sItuation every 3/4+ weeks |

## How the internet assists

Numerous sites have portfolio monitors or trackers. These usually relate only to stocks. Diagram 14.2 shows a typical portfolio. These are helpful in that you can see all the details for your stock in one place. Most update the price and volume of your stock.

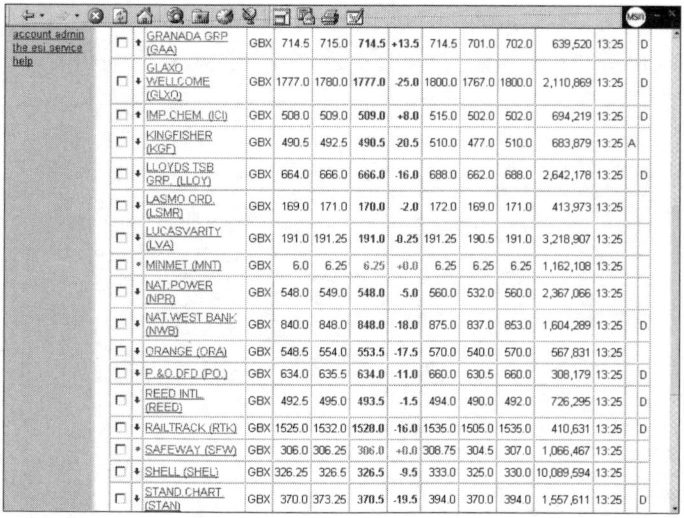

account admin
the esi service
help

| | | | | | | | | | | | | |
|---|---|---|---|---|---|---|---|---|---|---|---|---|
| GRANADA GRP (GAA) | GBX | 714.5 | 715.0 | 714.5 | +13.5 | 714.5 | 701.0 | 702.0 | 639,520 | 13:25 | | D |
| GLAXO WELLCOME (GLXO) | GBX | 1777.0 | 1780.0 | 1777.0 | -25.0 | 1800.0 | 1767.0 | 1800.0 | 2,110,869 | 13:25 | | D |
| IMP.CHEM. (ICI) | GBX | 508.0 | 509.0 | 509.0 | +8.0 | 515.0 | 502.0 | 502.0 | 694,219 | 13:25 | | D |
| KINGFISHER (KGF) | GBX | 490.5 | 492.5 | 490.5 | -20.5 | 510.0 | 477.0 | 510.0 | 683,879 | 13:25 | A | |
| LLOYDS TSB GRP. (LLOY) | GBX | 664.0 | 666.0 | 666.0 | -16.0 | 688.0 | 662.0 | 688.0 | 2,642,178 | 13:25 | | D |
| LASMO ORD. (LSMR) | GBX | 169.0 | 171.0 | 170.0 | -2.0 | 172.0 | 169.0 | 171.0 | 413,973 | 13:25 | | |
| LUCASVARITY (LVA) | GBX | 191.0 | 191.25 | 191.0 | -0.25 | 191.25 | 190.5 | 191.0 | 3,218,907 | 13:25 | | |
| MINMET (MNT) | GBX | 6.0 | 6.25 | 6.25 | +0.0 | 6.25 | 6.25 | 6.25 | 1,162,108 | 13:25 | | |
| NAT.POWER (NPR) | GBX | 548.0 | 549.0 | 548.0 | -5.0 | 560.0 | 532.0 | 560.0 | 2,367,066 | 13:25 | | |
| NAT.WEST BANK (NWB) | GBX | 840.0 | 848.0 | 848.0 | -18.0 | 875.0 | 837.0 | 853.0 | 1,604,289 | 13:25 | | D |
| ORANGE (ORA) | GBX | 548.5 | 554.0 | 553.5 | -17.5 | 570.0 | 540.0 | 570.0 | 567,831 | 13:25 | | |
| P.&O.DFD (PO.) | GBX | 634.0 | 635.5 | 634.0 | -11.0 | 660.0 | 630.5 | 660.0 | 308,179 | 13:25 | | D |
| REED INTL. (REED) | GBX | 492.5 | 495.0 | 493.5 | -1.5 | 494.0 | 490.0 | 492.0 | 726,295 | 13:25 | | D |
| RAILTRACK (RTK) | GBX | 1525.0 | 1532.0 | 1528.0 | -16.0 | 1535.0 | 1505.0 | 1535.0 | 410,631 | 13:25 | | D |
| SAFEWAY (SFW) | GBX | 306.0 | 306.25 | 306.0 | +0.0 | 308.75 | 304.5 | 307.0 | 1,066,467 | 13:25 | | |
| SHELL (SHEL) | GBX | 326.25 | 326.5 | 326.5 | -9.5 | 333.0 | 325.0 | 330.0 | 10,089,594 | 13:25 | | |
| STAND.CHART. (STAN) | GBX | 370.0 | 373.25 | 370.5 | -19.5 | 394.0 | 370.0 | 394.0 | 1,557,611 | 13:25 | | D |

***Diagram 14.2 Online portfolio monitor***

## What to look for when seeking an online portfolio tracker

- Does it recalculate the value of your total holdings?
- How many stocks can you list in one portfolio?
- How many portfolios can you have at one site?
- How often is the portfolio updated?
- Does the portfolio tracker alert you about news, earnings or other related items which may affect your stock?
- Does it monitor and alert you to a change in the technicals of your stock?

## The sites

## Interactive Investor International ***

www.iii.co.uk

It's free, it's easy and it allows UK, US and other country stocks on the portfolio.

## E*TradeUK ***

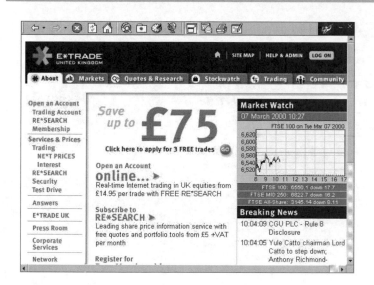

www.etrade.co.uk

This one has all the features you would expect – could do with more graphics though.

## MoneyNet ***

www.moneynet.com

This Reuters site adds graphical depictions of your profits and losses and makes things more interesting than most e-brokers.

## ClearStation **

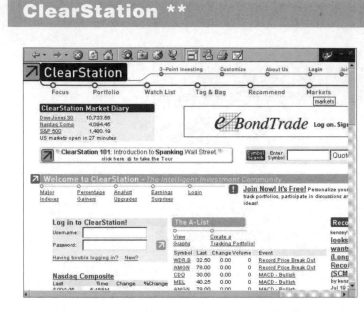

www.clearstation.com

A good, if occasionally fiddly, portfolio. The site goes offline a bit too often to be totally reliable.

## Summary

We have now examined what a professional approach to trading requires in terms of monitoring open and potential positions.

- With both the trading strategy and the trading tactic in hand, monitor both the open and the potential positions.

- Frequency of monitoring depends upon how close the target or stop is and generally on how quickly we expect to enter and exit.

- Portfolio monitors which can help reduce the workload.

# 15

# Keeping abreast: education

## In this chapter

Okay, so you have made and executed your order, but before you are ready to go on to making more decisions there is something else that you need to do. No matter what product interests you, whether it is Nasdaq stocks or pork belly futures, you may want to keep abreast of certain market-related information.

In this chapter we examine sources of further information which many traders use to supplement their analysis and which add to an overall professional and thorough approach. We examine the types of information available and its uses.

## Objectives

■ **Understand why and how to use market commentary and online magazines.**

■ **Learn how to choose newsgroups and newsletters.**

■ **See how to incorporate these into an action plan.**

## Market news and commentary

Almost all traders, whatever form of analysis they use and whatever product they trade in, whether bonds or shares, will want to examine daily market news and commentary, as these provide a context for all trading. It is the background against which all trading occurs. Even if you attach little weight to the market commentary it is an important aspect of trading.

The market commentary may relate not only to what is happening to the world economy, but also to the particular product in question. So, for instance, a futures

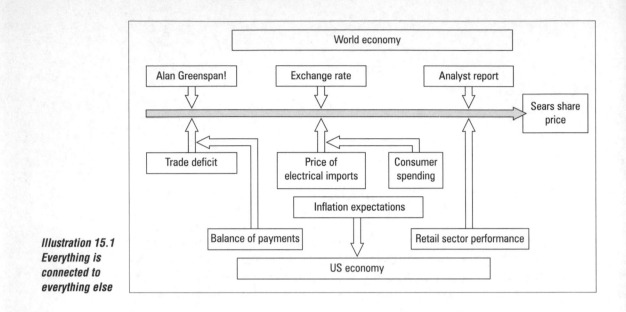

*Illustration 15.1*
*Everything is*
*connected to*
*everything else*

trader in currencies may want to know what is happening to the US macroeconomy and may also want commentary on currencies and currency futures generally.

If you trade UK stocks you may think it safe to ignore market commentary related to US non-farm payrolls, but you will then have missed why, on so many occasions, stocks with little US exposure, such as domestic electricals, are affected each month when the US non-farm payroll data are revealed. What happens is that the market often uses those data to gauge the likely changes in US interest rates, which in turn affects whether more funds are likely to flow into London or New York; that in turn can affect the share price of companies that have little to do directly with the US. The key rule is that everything is connected to everything else (see Illustration 15.1).

This does not mean you have to be an economics whiz to trade, but it does mean that the better informed you are about what the market is examining the more likely you are to make better trading decisions. In any event, few people would argue that more information can do harm. Here endeth the case for following market news and market commentary.

Criteria for including market news and commentary sites in the skeleton plans are:

- the news providers have to be well known, widely respected and with ample resources
- quality commentary on the markets

- categorized news, such as industry, business, commodity, etc. for ease of searching
- regular updates during the day.

## News sites

These are the sites I find particularly useful for keeping abreast of market news. However, broker sites often have such useful market commentary nowadays that you may not need these.

## BBC News ***

news.bbc.co.uk/hi/english/business

### How to use this site and what for
This one is good for world news as well as a general overview of market news. If you are looking at macroeconomic and political considerations then use this site.

## CBS MarketWatch ***

cbs.marketwatch.com

### How to use this site and what for
Great value this free site. Use it for the latest market stories as well as more in-depth research too. There is so much on this site that if you do use it, then you shouldn't need to go to another news site regularly, because you may end up spending too much time on just background material. Tom Calandra is a key feature to visit and is much followed. Also see the following links:

- **Investing Tools and Data**
- **Free Shop's Top Ten Free Offers**
- **Headlines** (updated every minute)

*Hot tip*

***Learning the markets***
*One of the best ways to learn about the markets and get a feel for them is to follow daily commentary on what happened in the markets and explanations for these events. This should give you an idea of 'what is on the market's mind.' What data do the market commentators say dealers are focusing on? This is not to say you should try to second-guess them, but rather get to appreciate what moves markets. PS. Nobody ever figures it out – not even the best.*

## Bloomberg \*\*\*

www.bloomberg.co.uk
www.bloomberg.com

### How to use this site and what for

World-beating provider of up-to-the-minute financial news. When using it for market news and general background just focus on the headline stories on the home page. Click on the **Columns** link and there you will see not only the columnists, but reports for all world markets – a really convenient way to get the low-down quickly. The **News** link is self-evident. I use the technology link a lot because I invest in technology stocks – it is very useful generally too. Also, if you click on the **TV** link you will be able to watch Bloomberg TV!

## CNBC \*\*\*

www.cnbc.com

### How to use this site and what for

The most useful things about this one are the news updates and the archived interviews, which can be helpful when researching a company. See the stock picks too – they tie in with what TV guests have recommended and can be a useful pointer.

## Financial Times ***

www.ft.com

### How to use this site and what for

Use the drop-down menu to get market news for various sectors and regions of the world. That is probably the feature most useful to traders. Other things like the portfolio are okay but you will probably use the one your broker provides.

## Wall Street Journal ***

www.wsj.com

### How to use this site and what for

This site is divided into WSJ Europe, US and Asia. Use it for market news and use the columns for a bit more analysis.

## Market newsletters

Many traders subscribe to one or more newsletters for the particular product they are interested in.

## What are they?

Essentially a market newsletter will contain recommendations as to what to buy and sell. The individuals who write them are often termed gurus. I suppose priest, rabbi and imam would be plausible alternatives as well.

## Why use them?

A typical newsletter will contain analysis of why a particular stock or other product is recommended. Most traders, if they use newsletters, do so to get a second opinion on their own analysis or to gain ideas. Sometimes a newsletter is a confidence builder for those a little tentative or unsure of their own analysis.

Before you choose to subscribe to any particular newsletter there are some important things to bear in mind.

*Hot tip*

***Using newsletters***
*Do not merely follow a newsletter: you may as well give your money to the newsletter author – and if you are willing to do that then why not give it to a professional fund manager? Remember, Soros and Buffet do not write newsletters. In other words, the truly successful trade: they do not recommend trades. So I would recommend that you do your own analysis before or after looking at the newsletter you have subscribed to and form an independent view as to the trade.*

## Product

Make sure the newsletter trades in the same products as you! Seems obvious – it is! But it also means that if you trade stock options, it will almost certainly be better to have a newsletter making stock option recommendations than one making purely stock recommendations.

## Strategy

Are the strategies the newsletter recommends ones with which you are comfortable? For instance, the newsletter may specialize in shorting stocks or spread trading.

## Your analysis and your guru's analysis

You need to be aware of the type of analysis you believe in and ensure the newsletter follows a similar form. For instance, if you tend to follow earnings surprises and do not care much for technical indicators then it would be perverse for you to subscribe to a newsletter that selected recommendations based on technicals.

## Time frame

You ideally want a newsletter that selects recommendations on a time frame you yourself like to trade to. An extreme example of a mismatch would be if you prefer to enter and exit trades on a weekly basis and the newsletter is monthly. Its value to you would be limited.

## Method of delivery

Are you happy with the mode by which the newsletter is delivered: e-mail, fax or snail mail?

## Comprehensible?

The issue here is do you like the layout and can you understand why the guru is recommending a stock? One thing that will ensure a wasted subscription is if you cannot understand the guru's choice. If you do not fully comprehend how he selects his recommendations you cannot critically analyze them and so are following blindly.

# You pays your money and you takes your choice

As Table 15.1 makes clear, there are an enormous number of factors that determine the type of newsletter best suited to your particular needs. Moreover, for every possible demand there seem to be several suppliers. That being so it would be ridiculous and unhelpful to list and review each and every available newsletter. Instead the sites listed are 'umbrella' sites which do precisely that. Furthermore, because they are net sites, they are going to be more up to date.

*Table 15.1 Checklist of factors for consideration*

|  | My choice | Newsletter 1 | Newsletter 2 | Newsletter 3 |
|---|---|---|---|---|
| Product |  |  |  |  |
| Strategy |  |  |  |  |
| Analysis |  |  |  |  |
| Time frame |  |  |  |  |
| Method of delivery |  |  |  |  |
| Comprehensibility (score) |  |  |  |  |
| Trial period |  |  |  |  |
| Cost |  |  |  |  |

To give you some idea of the plethora of choices, the list that follows contains just some of the newsletters I came across in the first 30 minutes of researching the issue.

The Addison Report
The Aden Forecast
Adrian Day's Investment Analyst
All Star Funds
Analyst Watch
Asset Allocator
BI Research
Beating the Dow
Bert Dohmen's Wellington Letter
The Big Picture
The Blue Chip Investor
Bob Brinker's Marketimer
The Bowser Report
The Buyback Letter
The Cabot Market Letter
California Technology Stock Letter
The Chartist
The Chartist Mutual Fund Timer
The Clean Yield
Closed-End Country Fund Report
Closed-End Fund Digest
The Contrarian's View
Crawford Perspectives
Dennis Slothower's On The
    Money
The Dines Letter
Donoghue's Wealthletter
Dow Theory Forecasts
Dow Theory Letters
Elliott Wave Theorist
Emerging & Special Situations
Equities Special Situations
Equity Fund Outlook
F.X.C. Investors Corp.
Fabian Premium Investment
    Resource

Fidelity Forecaster
Fidelity Independent Advisor
Fidelity Insight
Fidelity Monitor
Financial World
Ford Investment Review
Foreign Markets Advisory
Fund Exchange
Fund Kinetics
Fund Profit Alert
Fundline
Funds Net Insight
Futures Hotline/Mutual Fund
    Timer
Garzarelli Outlook
Gerald Perritt's Mutual Fund
    Letter
Global Investing
Good Fortune
The Granville Market Letter
Graphic Fund Forecaster
Ground Floor
Growth Fund Guide
Growth Stock Outlook
Growth Stock Winners
Growth Stocks Report
Hot Funds Analyst
Hussman Econometrics
Income Fund Outlook
Independent Adviser for
    Vanguard Investors
Individual Investor Special
    Situations Report
The Insiders
The International Harry Schultz
    Letter

InvesTech Market Analyst
InvesTech Mutual Fund Advisor
Invest With The Masters
Investment Quality Trends
The Investment Reporter
Investor's Guide to Closed-End
    Funds
Investor's World
Investors Intelligence
The Jupiter Group, Inc.
Kinsman's Stock Pattern
    Recognition Service
LaLoggia's Special Situation
    Report
Louis Rukeyser's Mutual Funds
Louis Rukeyser's Wall Street
The Low Priced Stock Survey
MPT Review
Margo's Small Stocks
Mark Skousen's Forecasts &
    Strategies
Market Logic
The Marketarian Letter
Medical Technology Stock Letter
Moneyletter
Morningstar Mutual Funds
Motley Fool
The Mutual Fund Advisor
Mutual Fund Forecaster
Mutual Fund Investing
The Mutual Fund Strategist
Mutual Fund Technical Trader
NAIC Investor Advisory Service
National Trendlines
Natural Contrarian
New Issues

The Ney Stock and Fund Report
No-Load Fund Analyst
*NoLoad Fund*X
The No-Load Fund Investor
No-Load Mutual Fund Selections
    & Timing Newsletter
No-Load Portfolios
ODDS OEX Fax Hotline
OTC Insight
The Oberweis Report
The Option Advisor
Option Selections & Timing
The Outlook
Overpriced Stock Service
The Oxford Club
P. Q. Wall Forecast, Inc.
The PAD System Report
PEcom Stock Valuation
Personal Finance
The Peter Dag Portfolio Strategy &
    Management
The Professional Tape Reader

Professional Timing Service
Prudence and Performance
The Prudent Speculator
The Pure Fundamentalist
The Red Chip Review
Richard E. Band's Profitable
    Investing
Richard Geist's Strategic Investing
The Ruff Times
Scientific Investment
Sector Funds Newsletter
Short On Value
Sound Advice
Sound Mind Investing
Stockmarket Cycles
Strategic Investment
Switch Fund Timing
Systems and Forecasts
Timer Digest
Todd Market Timer
The Turnaround Letter
US Investment Report

United & Babson Investment
    Report
Utility Forecaster
The Value Line Convertibles
    Survey
The Value Line Investment Survey
The Value Line Investment Survey
    – Expanded Edition
The Value Line Mutual Fund
    Survey
The Value Line OTC Special
    Situations Service
Vantage Point: An Independent
    Report for Vanguard Investors
VectorVest Stock Advisory
Vickers Weekly Insider Report
The Wall Street Digest
World Investor
Zweig Performance Ratings
    Report

## Investools **

www.investools.com  US

**Search** according to strategy, product and analysis (e.g. charts)
**Free** issues of some of the listed newsletters

### How to use this site and what for
A wide selection of newsletters here, but no ranking except by a link to Hulbert
Financial.

## Hulbert Financial ***

www.hulbertdigest.com **US**

**Analysis** of investment approaches of newsletters
**Profiles** of strategy and methods used for recommendations
**Addresses** of all listed newsletters
**Ranking** of past performance of all newsletters

### How to use this site and what for

Hulbert Financial is well known for its ranking of newsletters. It is a very comprehensive service; however you will have to pay for it.

## Newsletter Network **

**Diamonds in the dirt**
*Many prospectors for newsletters think that if they find some esoteric and little known newsletter they may find something everyone else has missed and so strike it rich. Don't kid yourself: the newsletter writer wouldn't be writing the letter if he or she was sitting on a potential diamond-field!*

Your Premier Source for Investment News & Analysis

Get FREE Trials or newsletter listings by:
Category, Publisher, Author, or Alphabetically.

| Amazon Investment Books | Fraser Books of Wall Street | Supertrader Books |

Click Here    FIRST ADVISORS    *FREE!*
Professional Money Management    QUOTES & PORTFOLIO
for the Individual Investor    CENTRAL·CORNELL·GABELLI·HEBERT·LOCKE·OXFORD

*A service of Newsletter Technologies, Inc. (Info: Author, Co-Brand, Corporate)*

**Institutional Research:**

Go to    Institutional Research Index

**Select Publisher:**    Go to    Publisher Index

**Or, Select Author:**    Go to    Author Index

www.margin.com  **US**

**Search** the extensive database according to publisher, letter and author
**Free** samples

### How to use this site and what for

Similar to Investools and it may be that the sites do not cover exactly the same newsletters, so it is worth using both sites as search tools.

## Chatting to a virtual community: newsgroups

## What are they?

A newsgroup is simply a collection of messages posted by individuals to a news server. Posting is the act of putting your message on to the server. News servers are just big computers that host (i.e. store) lots of newsgroup messages for people to view.

You read and post messages using a news reader. A news reader is software much like a browser and the best news is that most browsers include news readers that launch automatically when you want to go to a newsgroup. With Internet Explorer 4 for example the news reader is bundled with the e-mail reader called Outlook Express. In Netscape Navigator it is called Netscape News.

There are some web sites that provide their own news readers and so permit web-based 'newsgrouping' (see later) which can be easier for the novice.

There are newsgroups on virtually every topic under the sun from investments to sadomasochism (the dividing line between investment and sadomasochism can be a fine one at times). Some newsgroups are monitored or moderated, which means someone sifts through them to ensure the content meets certain quality standards and is not generally scurrilous, libellous or outrageously offensive.

## Adding a news server

To add a news server you will need the name of the server and your account name and password.

In Internet Explorer 4:

■ In Outlook Express click on **Tools** and then **Accounts** and next on **News** and finally follow the on-screen instructions.

In Netscape Navigator:

■ In the browser click on **Options** then select **Mail and News Preferences** and click on **Servers** (you may need to click on **News** first if this tab is available). Next enter the server name in the **News (NNTP) Server** box and follow the instructions.

## Subscription

The act of 'joining' a newsgroup is called subscription. You do not need to have subscribed to a newsgroup to be able to read and post messages. Subscription just means your news reader creates a special folder for that newsgroup and you can more conveniently send and receive messages by clicking on the icon. No fees are due and there are no membership lists. Before you can subscribe to a newsgroup:

1  Your ISP must have a link with the newsgroup's news server.

2  You have to have set up an account with the news server using your news reader.

Your news reader will usually download a list of newsgroups available on your news server when you connect. When you see one you may click on it to view a selection of messages and decide whether or not to subscribe (Diagram 15.1).

*Hot tip* 👉

**Web-based newsgroups**
*One of the easiest way to use newsgroups without all the trouble of linking to servers and fiddling with browsers is to go to* **www.infoseek.com**. *From there you can search for newsgroups and download the **My Deja News** news reader and subscribe to lots of newsgroups.*

*Diagram 15.1
Newsgroupies,
newsgrouping*

## Viewing a newsgroup

In your browser simply type in the URL box **news:name of newsgroup**, e.g. news:misc.invest.

## Quality of trading newsgroups

The major problem with newsgroups, which even a short visit will demonstrate, is that:

**1** They often get used by a small clique of users who are in fact just talking to each other, with outside messages not replied to readily.

**2** The focus of the clique can be quite narrow.

**3** The messages can get abusive and personal.

**4** Unregulated groups often get postings from unwelcome 'get rich quick' schemes.

**5** Investors often try to talk up positions they may be holding, so the information is often biased and not credible.

Consequently, for anyone coming to a newsgroup, it can be a little like going to a drinks party and trying to join in a conversation being held by a circle of individuals who have been chatting away for a few hours. My advice would be to use newsgroups only for asking questions, and be wary of the replies even then. They are not, in my opinion, a good source of investment advice on the whole, but better as a source of exchanging knowledge-based background information, such as, say, on the usefulness of stochastic indicators in technical analysis.

**Hot tip**

***Alternative advice***
*If you have an investment query, rather than seeking the amateur advice of a newsgroupie, you could always go to a web site dealing with the area of your query (e.g. bonds, etc.) and seek out e-mail addresses of people on them. Often, the advisers who produce the site provide their e-mail addresses and they can be a useful source of free advice on an issue.*

# Newsgroupie or web chatterer?

Many web sites specializing in trading have equivalents to newsgroups but are web-based (Diagram 15.2). These often provide higher-quality content and are a good alternative to free-for-all newsgroups.

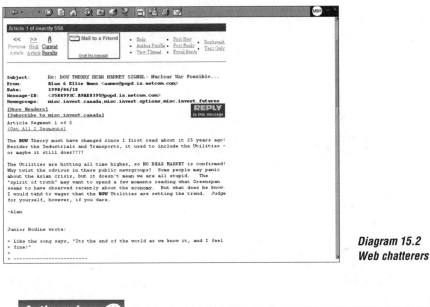

*Diagram 15.2*
*Web chatterers*

## Action plan

- Log on to the internet.
- Go to My Deja News.
- Register.
- Visit a financial newsgroup of your choice.
- Post a question.

*Table 15.2  Newsgroups from a general internet search*

| Name | Content |
| --- | --- |
| alt.invest.penny-stocks | Low-priced stocks talk |
| misc.invest | Investments |
| misc.invest.commodities | Commodities |
| misc.invest.emerging | Emerging markets |
| misc.invest.forex | Foreign exchange |
| misc.invest.funds | Mutual funds |
| misc.invest.futures | Futures |
| misc.invest.stocks | Stocks |
| misc.invest.technical | Technical analysis |
| uk.finance | UK personal finance |

*Table 15.3  Major web-based discussion sites*

| Name and web address | Stocks | Mutual funds | Futures | Options | Bonds | Technical analysis | Fundamental analysis |
|---|---|---|---|---|---|---|---|
| Avid Traders Chat<br>avidinfo.com | ✓ | | | | | ✓ | |
| The Financial Center On-Line<br>www.tfc.com/chat | ✓ | ✓ | ✓ | ✓ | ✓ | ✓ | ✓ |
| Investors' Free Forum<br>www.investorsforum.com | ✓ | ✓ | ✓ | ✓ | ✓ | ✓ | ✓ |
| The Motley Fool<br>www.fool.com | ✓ | | | ✓ | | | |
| Quicken People & Chat<br>quicken.excite.com/forums | ✓ | ✓ | | | | | |
| The Stock Club<br>www.stockclub.com | ✓ | | | | | | ✓ |
| Yahoo! Finance Message Boards<br>messages.yahoo.com/yahoo/<br>Business_and_Finance/ | ✓ | ✓ | ✓ | ✓ | ✓ | ✓ | ✓ |

## Some popular web-based discussion forums

Table 15.3 lists major web-based discussion sites and their properties (see also Diagram 15.3).

One of the best collections of web-based discussion is located within Yahoo! at: *messages.yahoo.com/yahoo/Business_and_Finance/Index.html.*

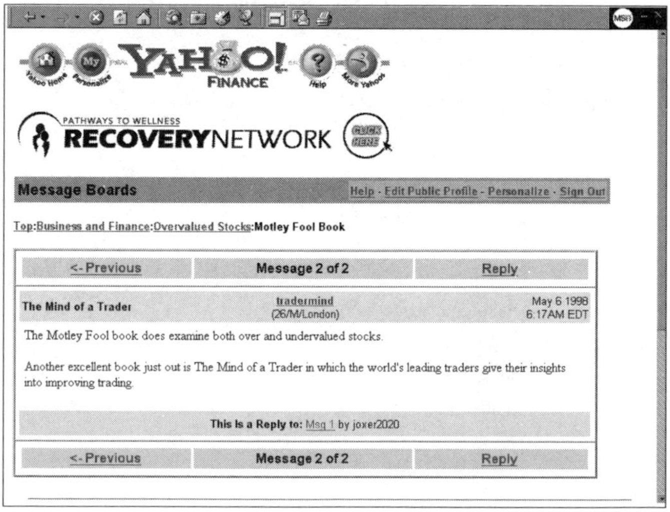

*Diagram 15.3*
*Yahoo*

Newsgroups exist on:

- brokerages
- market trends
- mutual funds
- options
- overvalued stocks
- short-term trading
- stocks (financial, consumer, energy, healthcare, service, technology, transport, utilities)
- specific companies, so you can discuss a single stock in splendid isolation.

## The very unboring boardsters

This first posting (below) is an excellent tip from someone who has been to the battlefront and come back alive.

### Trading keys

**Trading keys – for me – FWIW [for what it's worth]**

1 Limit your stocks for a particular day to one or two, if possible. And learn their chart action like the back of your hand. Know where support and resistance levels are.

2 Get a sense of the general market's movement for the day. Watch the bond yield and the foreign markets and get a good read on the 'perception' of the market in general, as well as the perception towards your stocks and their sector. Often stocks follow a daily pattern in a particular market environment (i.e. gap and trap etc.). Don't fight the pattern. No one wants to sit on a losing position all day long.

3 Be as up-to-the-minute as possible on *any* news items that may affect your stocks' (or their industry's or even sector's) movement. Know how seemingly unrelated news may affect your stocks. Economic news. Fed news. Legal news. SEC filings. Insider action. Institutional buying. Rumors. CNBC or CNNF plug.

4 Know which stocks in the industry trade along with your stocks. Which lead the group. And which lag. This, often, is a vital tool.

5 Watch the specific trading patterns of your stocks (on level II if Nasdaq issue). Which banks

seem to buy the rallies. Which sell into them. Note how the daytraders are playing it. They can often be found on Island … and they often trade on perception.

**6** Be ready to move in a millisecond's time.

**7** Sell losers fast. Losers can rack up larger than winners. That's because you'll tend to wait them out longer. Don't do it. Sometimes there's a reason a stock is dropping … and others aren't. Punt it fast. You don't *ever* want to get caught in a plunge and be forced to sell into it with a market order.

**8** Never look back with regret. After a losing trade (or a winning trade you sold too early), move on to the next trade. Don't be tempted to jump back in because you think you are 'missing the big run.' There will be others. There always are.

**9** Which brings me to the most important rule: *be patient.*

These are all off the top of my head. I'm sure there are many others, too.

This posting succinctly advises on the winning traits of winning traders.

## Winning traits

### Common traits of winning traders

**1** All those interviewed had a driving desire to become successful traders – in many cases, overcoming significant obstacles to reach their goal.

**2** All reflected confidence that they could continue to win over the long run. Almost invariably, they considered their own trading as the best and safest investment for their money.

**3** Each trader had found a methodology that worked for him and remained true to that approach. It is significant that discipline was the word most frequently mentioned.

**4** The top traders take their trading very seriously; most devote a substantial amount of their waking hours to market analysis and trading strategy.

**5** Rigid risk control is one of the key elements in the trading strategy of virtually all those interviewed.

**6** In a variety of ways, many of the traders stressed the importance of having the patience to wait for the right trading opportunity to present itself.

**7** The importance of acting independently of the crowd was a frequently emphasized point.

**8** All the top traders understand that losing is part of the game.

**9** They all love what they are doing.

This next posting reflects not only some of the gems you can find on boards but also the quality of this particular site. Of course there will be those miserable bleeders who will complain that all such tips are too general. If it appears too general then you may just not 'get' trading.

## Time-tested tips

This is a list of classic trading rules that was given to me while on the trading floor in 1984. A senior trader collected these rules from classic trading literature throughout the twentieth century. They obviously withstand the age-old test of time. I'm sure most everybody knows these truisms in their hearts, but this list is nicely edited and makes a good read.

1   Plan your trades. Trade your plan.

2   Keep records of your trading results.

3   Keep a positive attitude, no matter how much you lose.

4   Don't take the market home.

5   Continually set higher trading goals.

6   Successful traders buy into bad news and sell into good news.

7   Successful traders are not afraid to buy high and sell low.

8   Successful traders have a well-scheduled planned time for studying the markets.

9   Successful traders isolate themselves from the opinions of others.

10   Continually strive for patience, perseverance, determination, and rational action.

11   Limit your losses – use stops!

12   Never cancel a stop loss order after you have placed it!

13   Place the stop at the time you make your trade.

14   Never get into the market because you are anxious of waiting.

15   Avoid getting in or out of the market too often.

16   Losses – not profits – make the trader studious. Take advantage of every loss to improve your knowledge of market action.

17   The most difficult task in speculation is not prediction but self-control. Successful trading is difficult and frustrating. You are the most important element in the equation for success.

18   Always discipline yourself by following a pre-determined set of rules.

19   Remember that a bear market will give back in one month what a bull market has taken three months to build.

20   Don't ever allow a big winning trade to turn into a loser. Stop yourself out if the market moves against you 20 per cent from your peak profit point.

**21** You must have a program, you must know your program, and you must follow your program.

**22** Expect and accept losses gracefully. Those who brood over losses always miss the next opportunity, which more than likely will be profitable.

**23** Split your profits right down the middle and never risk more than 50 per cent of them again in the market.

**24** The key to successful trading is knowing yourself and your stress point.

**25** The difference between winners and losers isn't so much native ability as it is discipline exercised in avoiding mistakes.

**26** In trading as in fencing there are the quick and the dead.

**27** Speech may be silver but silence is golden. Traders with the golden touch do not talk about their success.

**28** Dream big dreams and think tall. Very few people set goals too high. A man becomes what he thinks about all day long.

**29** Accept failure as a step towards victory.

**30** Have you taken a loss? Forget it quickly. Have you taken a profit? Forget it even quicker! Don't let ego and greed inhibit clear thinking and hard work.

**31** One cannot do anything about yesterday. When one door closes, another door opens. The greater opportunity always lies through the open door.

**32** The deepest secret for the trader is to subordinate his will to the will of the market. The market is truth as it reflects all forces that bear upon it. As long as he recognizes this he is safe. When he ignores this, he is lost and doomed.

**33** It's much easier to put on a trade than to take it off.

**34** If a market doesn't do what you think it should do, get out.

**35** Beware of large positions that can control your emotions. Don't be overly aggressive with the market. Treat it gently by allowing your equity to grow steadily rather than in bursts.

**36** Never add to a losing position.

**37** Beware of trying to pick tops or bottoms.

**38** You must believe in yourself and your judgement if you expect to make a living at this game.

**39** In a narrow market there is no sense in trying to anticipate what the next big movement is going to be – up *or* down.

**40** A loss never bothers me after I take it. I forget it overnight. But being wrong and not taking the loss – that is what does the damage to the pocket book and to the soul.

**41** Never volunteer advice and never brag of your winnings.

**42** Of all speculative blunders, there are few greater than selling what shows a profit and keeping what shows a loss.

**43** Standing aside is a position.

**44** It is better to be more interested in the market's reaction to new information than in the piece of news itself.

**45** If you don't know who you are, the markets are an expensive place to find out.

**46** In the world of money, which is a world shaped by human behavior, nobody has the foggiest notion of what will happen in the future. Mark that word – *nobody*! Thus the successful trader does not base moves on what supposedly will happen but reacts instead to what does happen.

**47** Except in unusual circumstances, get in the habit of taking your profit too soon. Don't torment yourself if a trade continues winning without you. Chances are it won't continue long. If it does, console yourself by thinking of all the times when liquidating early reserved gains that you would have otherwise lost.

**48** When the ship starts to sink, don't pray – *jump*!

**49** Lose your opinion – not your money.

**50** Assimilate into your very bones a set of trading rules that works for you.

This next posting reveals the correct perspective for trading and systems.

## Execute the plan

Many people think that a winning trade is a good trade, and a losing trade is a bad trade. This can be a very unprofitable and naïve view.

A more successful way to look at your trades (IMHO [in my humble opinion]) is to view a good trade as *any* trade in which you *followed* your trading plan *precisely*. Of course, you must also have confidence that your trading plan is sound, and will be profitable over the long term.

A bad trade is *any* trade in which you *did not* follow your trading plan, regardless of whether the trade was profitable or not. This is a very important point. The most dangerous trades are trades in which you did not follow your trading plan, but managed to close out profitably. Why are these dangerous? They reinforce the idea that you can 'wing it' or ignore your stop-loss limit or wait a little longer for the market to turn when *your* system tells you to get out! *By ignoring your system, you have failed.* By ignoring your system, you have lost your structured plan which ensures that you can trade reproducibly day after day without emotion. In short, by not following your well-thought-out trading plan, you have given in to the emotion of the moment. This is a dangerous and losing path to follow.

Conversely, by following your plan, you have eliminated emotion from your trading. Over time, you can *modify* your trading approach to reflect your increased understanding of the market and to build in the lessons you have learned from your previous winning and losing trades. However, you will modify your trading plan when the market is *closed*, after carefully reviewing your reasons for the change. You will not be giving in to emotion by changing your trading plan 'on-the-fly' during the trading day on a whim.

Hopefully, this concept is clear. A 'losing' trade can be a 'good' trade. Simply follow your plan. Assume you enter a long position in WXYZ at a price of 90⅝ and subsequently exit your position when your stop loss is hit at 90⅛. Immediately thereafter, the stock reverses and goes directly to 93 without even hesitating. Unfortunate? Yes. Annoying? Yes. But did you make a *mistake* by exiting? *Absolutely not*. The trade was exited per your trading plan. The stop loss in your trading plan was designed to protect your account balance against a devastating loss, and you followed your plan. It was a successful trade, a good trade. Pat yourself on the back for doing the right thing.

During the trading day, don't focus on whether individual trades are profitable or not. Instead, focus on making 'good' trades, i.e. *always follow your plan*. After the market is closed, you can work to refine or modify your trading plan as needed. But during the day, follow your rules!

# Chats and boards: come join our community

## Online trader problems

- How best to use online chat sites, if at all.
- Which are the key sites online traders use to talk trading?

The aim of this book, as with all good trading books, is to impart not just information but also knowledge and wisdom. The experience of others besides your humble yet omnipotent author is essential to such a task. In trying to maintain a community feel, boards and chat rooms are an essential source of information, making this an important chapter in the book.

A top chat room or board will create a genuine community feel with intelligent conversation, inclusive of all-experience-level users. Unfortunately such chat rooms are as rare as a Democratic president who doesn't philander (my lawyers inform me I have to add 'and whose name is not Carter and who was president since 1960')!

With a chat room you can talk real-time by typing and posting and seeing instant replies (if anyone is in the room and deigns to reply). With boards you post a message and wait for a reply at some future time. In this chapter we shall see some of the best ones, what 'best' means, and how to use them.

## Why and how they are used

- to pose questions about issues you are unsure of
- to get ideas about what to trade. Be very wary of using them for this. A lot of posters put the 'bull' into 'bulletin board'. Be especially concerned if anyone offers insider information; it is usually the last cry of someone stuck in a bad losing position.

- as an educational tool by learning from the experiences of others, for instance which orders to use at what time of day

- as a review of online trading sites. By this I mean many postings may review who are the best brokers, or the cheapest sites etc.

- just to 'chill' and bond!

---

**From: Sam, Sunday, June 6 1999, on Silicon Investor**

I have been to several chat rooms. I find that it is good for several things:

1 getting a read on general market perception

2 getting a heads-up on stock movements you are *not* following that day (i.e. momentum trades)

3 Feeling out others' thoughts on particular stocks, sectors, news releases, etc.

4 companionship.

But it is not good for getting picks in real time IMO [in my opinion].

That said, know your fellow posters. There will be those you trust, and those you don't. Most, unfortunately, are not to be trusted. Not that they are looking to screw you, but more likely (as with SI) they will only admit selective info. Thus, it goes without saying, don't ever follow the hype. Remember, if someone has made a move, you are already late to the party. Don't allow yourself to be buying their shares as they corral you into a foolish move. You are not in business to bail them out. But, *if* you can trust them, you can see what they are playing on any given day and *why*. But don't let it rule your day. That's just plain lazy. It is a learning tool – that's all. There's work to be done all day long. Research and analysis (as well as actual trading). Getting other people's picks should never be a priority.

---

## Glossary

You will need to know the following terms just so you too can appear dead cool by knowing what the board's hippest in-crowd are talking about. It's a sociological thing.

| | |
|---|---|
| B4 – before | IRL – in real life |
| BBL – be back later | J/K – just kidding |
| BCNU – be seeing you | LOL – laughing out loud |
| BFN – bye for now | NT – no text |
| BRB – be right back | NTR – not trading-related |
| BTW – by the way | OIC – oh, I see! |
| CUL8R – see you later | OTOH – on the other hand |
| F2F – face to face | OTT – over the top |
| FAQs – frequently asked questions | ROTFL – rolling on the floor |
| FWIW – for what it's worth | laughing |
| GBH&K – great big hug & kiss | TIA – thanks in advance |
| HHOK – ha ha only kidding! | TTFN – ta-ta for now |
| IM(H)O – in my (humble) opinion | |

Before I set you loose, you will also want to know the following:

**Flaming** – a nasty or rude response to someone who breaches netiquette, e.g. by posting adverts, thereby treating the board members like buffoons.

**Posting** – the act of placing a comment on a board.

**Thread** – a line of discussion on a board with one person making a posting and the replies being the threads. (Also a thin piece of material used to keep garments together.)

## What to look for and watch out for on chat and board sites

When considering which chat and board sites to make your regular hangouts, you should consider the following issues.

### Size

When it comes to boards, size matters. You obviously want a board with lots of subject matter and members to ensure you get the broadest views and are not sharing the site with a sad and lonely broker from Florida.

### Quality of postings

Some sites just have poor-quality postings for several reasons. It may have been taken over by a few 'bully' posters who cajole, intimidate or just try to poke fun at anyone who may not know as much as the bullies think they themselves do. Sometimes postings are poor because the people posting on them are simply not that good, and postings can degenerate into slanging matches and challenges to settle matters outside the board. Sometimes you get an invasion of ramping postings; those morons who inform you something is about to sky-rocket because they know a man who works for this woman whose husband's mistress's cousin's niece's stepmother's alien dog told her the stock was a good purchase.

## Topics

As well as a wide range of topics the boards should be divided into subgroups so you can get into a relevant topic in enough detail and quickly.

## Design and navigability

It can sometimes seem there are millions of messages on billions of topics posted every two nanoseconds. In fact it is worse than that. All this makes the design and navigation of a site especially important, otherwise you will never get to read about what you want to know or post questions or replies.

## Price

Ideally you want a free site. Failing that, a free trial period followed by a cheap subscription will have to do.

## The Silicon Investor ***

www.techstocks.com

Despite having a name that does not match its web address, this is probably one of the most famous online trading board sites. These are the stats they proudly proclaim to all visitors:

### Size

- 140,000+ messages are posted per week, and 580,000 messages posted per month.

- There are 10,769,922 *searchable* messages stored in the SI database. 29,788 discussion threads have been created by SI members.

- More than 120,000 people have become active members of Silicon Investor.

### Quality
Quite high, not much 'noise'.

### Topics
Topics include the following (with subtopics within these)

- Aerospace and Defense
- Banking and Finance
- Brokerages/Investment Resources
- Canadian Stocks
- Casinos/Gaming
- Coffee Shop
- Five Dollars and Under
- Food Processing and Agriculture
- Futures and Commodities
- Gold, Mining and Natural Resources
- Initial Public Offerings
- International
- Internet Financial Connection
- Iomega (IOM) and IMP (IMPX)
- Market Trends and Strategies
- Miscellaneous (Biotech/Medical)
- Miscellaneous (General)
- Miscellaneous (Technology)
- Mutual Funds
- Overvalued Stocks
- Puts, Calls and other Options

- Real Estate/REITs
- Short-Term Traders
- Specialty Retail
- Transportation
- Web/Information Stocks
- Welcome to SI
- Year 2000 Stocks & Discussion

### Design and navigability

Its design is probably what a website may have looked like in the 70s if they had had the modern internet then. Nevertheless it is relatively easy to find topics, and some helpful chaps collect the best postings for a particular topic and archive them – I love that idea.

### Price

Reading is free, posting costs. There is a free trial membership plan for a fortnight and also a subscription fee of $100 for a year and $200 for life (best not take out the latter if you're 101 years old, then).

## Investorville ***

www.investorville.com

This site reeks of good ideas. It is easily one of the best chat sites on the web. Here's why:

### Size

Lots of members and postings – no worries there.

### Quality

High-quality content. Editing by the Mayor of Investorville ensures that adverts and bad postings are deleted. In fact I could not find a poor-quality posting!

### Topics

As well as covering topics by stocks, there is also a 'user-created' forums section which ensures relevance to online traders, discussing the issues most relevant to them. There is an 'ask a question' forum for all those questions which may not be answered elsewhere, but it also ensures there is a welcoming place for the novice. Now, that's my kind of community.

An excellent 'overheard' section lists and links to all the best, most perceptive and intelligent postings. Yet another good idea. Another section worth a mention is 'hot boards' which lists the most popular boards so you can instantly get a feel for where the most vibrant discussion and latest issues may be being discussed. The 'new posts' section lets you quickly keep up to date with the most recent new discussions.

### Design and navigability

Very easy to read and navigate. I cannot think how it could be simpler. Yeah, I know I am heaping praise on it, but when I see something I like, I just gotta let ya know. There are no annoying reference codes, which clutter threads, as on so many other sites.

### Price

Free as air, and twice as sweet.

## The Stock Club **

www.stockclub.com

This site offers real-time chat as well as boards. Specializes in stocks alone.

### Size

I got the impression there are a few people there but not as many as on, say, Silicon Investor.

### Quality

About average.

### Topics

Stocks are covered in alphabetical order and can be searched by industry group, which is helpful. But they should have industry-based discussion too.

### Design and navigability

The design and navigability are fine: not too bad but not too great. Since they focus on particular stock talk, there is very little you could do to improve it. They could have a 'hot boards' section which lists those stocks with the most postings.

### Price

Free, but you have to become a member even to read messages.

## Marketforum **

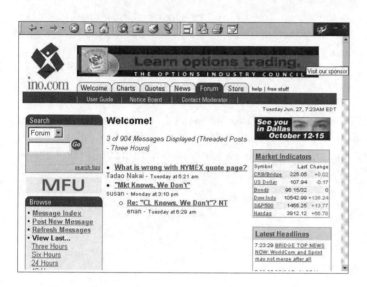

www.marketforum.com

This caters for futures and options and not stock traders.

### Size
The site claimed 3,676 messages in the previous two days when I did a search under 'online'.

### Quality
A very high-quality site with 'serious' talk.

### Topics
Topics are restricted to talk about commodities at an intermediate level.

### Design and navigability
Not too bad a design, though navigation was a bit difficult and it might have been easier to see a long list of articles than having to search by topic.

### Price
Free.

# E-zines: electronic magazines

'E-zine' can be used as a loose term for internet magazines. These may be either internet-only or online versions of offline magazines. Some of the best-known and best-quality e-zines are listed below.

## Why bother?

The main reasons behind visiting e-zines and then selecting one or two as ones you will visit regularly are the same as for following market news and commentary: they provide analysis of the market background against which all trading takes place. Moreover they are an excellent source of education.

## The listed sites

The sites included are ones which:

- are highly respected
- provide excellent quality
- represent quality online financial magazines.

### Action plan ⏱

- Surf sites which you feel meet your needs best in the light of what you have read here.
- Choose a site or sites which you like the best, bearing in mind the amount of time it would take to visit each one on a regular basis.

Online magazines are becoming better than offline ones. They are more quickly updated and have unlimited space to explore a topic. Hyperlinks to previous columns on the same subject can mean a good e-zine keeps you up to date in any particular area. If for instance you invest in technology stocks, then clearly Red Herring is a must to give you an investment edge. Use all of these sites as educational tools, occasionally to give you trading ideas and to separate the boy and girl traders from the adults.

# The top e-zines

Table 15.4 lists the top e-zines and their addresses (see also Diagrams 15.4–15.6).

*Table 15.4  The top e-zines*

| Name | Address |
| --- | --- |
| Applied Derivatives Trading | www.adtrading.com |
| Business Week Online | www.businessweek.com |
| The Economist | www.economist.com |
| Forbes | www.forbes.com |
| Fortune | www.fortune.com |
| Inc. Magazine | www.inc.com |
| InvestorGuide Weekly | www.investorguide.com |
| Red Herring Online | www.herring.com |
| Shares | www.sharesmagazine.com |
| Stocks & Commodities | www.traders.com |
| US News Online | www.usnews.com |
| Worth | www.worth.com |

*Diagram 15.4*
*Red Herring Online*

*An excellent publication. The magazine is a must if you trade in technology issues. The online version is packed full of informative, investigative and well-written pieces.*

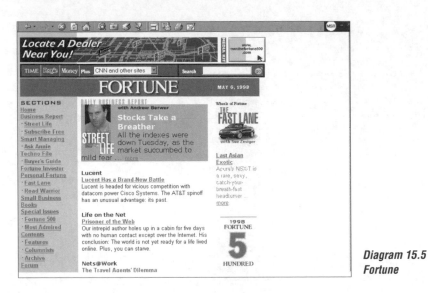

**Diagram 15.5**
**Fortune**

**Diagram 15.6**
**Shares**

## Summary

As you will have guessed, I am not a great fan of newsletters. But at least with the resources described in this chapter you have more information than ever before about how good they are. At least your choice will be informed.

Although the quality of content can vary widely in newsgroups and web-based discussion groups they can be a useful source of second opinions. Remember to always query motives of those posting messages. Their opinions carry more weight if independently verifiable (e.g. a news item you may otherwise have missed), rather than hope or spurious argument. Overall, the web-based discussion groups are of a higher quality than the newsgroups and my advice would be to choose 1 or 2 at the most, otherwise you will not be able to keep abreast of them all.

Always read a couple of e-zines focusing on general market issues. Next find a couple that focus on sectors or industries you invest or trade in frequently, such as telecoms or retail. The latter will provide an insight into stock performance.

What has been learnt about analysis can be added to fruitfully by examination of market commentary, newsgroups, e-zines and newsletters. These are all useful sources of supplemental analysis. However, with newsgroups and newsletters you must take great care in selection and with newsgroups great care in interpretation.

# 16

# Bonds and only bonds

**❝** *There are others as well who put their balls on the line but aren't good traders and they promptly have them taken off them* **❞**

**David Kyte**  Chairman, Kyte Group

## In this chapter

The problem with bonds is that the term covers a multitude of products and time frames. There are treasuries, long-dated, emerging market, company, mortgage-backed, asset-backed, repos and municipal bonds, to name just the most popular types. If you are interested in bonds, given their specialist nature, you will probably already have an idea of the area you are interested in. If you are a novice wanting to know more about this area then the educational sites and the recommended reading will undoubtedly come in handy.

## Good bond sites

A good bond site should have the following characteristics for which they are the most useful.

### Quotes
Delayed and historical quotes are, of course, very helpful.

### Commentary and charts
Market analysis from reputed analysts, in terms of both past movement and prospective market changes, adds considerable value.

### Search engine
The ability to search for bonds based upon numerous variables is an added bonus. This can be considered the same as filtering or screening.

### Credit rating
A site providing credit rating from a reputable source is a good bonus.

## Discussion forum

A discussion forum is a definite bonus. Use this to post queries, get ideas or just learn from what other people are talking about.

## Bonds Online ***

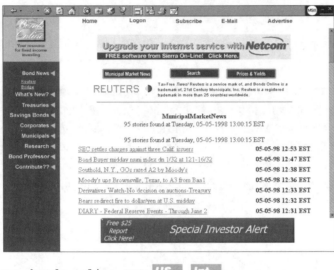

www.bonds-online.com US Int

### How to use this site and what for

The credit rating information available here is exceptional. Overall, the site is very slick and the information diverse and of a high standard. The Bond Professor is an excellent source of information if you have queries regarding bonds. Also, a lot of reasearch is aggregated from other sources, which can be convenient.

## Brady Net **

www.bradynet.com  US   Int

### How to use this site and what for

As can be discerned from its name, this site specializes in emerging-market bonds. It is a good site with good-quality information and worth a visit if your particular fetish is the emerging market. Use the chat room too as it is an especially useful resource on this site.

## PC Trader **

www.fixedincome.com  US   Int

### How to use this site and what for

The quotes for this site are from GocPX, a popular and reliable source. The market news and commentary are very good and professional (hence some are fee-based).

## Investing in Bonds

`www.investinginbonds.com`

**How to use this site and what for**

Use this site for its educational materials but not much else.

## Summary

I was pleasantly surprised at the quality of bond sites. Although some were very technical, most were very generous in the information they provided.

# The truth is out there

# 17

# Net trawlers: search engines

**❝ If you meet a trader who is very, very successful, and he truly, honestly believes it is because he is smarter and faster and more insightful and more aggressive than all of his peers, I don't believe him. I truly don't ❞**

**Bill Lipschutz** Former Global Head of Foreign Exchange, Salomon Brothers

## In this chapter

We here examine one of the most used methods of finding information on the internet: the search engine. For most people, this chapter will be too basic, although there are one or two search tricks that even the most advanced user will find helpful.

## Objectives

- Familiarize ourselves with the workings of search engines.
- Know when to use searches.

## What is a search engine?

A search engine is simply a site that 'searches' other sites depending on keywords entered by a user (Diagram 17.1).

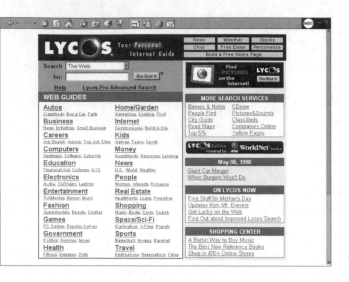

*Diagram 17.1*
*A search engine*

## Some things to know

■ Since pages on the internet change quickly, a search engine is unlikely to be up-to-the-minute, and some results returned may be outdated.

■ Just because an engine does not find a site this does not mean it does not exist.

■ Because of the different way each engine works each will return different results.

■ Results are ranked according to how close the match is to your request, and not, of course, according to best available site in terms of content.

■ If you are not satisfied with the results try a different engine.

## How to search

Very simply: type in the keyword and press enter. If you want to be technical, most search engines will have options which allow you to specify whether the engine is to provide results that contain the keywords as a phrase or any one of the keywords.

## Advanced searching

■ To search for sites that are country-related, go to the search engine's home page and look for the link to the appropriate country, usually at the foot of the page, or try typing **domain:country code**, e.g. in the search box for AltaVista **domain:de** lists web sites which display the domain **de** (Germany).

■ The asterisk (*) can often be used as a wild card, e.g. trad* would look for 'trader', 'trade', 'traditional', etc.

■ In the keyword box of the search engine if you enter two words then be careful as to what you are looking for (see Table 17.1).

Beyond this, different search engines will all have their own language to assist searches, but in most cases the pure and simple keywords will do.

*Table 17.1 Keywords and sample results*

| Keyword | Result |
| --- | --- |
| Dow Jones | All sites containing somewhere in them the words Dow or Jones or both, not necessarily together |
| Dow AND Jones | All sites containing somewhere in them the words Dow and Jones, not necessarily together |
| Dow OR Jones | All sites containing somewhere in them the words Dow or Jones or both, not necessarily together |
| "Dow Jones" | All sites containing somewhere in them the words Dow Jones together |
| +Dow -Jones | All sites containing the word Dow but not those containing the word Jones |

## Top search engines

Table 17.2 lists the major search engines with addresses and ratings (see also Diagrams 17.2, 17.3, 17.4).

*Table 17.2 Major search engines*

| Name | Address | Rating |
| --- | --- | --- |
| AltaVista | altavista.digital | *** (recommended) |
| Excite | excite | *** |
| Lycos | lycos | *** |
| Yahoo! | yahoo | *** |
| Deja News | dejanews | *** |
| InfoSeek | infoseek | *** |
| WebCrawler | webcrawler | ** |
| MetaCrawler | metacrawler | ** |

*** Means the search engine lists a very large number of sites, the amount of information displayed can be altered, supports complex searches, includes directories and other category-based searching links.

** As above but fewer results and category links may not be as good.

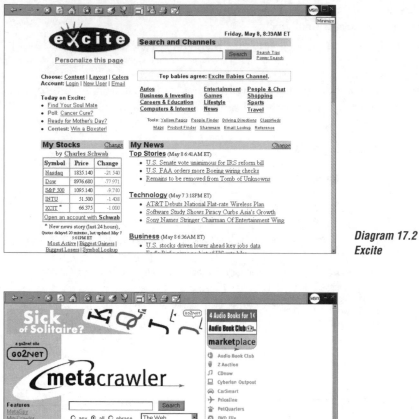

*Diagram 17.2*
*Excite*

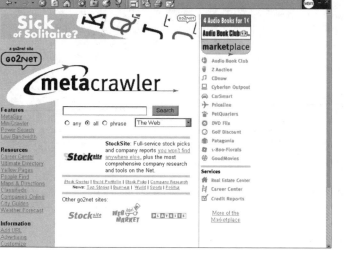

*Diagram 17.3*
*MetaCrawler*

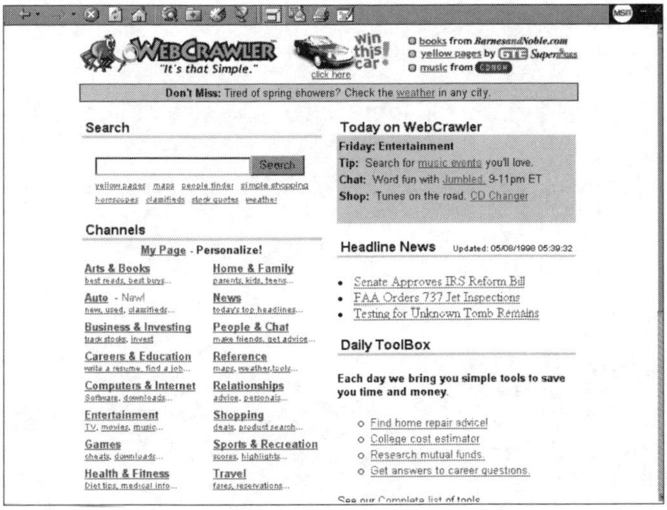

*Diagram 17.4*
*WebCrawler*

## Summary

We have seen the basic operation of search engines. Today they are sophisticated sites providing a wealth of information beyond merely search facilities. They are worth checking out for that alone. Next, we move on to directories of sites, which may further assist in finding information on the internet.

# 18

# The directory approach: web financial directories

*❝ One has to have an interest to understand what is going on in the market. That is a characteristic which very few people have ❞*

**Bernard Oppetit**  Global Head of Equity Derivatives, Banque Paribas

## In this chapter

Continuing our examination of tools that will help us effectively and efficiently find trading information and sites we examine internet financial directories (as we have seen, sometimes referred to as umbrella sites – maybe because they contain everything under the sun).

## Objective

■ **Gain familiarity with directories as means of research.**

## What a directory is

An internet directory simply organizes and lists sites according to category (Diagram 18.1).

The downside is that they rarely rank, review or give much detail about sites. Nevertheless, they can add more focus to a search than a search engine necessarily can.

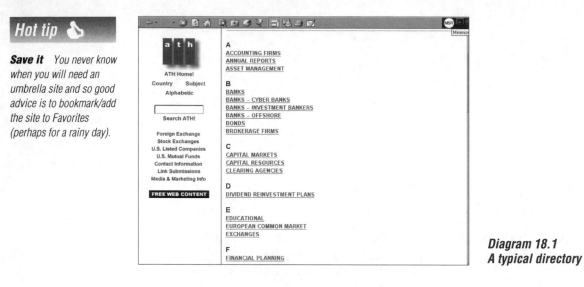

*Diagram 18.1*
*A typical directory*

## Which directories?

Some of the best directories are listed in Table 18.1. They are all worth visting and possibly even bookmarking for a rainy day. It can be great fun just surfing these. I consider them the internet equivalent of a candy store – you walk in and there is so much to try – but without the plaque.

*Table 18.1  Leading finance directories*

| Directory | Address | Ranking |
|---|---|---|
| AltaVista | altavista.looksmart.com | *** |
| Dow Jones Business Directory | bd.dowjones.com | ** |
| Finance Wise | www.financewise.com | ** |
| Finance Watch | www.finance.wat.ch | *** (recommended) |
| Investorama | www.investorama.com | *** |
| Yahoo! Finance | quote.yahoo.com | *** (recommended) |
| Investools | www.Investools.com | *** |

*** An excellent selection of categories and links. Comprehensive, diverse and easy to navigate.
** Many good features and a fair selection of sites and categories.
Anything lower than ** is not included because the standard is so high.

## AltaVista ***

`altavista.looksmart.com`

### How to use this site and what for

The tree structure to this directory is very useful: you can see where you have been, what else is available and where you may want to go next. It saves a lot of time, avoiding the need to go back and forth in the browser. The directory content itself is also pretty extensive. Use this one for First Call's earnings content too.

## Dow Jones Business Directory **

`bd.dowjones.com`

### How to use this site and what for

The chief benefit of this directory is that unlike virtually any other finance site it actually ranks each site and describes them in some detail. However, it does include relatively few sites.

# FinanceWise **

www.financewise.com

## How to use this site and what for

FinanceWise provides both a search engine and a directory. The directory is not too bad and does have categories others do not. Covers both finance and trading well.

## Finance Watch **

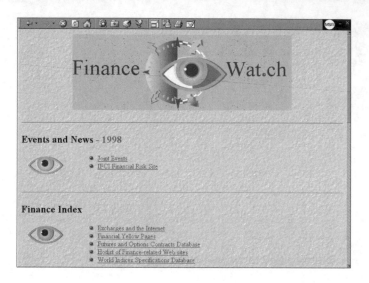

`www.finance.wat.ch`

### How to use this site and what for

This Swiss-based site (hence the .ch) is massive, nay, it is humungous. I used to say, 'If it ain't 'ere, it ain't nowhere!' but it *has* gone just a little bit downhill in the last couple of years.

## Investorama***

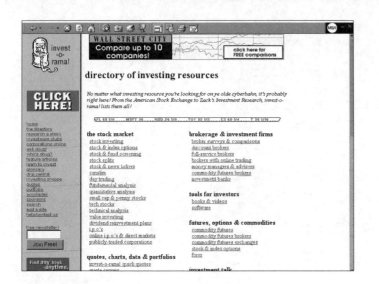

www.investorama.com

### How to use this site and what for

This directory has a vast number of categories and because the structure is fairly flat (i.e. there are few sub-directories) you can quickly get a very good overview. Use it for a comprehensive one-stop shop with easy access.

## Yahoo! Finance ***

quote.yahoo.com

### How to use this site and what for

This is how a web site should be designed. The amount of information on the screen without the need for excessive scrolling, eye strain or clutter is remarkable. The financial directory is also comprehensive for a non-finance company. Excellent. I think I'll buy me some shares in Yahoo! [Update to version 2.0 – and didn't those shares do well since I first wrote this! I think I'll IPO myself – see you at version 3.0, same place!]

## Investools ***

www.Investools.com

### How to use this site and what for
Some of the most useful things in this very comprehensive site are the screeners and personal portfolios. Very good.

## Summary

In this chapter we have seen some of the powerful and useful service provided by directories as a potential source of trading information and research. While their listings can be extensive we nevertheless need to monitor for quality.

# 19

# Be an online bookworm

**❝** *Another way [to improve trading] is reading books and reading magazine articles to see which trader has a style that would work for you* **❞**

**Jon Najarian** Chairman and CEO, Mercury Trading

## In this chapter

One of the major problems we traders face is accumulating a lot of knowledge about a topic, without having the luxury of being taught it at our merchant bank – unlike the institutional traders! I always advise online traders to read as much as possible about a subject before ploughing their ill-gotten gains into the market. When you want to research a trading topic a little deeper, sometimes it is worth considering non-internet resources, namely books. Online bookstores can very often undercut normal bookstores because of lower operating costs. In this chapter we examine looking for and buying books online.

## Objective

- **If thinking of entering a new market, trading a new product (e.g. futures) or trading a new time frame, get lots of information from experts and build on their experience.**

## Online stores

The best sites have several features:

### Search

All the sites permit you to search for books. The better sites permit searches based on:

- author
- title
- subject
- publication date
- publisher
- ISBN.

## Categories

Many of the online bookstores have books listed according to categories, which can help surfing if you are not quite sure what you want.

## Jacket pictures

Always helpful.

## Reviews

Reviews of the book either from online readers or taken from the jacket are a useful feature.

## Table of contents

Sadly, few include this but many should, given that in a bookstore this is really the first thing one will often examine.

## Synopsis

Vital, unless you know what the book is about already.

## E-mail notification

Some sites monitor titles similar to ones that you tell them interest you and notify you of new releases. This can be useful, or sometimes tedious.

## Other

Since some internet bookstores are massive businesses they will often have lots of other features: guest speakers, best-seller guides, reviews from magazines, 'books in the news' etc. With other sites you can pay in several different currencies. Most deliver anywhere in the world.

## Things to bear in mind

When buying books online there are several pieces of advice worth bearing in mind:

### Check out several sites

The price of a book between online stores can vary significantly. Bookmark or add to Favorites all the bookstores listed below and check them out if you are making a purchase. Another reason to check out different stores is that the amount of information varies from site to site.

### Beware p&p

Prices quoted exclude postage and packaging, but some sites only tell you those charges after you have placed a provisional order. Remember to factor in the cost. Most sites offer a variety of delivery times, and if you are not in a hurry, take the slow and cheap option.

### Delivery

Find out what the delivery times are. Sometimes online books can take up to three months to be delivered.

### Worried about giving credit card details online?

All the sites below if viewed through Internet Explorer or Netscape Navigator should encrypt and keep secure your credit card details. You can also visit the sites and view their reassurances on online security if not convinced. Some sites provide a phone number for phoning or faxing orders. Alternatively if you are still unhappy, look for the book online and ask your local bookstore to order it from its supplier – of course it won't be as cheap as the online order.

## Comparisons

As you can see from Table 19.1, the price of a book can vary between sites greatly, some offering the same book at double the price. This led me to recommend Shopping.com for price. However, the cheaper giants, like Shopping.com and Amazon.com, often do not have as many titles on trading as the more specialist stores. Many a time I have found the title I have been looking for on Global Investor when I failed to find it elsewhere.

*Mix and match*
*Since the prices of books and information about a book vary between sites, why not get all you want to know from one site and place the order with another site?*

*Table 19.1  Online stores*

| Name & address | Ranking | Price of *Trading Online* | Search | E-mail notification | Categories | Jacket pic | Reviews | Table of contents | Synopsis |
|---|---|---|---|---|---|---|---|---|---|
| Global Investor www.global-investor.com/bookshop | *** (Recommended) | $39.36 | ✓ | ✓ | ✓ | ✓ | ✓ | ✓ | ✓ |
| Amazon www.amazon.com | *** | $21.56 | ✓ | ✓ | ✓ | ✓ | ✓ | ✓ | ✓ |
| Barnes & Noble www.barnesandnoble.com | *** | $21.56 | ✓ | ✓ | ✓ | ✓ | ✓ | ✓ | ✓ |
| Internet Bookshop www.bookshop.co.uk | ** | $22 (£13.81) | ✓ | ✓ | ✓ | ✓ | ✓ | ✓ | ✓ |
| Traders' Library www.traderslibrary.com | *** | $26.95 | ✓ | ✓ | ✓ | ✓ | ✓ | ✓ | ✓ |
| Shopping.com www.shopping.com (Recommended on price) | ** | $20.97 | ✓ | ✓ | ✓ | ✓ | ✓ |  | ✓ |

*** A model site, with deep discounts, excellent stock range, search facilities and book details.

** Good prices, fair range and reasonable search facilities.

# Global Investor ***

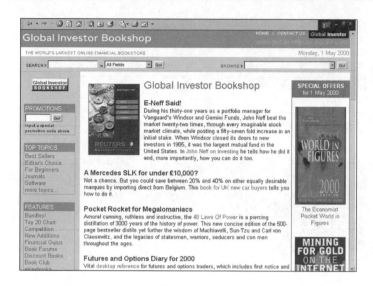

www.global-investor.com/bookshop

## Comment

A specialist site concentrating on trading books. Lots of innovative ideas such as book bundles that complement each other, comments from prominent people on books they recommend, and competitions. The site also gives you as much information as possible short of giving you the book. I would like to see extracts and customer comments though. An excellent site from which to buy your books. A useful currency converter ensures they have clients in over 100 countries worldwide. I use them myself.

## Amazon ***

`www.amazon.com`

### Comment

A small book company based in Seattle. You may have heard of them. They cannot provide some of the specialist content that a site like Traders' Library or Global Investor can, but do provide cheap books, customer comments and star ratings from readers.

# Barnes & Noble ★★★

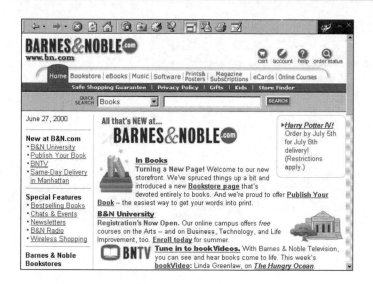

`www.barnesandnoble.com`

## Comment

Another small bookstore gone online. They have one or two real bookstores too, I believe. Price is the key attraction here again, but somehow they always seem one step behind Amazon in features.

## Internet Bookshop **

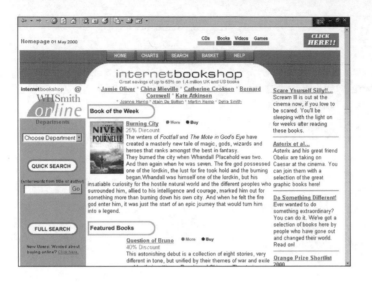

www.bookshop.co.uk

**Comment**

One of the earliest online bookstores outside the US. Medium-sized, not a specialist trading bookstore, but useful for UK book buyers.

# Traders' Library ★★★

www.traderslibrary.com

## Comment

This site has come a very long way in the past year. Like Global Investor, it seeks a competitive advantage to the big stores like Amazon on the basis that it has specialist expertise in its field. This strategy works, though you don't get the feeling with the site that it is provided by people with a lot of knowledge about trading.

www.shopping.com

### Comment

This is an Alta Vista company. It provides very cheap books on trading but with limited information about them. If price is king then this store sits on a throne. However, it often lacks some of the titles to be found at Global Investor and Traders' Library and doesn't have advance notice of new trading books as is found at those sites.

## Summary

Thankfully there are some excellent specialist trading bookstores on the web. It seems that there will continue to be a division between the supersites, such as Amazon, which have to try hard to add specialist content, and the more specialist sites like Global Investor. The latter live and breathe trading books and so as well as offering individual titles can anticipate traders' needs and offer bundles of books, competitions, newsletters, software etc. Unfortunately, the bigger sites have the clout with the publishers and distributors to be able to offer lower prices. Hopefully this will change soon.

# 20

# Scams, spams and other online trading pot-holes

*❝ Bulls make money. Bears make money. Pigs get slaughtered ❞*

**Anon**

## In this chapter

Online fraud seems to be increasing exponentially. In this chapter we examine some of the dangers and the sites if you want to explore matters further.

## Objectives

- Gain an awareness of scams on the net.
- Get details of some sites for more information.

## A growth industry

With the cases of Tokyo Joe and Whoofnet.com, the start of 2000 confirmed that as online trading grows, we can expect more online trading scams from fraudsters, hoaxers and plain desperate losing online traders, attracted by the prospect of duping the greedy and the unwary.

Not a good start to the year for some investors. So, what types of scams can we expect? What are the warning signs for online traders, and what precautions can the online trader take?

### Recent scams

Tokyo Joe was an online stock picker who, US regulators have alleged, fraudulently induced investors to pick his tips without disclosing his own holdings and then, once the price went up, sold those stocks himself at a profit. He charged as much as $200 a month for his picks.

Whoofnet.com was a scheme offering free shares to its service users. But to join the scheme you had to pay £400, which could be recouped by getting others to join; an e-pyramid scheme.

## Pump and dump

One of the most usual types of online trading scams is the 'pump and dump'. It comes in a variety of guises. For instance, it could be as unsophisticated as a private investor who makes a false claim in the expectation of manipulating the stock price. He may claim on a bulletin board that the company in question is about to release news of some new product, service or alliance. Our desperate investor is of course hoping other readers will buy the stock and pump the price. In any event he may well be distributing insider information, and trading decisions based on such information may also be criminal acts.

The problem is not gossip, guesswork or speculation – free speech enshrined somewhere in a European Convention permits that – rather, the problem is the intention to manipulate stock prices – which *is* illegal. The more philosophical may argue that it doesn't matter whether the information is true or false since either way it moves the market and the intention of the one individual concerned is irrelevant. For now, I will steer clear of the metaphysical.

More sophisticated 'pump and dump' scams involve stock newsletters. Unlike our desperate private investor, these newsletters, and similarly e-mail tips or website picks, carry an air of formality and authority making them more convincing.

## Warning bells

The warning signs for innocent online-trading bystanders are several: with ever more astute online traders on the most popular bulletin boards and chat forums, there tends to be a degree of self-regulation and it is worth reading the replies to any stock hyping to determine how sceptical everyone is.

Scamsters tend to focus on thinly traded stocks, usually AIM-listed ones trading less than 100p. These are the most likely to be moved by rumours, particularly since City brokers and market-makers often monitor the boards too. It is not always small companies that are prey to manipulation efforts. In 1999 Reckitt & Colman merger was illegally revealed on a message board.

Scamsters also tend to select stocks that are thinly researched by analysts or rarely followed by journalists. It is this vacuum of information that makes any information, regardless of source, all the more effective and vociferous.

On 'tips' from newsletters you should check the small print to see if they may be funded or sponsored or own stock in the companies they are tipping. Of course, fraudsters won't disclose this. In 1998, the *Daily Speculator*, a US tip-sheet was sued by the SEC for allegedly costing investors $5.8 million by hyping a stock in a company in which it had a 90 per cent shareholding.

## Conduct your own research

Conducting your own research before investing in a stock is of course a vital insurance policy against scams, as is diversification among holdings. Always check for news stories on news sites containing archives, such as FT.com. The excellent Stock Detective site (*www.stockdetective.com*) recommends examining the following:

- The stock sells at a much higher price-to-earnings multiple than its recent sales growth rate.

- The stock sells at a valuation of more than three times total revenues.

- The company's total market capitalization exceeds the size of the total market its products will serve.

- The company's income statement reveals unusually excessive general and administrative expenses.

- The company's cash flow statement shows losses from operations in contrast to net earnings.

- The company has nothing but a concept and generates no revenues.

Of course none of the above is fool-proof. You may still get caught out, or wrongly misjudge a true claim for a false one, or a sound one for a poor one. Given the business ideas behind some recent internet start-ups, it is definitely difficult to judge if the people behind them are genuine.

If you are intrigued by net scams, Internet Fraud Watch (*www.fraud.org/ifw.htm*) provides a guide for detecting scams. Both *www.nasd.com* and *www.sec.gov* provide 'anti-scam' advice. On the specific issue of stock fraud, the *www.defrauded.com* site summarizes recent allegations of stock fraud.

Feel safe to stroll those superhighways now.

## The sites

## Internet Fraud Watch ***

`www.fraud.org/ifw.htm`

### How to use this site and what for

A great little site offering some good tips and some more obvious ones on avoiding being caught by net scams. The site also has a fascinating section dealing with some popular and recent scams on the net. Covers more than online-trading-related scams, and concerns itself with those relating to magazine subscriptions and work-at-home schemes.

## Stock Detective ***

www.stockdetective.com

### How to use this site and what for

Unlike Internet Fraud Watch, this one focuses on trading-related scams. Use the list evaluating sites which may not be providing objective analysis but are sponsored without declaring it openly.

## National Association of Securities Dealers *

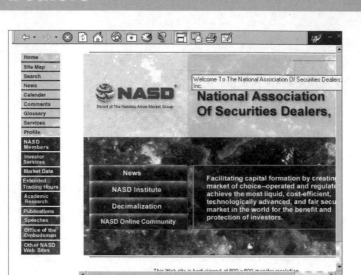

www.nasd.com

### How to use this site and what for

This is the security industry's own self-regulating body. Use it for information on arbitration procedures and processes; beyond that maybe a bit dull.

## Investor Rights Online **

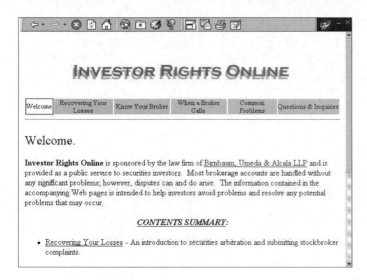

www.investor-rights.com

### How to use this site and what for

The site is the work of an LA law firm. Useful for tips on some of the top scams (such as churning, when the broker makes you over-trade in order to earn a commission) and how to avoid them. It can also be useful if you want to know how to handle cold-calling brokers.

## Nolo Law Center **

www.nolo.com

### How to use this site and what for

Use this one for more background information on the legal issues associated with
stock trading. Good if you have a problem and want more information before
taking further action, or if you are just curious.

## Securities Law **

`www.seclaw.com`

### How to use this site and what for

The site has content posted by a New York lawyer – yes, there must be one who does something gratis. It has lots of information about securities law and it will be more useful if you know a little law in the area already. Use it to get a feel for the common types of disputes arising between parties and to keep up to date with legal changes.

Section **4**

# Appendices

# Essential hardware and software

## In this appendix

You can't sky-dive without a plane and you can't trade online unless you are online. In this appendix, we look at the minimum hardware a trader needs for trading. You could, of course, go higher-spec: that's up to you.

## Objective

■ **Find out what gear is necessary to get up and running as an online trader.**

## Hardware

### Computer

**A PC and not a Mac is recommended**

For reasons best known to Bill Gates and Steve Jobs, most trading software is not Mac-compatible. It makes far more sense therefore for you to stick with a PC (which are always Windows-compatible) than buy a Mac and be disappointed.

**For trading, a classic 100 MHz Pentium processor is sufficient**

Although there are as many new processors produced each year as sex allegations against Bill Clinton, it remains the fact that old is best (when it comes to processors, at least). Newer, faster processors are great for games, but not necessary for trading.

**It is not necessary to buy the latest PC**

It will go out of date and you will be paying a premium. Instead, buy a cheaper PC and upgrade later.

### 32 MB RAM is minimum requirement

RAM is the temporary memory in which your computer runs programs, a little like room to play. The more room the computer has, the quicker it can get things done. However, 32 MB is more than enough. If you want you can buy more, but you do not strictly need it for your trading.

### 3 GB hard drive or larger is best

The hard drive is where all the programs and other things you save are stored. Storage space is useful as over the years we all tend to collect clutter, such as bric-a-brac, spouses, etc. A 3 GB drive would probably last most traders until they decide to upgrade their computers (and their spouses).

### Windows 98 operating system is recommended

When it comes to programming trading software, most programmers use the latest version of Windows.

### CD drive useful, x16 or faster

Most programs and much data are provided on compact disks. A 16-speed one is more than adequate although many computers now come with nothing slower than 32-speed. DVD players are not needed as yet.

### Soundcard and speakers

Soundcard and speakers can be useful for online news broadcasts and some trading software, such as metastocks using videos of advisors. However, they are not essential. Many internet sites provide live broadcasts, and a soundcard and speakers will add even more value to the internet. Fortunately, these are normally thrown in with new computers, or are available pretty cheaply.

## Modem

### Internal or external makes little difference

It does not matter from a trading point of view whether the modem is some electronic wizardry inside the computer, or a separate attachment outside it. The latter option may be better if you are not keen on opening up the computer.

### At least a 56k modem is recommended

You do not want to be waiting all day to receive trading news and information. The speed of your modem is important to ensure you can have an outside life, too.

### Consider ISDN or ADSL if you can afford it

These offer digital connection that is faster than a normal modem. They are lightning fast, but can be expensive.

## Monitor

### 15" minimum required

Beyond 15″ and monitors start getting very pricey. Less than 15″ and you start needing a magnifying glass. With 17″ screens becoming standard, you could even go to 19″.

### Anti-glare and anti-radiation filter essential

The radiation emitted from the trading screen that is on all day may cause you to grow a second head, but there is no evidence that two brains would improve your trading performance. So buy a filter, and keep your uni-head good looks.

## Printer

### Laser printer most expensive but best for drawing charts

These printers have dropped dramatically in price and are best when it comes to printing out all those trading charts and for reading text.

### Inkjet minimum requirement

If the purse strings are tight, an inkjet is likely to be adequate for printing charts and text.

# Internet service providers (ISPs) and access providers (IAPs)

## ISPs

ISPs not only provide access to the internet but they also have their own member-only content, rather like an online magazine. Many organize events like online special guest stars.

## IAPs

Unlike internet service providers, these do not have their own content, but only provide internet access. However, they are cheaper than ISPs and are sufficient for trading purposes.

## An unlimited online time plan is required

ISPs and IAPs usually have different charging plans, many charging by the number of hours spent using their services. Since we traders may spend a lot of time online, the cheapest pricing option is almost always the 'unlimited' time plan, since there is only a monthly flat fee for access.

### Take a free trial

Try before you buy is the advice here. Almost all ISPs and IAPs permit a one-month free trial, and it is best to use this to test their reliability.

### Compare providers

The web site *www.consumeratings.com* ranks providers according to numerous variables. It can be a good pointer for narrowing down the providers you would like to test before subscribing.

## Browsers

### Software

Browser software turns data into audio-visual content and so lets you experience sites in graphics, sound and video. Browsers are a great and essential part of trading, as important to trading as the remote control is to television viewing.

### The latest versions of Internet Explorer or Netscape Navigator are recommended

If you are looking for a browser then you want the most sophisticated one and one catered for by almost all internet sites. So Internet Explorer and Netscape Navigator are highly recommended. They are available free from cover CDs of most internet magazines.

### Bookmarks

It is essential to familiarize yourself with Bookmarks in Netscape Navigator or Favorites in Internet Explorer for the purposes of managing information.

## PC TV

If you are trading from home, then you could have a TV playing in a small section of your monitor, such as CNBC or Bloomberg, to keep you up to date with the markets. Not essential, but I like it, also great for watching *Simpsons* while you write books – only kidding: you, the reader, have my undivided attenti …

## Summary

This appendix has covered the basics for those already familiar with computers and the internet. Most entry-level PCs will accommodate all the aspects mentioned here and you will not have much to worry about. People with older systems may need to upgrade, however.

# The basics of futures

## In this appendix

Many people are intrigued by futures; this is a painless guide to those derivatives. Remember to see the recommended reading, the exchange sites in Chapter 12 and the futures and options sites in Chapter 10.

## Objective

- **A broad overview of futures with a view to finding out more and considering further whether to trade them online.**

## What is a futures contract?

A futures contract has several features:

- It is a legally binding contract.
- It is usually traded through a recognized exchange (e.g. Chicago Mercantile Exchange).
- One party agrees to *take* delivery and the other party agrees to *make* delivery are the underlying asset.
- The specific *quality* and *quantity* of the underlying asset to be delivered are agreed in advance.
- The *date* of delivery is fixed in advance.

■ The *price* of delivery is fixed in advance.

■ The *place* of delivery is fixed in advance.

In other words, a futures contract is simply an agreement to deliver a specific quantity and quality of an asset at a predetermined price, place and date. If you are 'long' a futures contract then you have bought a futures contract and so are the party that will take delivery. You may already have entered into very similar contracts; ever bought something and asked for it to be delivered? If you are 'short' a futures contract then you have sold a futures contract, and so are the party that will make delivery.

## The product range

Today futures are available on:

■ *metals:* silver, gold, copper, platinum

■ *energy:* crude oil, heating oil, natural gas, unleaded gasoline

■ *wood:* lumber

■ *indices:* NYSE Index, S&P 500 Stock Index, US Dollar Index, CRB Futures Index, Municipal Bond Index

■ *currencies:* British pound, US dollar, French franc, Eurodollar, Swiss franc, Deutschmark, Japanese yen, Canadian dollar

■ *interest rates:* treasury bonds, treasury bills, treasury notes, Eurodollars

■ *foods and fibres:* coffee, cocoa, sugar, cotton, orange juice

■ *meats:* live cattle, feeder cattle, hogs, pork bellies

■ *grains:* wheat, corn, oats, soybean complex.

For every futures contract the most important information is:

■ minimum contract size, e.g. 100 troy ounces of gold per contract

■ how the price is expressed, e.g. $ per ounce

■ effect of minimum tick movement, e.g. a $1 move in the contract price equals $100 difference in profit/loss per contract.

So, for example, a typical futures contract might look like this:

Cattle (CME); 40,000 pounds; cents per pound,
quoted at 72 for December delivery.

What this means is that each cattle futures contract on the Chicago Mercantile Exchange is for 40,000 pounds of live cattle, and prices are expressed in cents per pound. The price of 72 means 72 cents per pound. Therefore, a one-cent price move causes a $400 change in equity (i.e. 1 cent × 40,000).

Note, however, that only about 1 per cent of all futures contracts are held until delivery; they are usually 'closed' before then. That is, an equal and opposite futures trade is made which cancels out your delivery obligations. The reasons vary as to why most futures contracts are not held to delivery, but the major reason is that the futures contract is used for speculation and one does not care about the underlying asset, and also because the future is used as a hedge (see glossary).

## Example

Gold futures contracts are traded on the New York Commodity Exchange (COMEX).

Minimum contract size is 100 troy ounces.

Price expressed in $/oz.

Therefore, a $1 change in the contract is worth $100.

|  |  | $/oz | Contract value | Margin |
|---|---|---|---|---|
| **May 2** | Bought one contract COMEX gold June delivery | 342 | $34,200 | $2,000 |
| **May 23** | Sold one contract COMEX gold June delivery | 352 | $35,200 |  |

Profit is $1,000 on an initial margin of $2,000. That is, $10 per oz across 100 ounces that a contract consists of.

# Futures on the Dow Jones Industrial Average

Probably the most widely recognized index in the world is the Dow Jones Industrial Average (DJIA). Moreover, it is very easy to track, given that every newspaper and TV and radio station in the world that carries financial news carries news about the Dow, with the possible exception of the *All-Baghdad Finance Show*. Yet until quite recently you could not trade the futures on the index – they did not exist. Now for everyone who has an opinion on the future direction of the Dow Jones (and let's face it, who doesn't?) you can put your mullah where your opinion is.

## The DJIA

The Dow Jones Industrial Average represents a portfolio of 30 large cap blue-chip stocks traded on the New York Stock Exchange. It includes companies such as Microsoft and GE. They represent about one-fifth of the market value of US stocks!

## DJIA futures – salient features

### Unit of trading
$10 times the DJIA. So with the index at say 11,500, holding one futures contract is the same as investing $115,000 in the DJIA portfolio. So, for every point it rises the long, holder makes $10.

### Minimum price fluctuation
One point ($10).

### Trading hours
8.15am to 3.15pm Chicago time.

### Contract months
March, June, September, December.

### Last trading day
The trading day preceding the third Friday of the contract month.

### Ticker
DJ.

## S&P 500 futures

Like the Dow, the S&P is a very widely recognized and well-reported index. On this index, too, you can buy options. The S&P 500 Index is based on the stock prices of 500 different companies. The market value of these companies represents around 80 per cent of the value of all stocks on the New York Stock Exchange.

One S&P 500 futures contract is the same as owning $250 multiplied by the futures price. So, with the index at 1100, the value of the contract is $275,000. A change in the price by the minimum tick possible, $0.1, would change the value of the contract by 0.1 x $250 = $25.

## Why are there futures contracts?

In the US, between the Great Lakes and the grain-growing, livestock-rearing Great Plains, lies Chicago. A natural port for access to the world's markets for most American farmers, Chicago soon became and remains the home of the largest commodities exchanges in the world.

Picture Chicago in the 1850s. As a farmer growing wheat in rural America, each harvest I reap the rewards of my annual toils. I sell most of my wheat to a few livestock farmers who use it to feed their animals. Each year, I pray for wheat prices to rise, so that I may make greater profits when it comes to selling my wheat, and each year I worry that the prices might fall. Each year, the livestock farmers pray for bumper crops so that the price might fall and their costs drop, and each year they worry that the price might rise. Then, while in our respective fields, it occurs to us to fix our prices several months in advance so that we may plan ahead. While we are at it, we should also fix when, where, and what quality our wheat should be. What we have stumbled across is the futures contract.

Essentially, the futures contract was created to meet a business need. That need still exists today: the need for certainty in an uncertain world. The futures contract permitted hedges (i.e. protection) against adverse price movements by fixing the sale price today. Of course, it soon occurred to some non-farmers with stripy shirts, braces, slicked-back hair and fast red Italian and German sports cars that futures could also be used to speculate.

## How are futures prices fixed?

A future is a derivative. That is, its price is derived from the price of the underlying asset it refers to. A gold future's price is derived from the price of gold. The cash or spot price of the underlying asset is the price at which the underlying asset is currently being bought and sold in the market. The price of the cash asset changes with supply and demand. The futures price responds to changes in the spot price.

Obviously, at delivery, the futures price and the spot price are the same. If they were not then you could buy one and sell the other for instant profit (arbitrage). Before delivery, the futures price equals the cash price plus the cost of holding the cash commodity until delivery. A little thought makes it clear why this must be so. If it were not so, suppose the futures price of wheat is high relative to the cash price of wheat: you could buy the cash wheat – store it, and pay interest on the money you borrowed to pay for it – and sell ('go short') the future (i.e. promise to deliver the wheat in the future). Basically your costs (of buying and storing the wheat) would be less than your receipts (from selling the wheat) and you would make a profit:

| | |
|---|---|
| Price, above cash wheat price, of wheat future per bushel for delivery in 1 month | 20¢ |
| Costs of holding cash wheat per bushel for 1 month | 13¢ |

Therefore, sell the future and buy the cash stock. Deliver the cash stock against the future in one month. Locked-in profit = 7¢ per bushel

## What is margin?

*Initial margin* is a small fraction of the contracts value paid at the time the position is opened. For example, to trade a futures contract worth $20,000 may require initial margin of $2,000, just 10 per cent of contract value. A 5 per cent movement in the contract value, i.e. $1,000, would result in a gain or loss of 50 per cent of the sum invested. This is what is meant by leverage. Margin requirements are set by the exchange.

*Variation margin* is the further payments that need to be made if the price moves adversely.

## Speculation

A futures speculator is like a speculator in any other asset. He seeks to profit from price changes. How he comes to decide what price changes are likely is his business; there as many different methods as traders. A trader may think that the UN is about to relax oil sanctions against Iraq and so the price of oil likely to fall. As we saw earlier, all other things being equal, if the price of the cash commodity falls then the price of the future is also likely to fall. Consequently, our trader may short oil futures. However, he will have to be careful that there are not counter-vailing price-raising forces which may swamp the effects of the UN decision. The trader will also have to ensure that the expectation of an imminent fall in oil prices is not already discounted in the price, in which case when the event eventually occurs the price will be unaffected.

### Example

#### A successful speculation

|  |  |  | Margin |
|---|---|---|---|
| **April 10** | Buy one December copper contract at | $97.25 | $1,250 |
| **May 31** | Sell one December copper contract at | $102.25 | |

Here the speculator made a profit of 5¢ per pound or 5 × $250 = $1,250. That is a 100 per cent profit on the original margin from a 5¢ move. But losses can be equally spectacular.

Speculators also use spread positions. A simple spread involves a long and short position so that a gain on the long position is offset partly by a loss on the short position or vice versa. The spreader desires a net gain.

## Example

| March | Buy one May wheat contract at $2.85 per bushel, sell one July wheat contract at $2.80 per bushel |
| April | Sell one May wheat contract at $3.20 per bushel, buy one July wheat contract at $2.90 per bushel |

The net result is a gain of $.25 per bushel. Gain of $.35 on the long position and loss of $.10 on the short position.

# Why spread?

The major benefit of spreading is that the downside risk is reduced considerably compared to a net long or short position. Consequently margin is also reduced.

# The hedge

A hedge is a futures position that is roughly opposite and equal to the position the hedger has in the cash market. If you are long (own) the cash commodity, your hedge would be to short futures. The hedge is an insurance contract, in effect.

## Example

A farmer notes that the price of wheat is $2.85 per bushel in the cash market. He wants to ensure he can get that price in seven months when it comes to harvest.

|         | Cash market | Futures market            |
|---------|-------------|---------------------------|
| October | $2.85       | Sell wheat future at $2.90 |
| May     | $2.44       | Buy wheat future at $2.49  |

In May the farmer sells his crop in the cash market for $2.44. He also got a gain of $.41 per bushel from the futures hedge, i.e. he received $2.85 per bushel. Had he not hedged, he would only have received $2.44.

## Summary

The most basic thing to remember about futures is that you buy them (go long) if you think the price will rise, and sell them (go short) if you think it will fall. There is unlimited risk with futures and they should not be traded without a substantial period of paper trading for a full appreciation of the monetary risks.

# The basics of options trading and strategies

## In this appendix

For those of a technical persuasion, we shall examine some common technical indicators that can be found in all the major software packages. After briefly describing each one, there will be a description of how it is popularly interpreted. At the end I provide my list of what I consider to be the most popular indicators.

## Objective

- ■ **A thorough comprehension of options as the basis for further study.**

## What is an option?

An option is a contract between the holder and the grantor (called writer) of the option. A holder pays the writer a premium for entering into the contract. There are basically two types: call options and put options.

A call gives the holder the right, but not the obligation, to buy from the writer:

1 within a fixed period of time (the exercise period)
2 a fixed quantity of the underlying security
3 at a fixed price (being the exercise price or strike price).

**key terms**

*Writer*
*Strike price or exercise price*
*Exercise period or expiry date premium*

> **Example**
>
> In the UK, 'one contract of the Barclays July 1,100 calls priced at 67p' would give the holder the right to buy, any time before a fixed date in July, from the writer 1,000 shares in Barclays Bank at a price of 1,100 pence (or £11) each. To purchase the option in the first place the holder would have to pay the writer £670 (1,000 x 67 pence) as premium.

> **Example**
>
> ABC Corp. July 80 calls entitle the holder to purchase 100 shares of ABC Corp. common stock at $80 per share at any time prior to the option's expiration in July.

## What's the big idea 'ere?

The general idea is, of course, to make money! The flexibility of options provides many ways in which this can be done. One of the simplest ideas is (in the case of a call option holder) to buy shares in the future from the option writer at the fixed exercise price and then immediately sell them in the market at a profit, assuming the market price is greater than the exercise price. In the Barclays example, if the underlying price of the stock were 1,200 at expiry in July, the holder would call for his 1,000 shares (at a cost of £11 each) and then sell them immediately in the market at £12 each. Call holders therefore want the underlying share price to rise.

From the point of view of the writer or seller of the option, he is obliged, if 'called' upon, to sell the 1,000 shares in Barclays Bank, and would receive the £11 per share in return. The writer wants to profit from receiving his premium, and not having to have to sell the holder any shares in the future. The call writer therefore does not generally want the market price to rise above the strike price, otherwise he will have to sell to the call holder at a lower price than he could get in the market. In the Barclays example a call writer would have to sell at £11 under the option, when in the market he could otherwise have received £12. Call writers therefore do not want the underlying share price to rise.

Similarly, a put option provides the holder with the right, but not the obligation, for a fixed period of time to sell to the writer a fixed quantity of the underlying security at a fixed price.

Most people trade in traded options. That means they can sell the option contract itself to someone else if they so wish, without ever exercising it.

## Strike price

Each common stock will have numerous options with differing strike prices. The strike price for an option is initially set at a price which is reasonably close to the current share price. The exchange introduces other strike prices at fixed intervals from that initial strike price.

## Read the press

Premiums for exchange-traded options are often printed in major financial newspapers. Typically the listing may look like Table A3.1 (only calls have been shown).

**Table A3.1 Premiums for exchange-traded options**

| Option and closing price | Strike price | May | June | July |
|---|---|---|---|---|
| ABC | 105 | 7½ | 9¼ | 10⅛ |
| 112⅜ | 110 | 3 | 4¾ | 6¼ |
| 112⅜ | 115 | ¹³⁄₁₆ | 2⅛ | 3½ |
| 112⅜ | 120 | ¹³⁄₁₆ | ⅞ | 1¾ |
| 112⅜ | 125 | ¹⁄₁₆ | no option | ¹³⁄₁₆ |

In this illustration ABC May 115 calls are trading at ¹³⁄₁₆ or $81.25.

## How is the option price calculated and how can I profit?

The price at which an option is bought and sold is called the premium. In the Barclays example, the option premium was 67p. This is a little like a margin payment.

An option's premium has two components, the *intrinsic value* and the *time value*.

### Intrinsic value

A call option has intrinsic value if the underlying security price is greater than the option's strike price. A put option has intrinsic value if the underlying security price is less than the strike price.

**Key points**

**Intrinsic value**
In the money option
(an option with intrinsic value).
Out of the money option
(an option without intrinsic value).

(Share price) < (strike price) = put option has intrinsic value

(Share price) > (strike price) = call option has intrinsic value

So, in our example, if the price of Barclays shares was 1,110p then the option's intrinsic value would be 10p. That is, if you exercised the call you could buy Barclays shares from the writer at 1,100p (strike price) and sell them in the market at 1,110p (underlying security price). That is also why an option can never be worth less than its intrinsic value.

A call option would have no intrinsic value, and so only time value, if the underlying price was lower than the strike price. If an option has intrinsic value, it is *in the money*. If an option has no intrinsic value, it is *out of the money*. An option whose strike price is nearest to the underlying price is *at the money*.

(Share price) < (strike price) = in the money put / out of the money call

(Share price) > (strike price) = out of the money put / in the money call

## Time value

The second component of option premium is time value. It is the difference between the option premium and its intrinsic value.

Time value = premium – intrinsic value

See Diagram A3.1 for a diagrammatic representation of these two values.

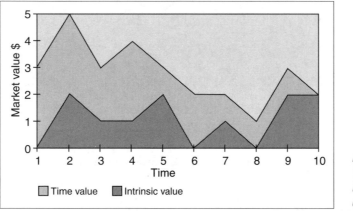

*Diagram A3.1*
*Time value and*
*intrinsic value*
*compared*

So, in our Barclays example time value would total 57p. Time value essentially represents the price the holder pays the writer for the uncertainty. It is the cost of risk which the writer faces. Time value erodes as expiry approaches. Therefore an option is a wasting asset in the hands of the holder.

Time value can be calculated using complex mathematical option-pricing models such as the Cox–Rubenstein model. The variables are risk-free interest rates, strike price, underlying security volatility, underlying security price and any dividends which would be paid if the underlying security were held (see Table A3.2).

*Table A3.2  Factors affecting time value*

| | |
|---|---|
| **Interest rates** | Higher interest rates tend to result in higher call premiums and lower put premiums |
| **Dividends** | Higher cash dividends imply lower call premiums and higher put premiums |
| **Volatility** | Volatility of the underlying stock places a greater risk on the writer that the stock will expire in the money and so volatility raises premium |

From this, then, it follows that at expiry (when time value equals zero) an out of the money option is worthless and an in the money option is worth its intrinsic value. Note that since an option cannot have negative intrinsic or time value the most an option holder can lose (and the most a writer can make) is the premium, no matter how much the underlying price changes.

# Relationship between option price and price of the underlying security

The most important thing to remember is that the price of a call tends to rise as the underlying security price rises and the price of a call tends to fall as the underlying security price falls. The price of a put tends to rise as the underlying security price falls and the price of a put tends to fall as the underlying security price rises.

So, why buy an option and not the security? Because an option is leveraged. This means that, for a given percentage change in the underlying price, the option price can change by a greater percentage. You get a bigger bang for your buck.

Going back to our previous example, if the price of Barclays moved from 1,110p to 1,150p, the option price may move from 67p to 97p. That means there would have been a 3.6 per cent change in the underlying price and a 44.7 per cent change in the option price. You could then decide to sell the option or, as before, exercise it. There would be more money to be made from selling it.

The price of an option rarely has a 1:1 correlation with the underlying security price. The *delta* is the rate of change of the option price to the rate of change of the underlying price. So, for example, a delta of 0.5 means that if the underlying price rises by, say, 10 cents then the option price will change by 5 cents. Obviously the greater the delta, the greater the bang for your buck. However, the delta is greatest for in the money options, i.e. those with the most intrinsic value and, therefore, the most costly options. Consequently, a balance has to be made when calculating potential returns between the delta and the price of the option.

An example will clarify the situation.

### Example

Barclays shares are trading at 1,110p.

July 1,100 calls are 51p; July 1,200 calls are 16p.

If tomorrow the price of Barclays shares were to be 1,200p then it may be that the July 1,100 calls trade at 123p (average delta of 0.8) and the July 1,200 calls trade at 22.5p (average delta of 0.25).

The return from the July 1,100s is 141 percent and from the cheaper 1,200s is only 41 per cent. Of course in this example we have only estimated deltas and have ignored costs and bid ask spreads. Nevertheless it gives you some idea of the balances that need to be drawn. For modest moves one is likely to profit most from just in the money options.

## Example of leverage

To own 100 shares of a stock trading at $30 per share would cost $3,000. By the same token, to own a $5 option with a strike price of $30 would give you the right to buy 100 shares for $30 at any time up to expiry. The option would only cost $500 ($5 × 100 shares).

If, one month after the option is purchased, the stock price has risen to $33, then the gain on the stock investment is $300, or 10 per cent. However, for the same stock increase the option may have increased to $7, for a return of $200 or 40 per cent.

Leverage has parallel downside implications, of course. If in our last example the stock fell to $27, the loss on the stock investment would be $300 or 10 per cent. For this $3 fall the option may now be worth $3 itself, i.e. a 40 per cent loss.

## Vive la différence

Options are in many respects similar to stocks for the purposes of trading for profit (see Table A3.3).

*Table A3.3  Vive la différence*

| Similarities | Differences |
| --- | --- |
| Orders to buy and sell are handled by brokers | Options have a limited life |
| Trading is conducted on regulated exchanges | There are fewer options than stocks |
| Pricing mechanisms are open and transparent | Option owners have no rights over a company; they are not shareholders |
| Investors have the opportunity to follow price movements second by second if they so wish | Option holders receive no dividends |

# Strategies

Although there are only two types of options, calls and puts, there are a lot of option strategies. With options you can protect your stock holdings from a price decline, you can prepare to buy a stock at a lower price, you can increase income on your current stock holdings, you can participate in a large market move, even if you are unsure beforehand which way the market is going to move, and of course you can participate in a stock rise or fall.

## Kids' stuff

The simplest strategy is to go long a call or a put. That means you buy to open a call or put. If you go short (write the option) then you sell to open a call or put. In the latter case, you have to post margin since your losses are potentially unlimited. It is a lot safer for the lay investor to be long puts than short calls even though on both you profit from falling prices. A common options strategy already discussed is to purchase calls to participate in an upward price movement.

## Locking in a price

Another popular use of calls is to lock in an attractive stock purchase price. Imagine that ABC is trading at $55 and you believe it is about to increase in value, but you do not have the funds to buy 100 shares. You know you will have the funds in six months, but you are afraid that if you wait that long the shares will already have increased in value.

You see that the option expiring eight months hence at the strike price of $55 costs $3, i.e. $300. If you buy one contract and then in six months the price of the stock is $70, you could exercise your option and buy the stock for $5,500 + $300. Whereas if you did not have the option and had to buy the option in the open market, it would have cost you $7,000. So you just made a saving of $1,200.

## Puts to protect unrealized profit in a stock position

Imagine you bought ABC stock at $50 and it is now trading at $70. You fear there may be a short-term fall in the price but do not want to sell your holding on the hunch. By buying an ABC put option with a strike of $70 for $2 you are assured of being able to sell your stock at $70 no matter what happens to the stock price. If the price does not collapse, then you will have lost the premium $2 × 100 = $200. Consider it an insurance premium.

But if the stock had fallen to, say, $55, you could have sold it at $70 per share, less $2 per share for the option premium. That means you would have earned $13 more per share with the option than if you had not taken out the insurance policy.

## Examples of option strategies

Option strategies are really beyond the scope of this book, but I will mention a few to give you some idea of what the professionals and experienced non-professional can do with options.

### Hedge

A hedge is a position where one position profits if the other position loses. So a hedge can be thought of as an insurance against being wrong. For example, a hedge against a long call: one could sell short a different call or go long a put.

### Straddle

Buy to open an at the money call and buy to open an at the money put. You profit by increased volatility in the underlying price irrespective of direction. The strategy is a 'guts' if the options are both in the money and a 'strangle' if they are both out of the money.

### Bull call spread

Long in the money call and short out of the money call. Profit from upward price movement. This becomes a bull call calendar spread if the short call is nearer month than the long call.

### Bear put spread

Long in the money put and short out of the money put. Profit from downward price movement. This becomes a bear put calendar spread if the short put is nearer month than the long put.

Various other strategies exist depending on one's views as to volatility, direction, and extent of risk one wishes to take. These strategies have some unusual names, e.g. butterfly, condor, iron butterfly (buy a straddle and sell a strangle because you expect a limited size move), combo, ladder, box, conversion, and reversal.

See the further reading section if you want to investigate options further.

## Summary

The essential things to remember about options are that they are leveraged and decrease in value the longer they are held; calls increase in value with the underlying asset, and puts do the opposite.

# Orders

## In this appendix

There are many different ways to place an order to enter or exit a trade. In this appendix we examine some of them.

## Objective

- **Familiarize ourselves with types of orders and usage.**

## All or none order

A command to 'fill' either the entire order, or none of it.

### Example
Buy 500 McDonald's at $59\frac{1}{2}$ all or none.

### When used
When you want to buy all 500 shares at the specified price, but not fewer, or want to average out at the price.

## Day order or good for day order

If the order cannot be executed before the end of the day, it is cancelled.

### Example

Buy 500 McDonald's at 59½ good for day. If the current price is 60–60⅛ and the bid price fails to reach 59½ then the order will not be executed.

### When used

If you want to enter at a specific price, but only for the day in question, because the next day you may revise the order.

## Good till cancelled order or open order

This order stands until the customer cancels it or it is executed.

### Example

Buy 500 McDonald's at 59½ good till cancelled. If the current price is 60-60⅛ and the bid price fails to reach 59½ then the order will not be executed until the price reaches 59½ or the order is cancelled by the customer.

### When used

As with the good for the day order except the customer wants to keep the order open until they cancel it.

## Limit order

An order to buy or sell at a specific price or a better price.

### Example

Buy 500 McDonald's at 59½ limit. This means the broker can pay a maximum of 59½.

### When used

Where the buyer or seller wants to place a limit on the price they want to buy or sell.

## Market order

The order to buy or sell at the best price available in the market.

### Example

Buy 500 McDonald's at market.

**When used**

When the buyer or seller wants to buy or sell as soon as possible.

## Stop order

An order that becomes a market order as soon as the price is reached. Can be buy stop or sell stop orders.

### Example

Buy 500 McDonald's at 59 stop.

### When used

When the buyer or seller wants the order executed at market price only after a certain price level has been reached.

## Summary

**Although many types of orders have been examined, most traders only ever find the need for one or two types, usually market and limit orders.**

# The bigger picture

## In this appendix

After all this talk of online trading, maybe you would like a detour to look at the bigger picture.

## Objective

- **An overview of the net and of how online trading works.**

## What drives the net?

Profits drive the net. We are here to make money. It is no wonder the full fruits and promise of the internet were realized first and foremost by Americans and they remain the most frequent users of it. Henry James once observed: 'To make so much money that you won't, that you don't "mind", don't mind anything – that is absolutely, I think, the main American formula' (*The American Scene*, 1907). James Bryce wrote in confirmatory tones when he said: 'How does Wall Street tell on the character of the people? They are naturally inclined to be speculative. The pursuit of wealth is nowhere so eager as in America, the opportunities for acquiring it nowhere so numerous' (*The American Commonwealth*, 1888).

Sure, there are the idealists who proclaim the internet a great democratizer, a leveller, where the most humble can cast the shadow of a giant by setting up a home page next to that of General Electric or IBM or any other Fortune 500 company. But they are not what drive the internet. Theirs are not sites of popularity. They are indulging in a self-gratifying ego-massage.

And, to be sure, the availability of information drives the net. Information sources are the most popular and lucrative sites on the internet, but their *raison d'être* is not altruism. Search engine Yahoo! is a listed company with shareholders making money from selling 'advertising virtual estate' (i.e. internet real estate). The internet provides information; that is provided for the purpose of profit and profit is the purpose of the internet. As Walter Wriston, former chairman of Citibank, noted: 'Money is just another form of information' (*Risk and Other 4-letter Words*, 1986). Despite the praise heaped upon it, the internet has not prevented man, woman or corporation from remaining economic agents out to make a buck.

## Why do we want so much information?

To profit. Information about stocks, information about cars and information about cinema tickets is sought because we perceive the benefit to outweigh the costs of obtaining the information – i.e. a personal profit. But that leads us to the most interesting issue of all: what is the importance of the internet – for us as people and for the economies in which we live?

## The consequence of all this information

### Inadequate information stifles trade

Asymmetric information between buyer and seller results in a no sale or fewer sales than would have been the case with perfect information. The result is an inefficient market, i.e. one in which both parties would have benefited from the trade but it failed to take place because of inadequate information, and they did not get the information because the costs of obtaining it would outweigh the benefits of doing the trade.

I am far less likely to buy a second-hand car from you if I have no way of knowing its quality. That is why you permit me to inspect it visually. That low-cost method of obtaining information about the subject matter of the trade results in my buying it. Inadequate information is the reason why brand new cars depreciate as soon as they are taken from the showroom, because as soon as they have an owner, any future buyer will have inadequate information about the car and be less willing to buy it, so the owner is forced to reduce the price to entice buyers.

The internet is a source of cost-effective information about a host of goods and services. Whereas before there may have been inadequate information stifling trade, now the internet provides low-cost information facilitating trade. The seller wants to provide the information because he wants a sale and the purchaser wants the information because he wants to buy.

Consider stocks: is it any wonder that trading online is one of the success stories of the internet when you consider that people are more likely to buy stocks when they can research them than when they cannot? I will not buy a stock if my information is inadequate. Hey presto! Along comes an internet broker and provides free information about a stock. Why? Because he gets the benefit of a sale. Remember: profit not altruism drives the internet.

The chain of reasoning is simple: the cost of obtaining information from the internet is lower than the benefit of doing the trade and therefore the internet helps those trades which would otherwise not have occurred. The internet makes an inefficient market more efficient. The internet increases trade.

The internet is a remover of inefficiencies. To test if something can work on the net, consider the current way it is done and any inefficiencies associated with it, and then consider if the internet would reduce those inefficiencies without increasing costs so as to wipe out benefits of the trade. If so, all other things being equal, it will work on the internet.

## Transaction costs: another inhibitor of trade

Consider another inefficiency of most markets: transaction costs. The labour market has a transaction cost: the cost of commuting. Hence, with the advent of computers we have telecommuting, removing the inefficiency but delivering labour nevertheless.

Brokerage commissions are another transaction cost. The result? Deep-discount brokers. But why not a step further? Why not connect my computer directly to the order book so buyer and seller can meet? Already happened. The NYSE and International Petroleum Exchange are on to it. Charles Schwab is on to it. (Let us not forget online banking and the transaction costs of traditional banks maintaining a building, paying staff, etc. And look at the transactional costs of the traditional bookstore!)

Again the simple test applies: transaction costs are reduced, so I trade where before I may not have. Trade increases. The equation for me is whether my transaction costs are reduced sufficiently so that I enter a trade which I would not otherwise have entered. The equation for the person facilitating the reduction in transaction costs is whether the benefits of trades as a result of his activity outweigh the cost of reducing transaction costs.

The questions are:

- What are the information and transaction costs?
- Will the internet reduce them to such an extent that trade is increased?
- Does the increased trade offset the costs to the service provider?

Put another way: can I get marginally more benefit than before per unit cost?

## The result?

The result of increased trade through improved information is increases in growth on a macroeconomic scale. Reduced transaction and information costs mean increased productivity. Reduced costs alone should lower inflation.

A report by the US Department of Commerce, entitled *The Digital Economy* (1998), implies that inflation in the US would have been 1 per cent greater if not for the online economy. Is it coincidence that the internet heralded the commencement of the Goldilocks economy? We must be aware that the internet does not imply a guarantee of lower inflation: a mismanaged economy can lead to recession. But the internet has resulted in possibly an important structural change in the global economy: releasing the benefits of lower inflation and higher trend growth through making more markets efficient with the resultant increase in global trade and hence wealth. That is the glory of the net.

In terms of market efficiency the internet is similar for world trade to what the derivatives market in Chicago was for farmers. The latter reduced transactional costs of search and delivery and informational costs by contract standardization, thus increasing trade, not only for the farmers, but also for the US. The internet is more like a stock or derivatives exchange in that it is a near perfect market.

## Happy now?

Will the reduction of transaction and information costs mean more leisure time? No: that is what we naïvely thought 20 years ago. We believed computers and technology would mean that the same work could be done more quickly and, therefore, that there would be more time for leisure. But as we know, man, woman and corporation are not altruistic. Profits run markets, and if the same amount of work can be done in half the time then twice as much can be done in the same time. More profits.

As T.S. Eliot pointed out:

*Where is the Life we have lost in living?*
*Where is the wisdom we have lost in knowledge?*
*Where is the knowledge we have lost in information?*
                                        *The Rock, 1934*

## So is it raining money if you provide information?

All the statistics about billions of dollars streaming through the internet and its huge popularity do not mean that you have only to set up a site and money will follow. Many sites on the internet fail to meet the strategies already discussed. How many sites are just plain old difficult to navigate, making their product unpalatable? Moreover, if someone else is doing the same thing on the net, but better, you will be beaten to the finishing line anyway.

It is no wonder that whole books have been written on designing internet sites. Information is not enough. Presentation is all. If information were the point of arrival, there would be no lawyers. The client could place the depositions on the judge's table and leave. Presentation of information is one direction in which the future of the internet is going. How can we convey information to the end user better? That is why so many web sites allow customizable pages. We are all artists and psychologists now.

## No more big boys?

Does all this information mean that the playing field for traders is now level, or at least more level? Does all this information mean that the individual investor and the professional trader are similar? No more so than placing an individual in a law library makes him a lawyer, or placing him in a medical library makes him a surgeon. If the provision of information was all, then this book would not find a market; you would just go to the internet.

The trading playing field is not level, but the slope is a little gentler. Information is not knowledge and is even further removed from experience and further still removed from wisdom. The internet provides the private investor with information, some sites provide knowledge, and some, through trading games, may provide experience, but the professional trader remains at a significant advantage. Were it not so, Merril Lynch would not spend hundreds of thousands of pounds on training programmes for its traders; it would just give them access to the internet.

Individual traders are bound in ignorance to think they can compete with the big boys based on information alone. It has been an objective of this book to impart knowledge and wisdom: how the information is to be used, not only where to find it. The internet is not good at genetically engineering talent. Nor is it good at training; the classroom and personal effort remain the most efficient ways of doing that.

And so it is not the case, as is commonly predicted, that the middleman, the intermediary, in all things will vanish because of the internet. Sure, their roles will change, but they will remain because:

- Information in the hands of the private investor will not guarantee profit without training and talent. So an adviser or fund manager may still have a job!
- The division of labour is a market efficiency not an *in*efficiency. It makes more sense for me to pay my adviser $100 to do something which would cost me $200 to do, and so while he is doing it I can go away and earn $300.

## Summary

The internet does not mean no more losses for the trader, for information alone is not the answer. It is the purpose of books such as this to provide another field-leveller: knowledge.

*Appendix* **6**

# Speeding things up

We examine some quick tips which may help tune up your computer and squeeze that extra iota of performance out of it and the browser.

**Objective**

- **Learn some quick ways of speed surfing.**

## Clear cache

The sites you visit are stored on your computer's hard disk. To speed things up when downloading web pages you can:

- In Internet Explorer 4 (Diagram A6.1) click on the **View** drop-down menu and then on **Internet Options**; on the **General tab** click on **Delete Files** and on **Clear History**.

- In Netscape Navigator (Diagram A6.2) click on the **Edit** drop-down menu and go to **Preferences** and **Navigator**, then click on **Clear History**; under **Advanced** go to **Cache** and then click on **Clear Memory Cache** and **Clear Disk Cache**.

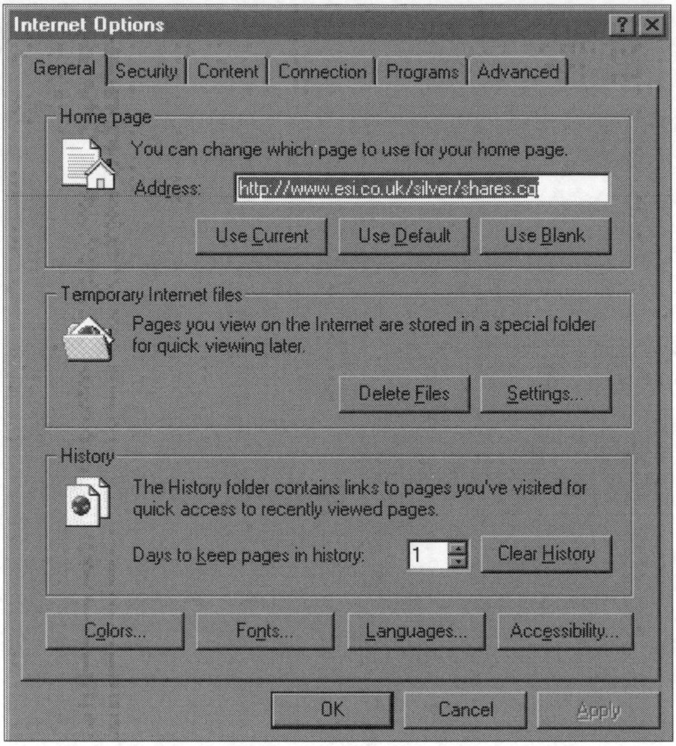

*Diagram A6.1
IE4 with Options
folder open*

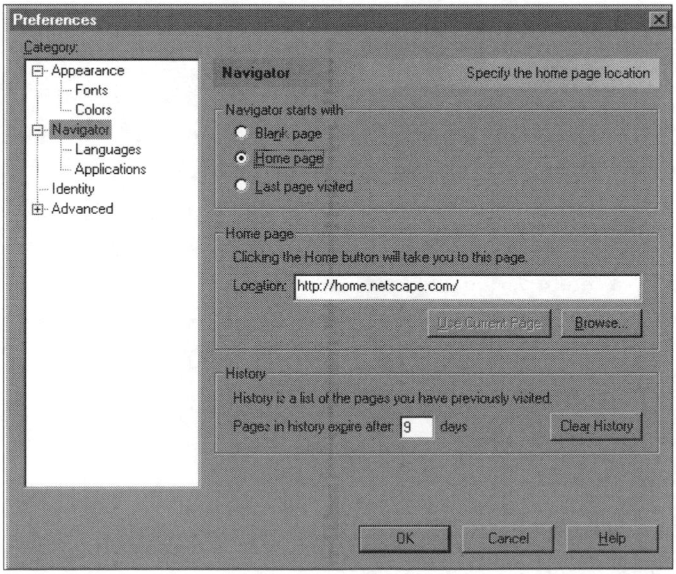

*Diagram A6.2
NN4 with Preferences
folder open*

# Turn off graphics

Pages load a lot faster if you are not downloading graphics:

- In Internet Explorer 5 click on the **View** drop-down menu and then on **Internet Options**; on the **Advanced** tab scroll down to **Multimedia** and clear the **Show Pictures** box.
- In Netscape Navigator click on the **Edit** drop-down menu and go to **Preferences** and under **Appearance** then click on **Text Only**.

# Consider an internet accelerator

Go to any software vendor and they will have some software called an internet accelerator. Most of these download links which lead off your current page when your modem is not doing anything else and you are reading a particular page. That way, when you click on one of the links, hey presto! the page is already downloaded (see Table A6.1).

I am dubious about their value for money but they occasionally speed things up marginally.

*Table A6.1  Selection of internet accelerators*

| Name of accelerator | Address |
| --- | --- |
| Blaze | www.xspeed.com |
| Net Accelerator | www.imsiuk.co.uk |
| Peak Jet | www.peak-media.com |

# Open multiple windows

Remember you can launch multiple copies of your browser simultaneously, so while surfing one page you can wait for another to download.

# Time your time online

Internet speed slows down around 7–10 a.m. EST (US) and 4–7 p.m. EST (US) when internet traffic is horrendous. Browse around 3 a.m. EST for best results!

# Increase cache size

Pages you have visited already are saved on your hard disk and loaded from there before being downloaded by your browser if you visit them again. Since downloading from a cache is quicker than from the internet you should increase the size of your memory cache:

- In Internet Explorer 4 click on the **View** drop-down menu and then on **Internet Options**; on the **General** tab click on **Settings** and adjust size of cache.

- In Netscape Navigator click on the **Edit** drop-down menu and go to **Preferences** and **Advanced** and then **Cache** and **Increase size**.

## Defrag

Downloaded web pages get scattered around on your hard drive, which means your computer gets slower and s-l-o-w-e-r at finding them from the cache. Defragment your hard drive to reduce this and speed things up.

In Windows 95 click on **Start** then on **Programs**; next go to **Accessories**, then **System Tools** and **Disk Defragmenter**.

## Summary

There are various things you can tweak on your browser to make things happen a little faster. We have explored them in this appendix. Most internet magazines, and the help files in browsers, usually contain a good splattering of tips and tricks too.

# Recommended reading

## Key

★★★ Excellent; comprehensible and comprehensive as well as value for money. Should be on your bookshelf

★★ A useful read with very much to offer

★ A good read if, having read the others, you want to continue looking into the subject

# Online trading

### Trading Online ★★★
**Alpesh B Patel**
*FT Prentice Hall 2000*

New and revised version of the best-seller covering all the steps to trading from getting set up to monitoring positions.

### The Complete Idiot's Guide to Online Investing *

D Gerlach

*Que 1999*

Que are known for their computer books and this venture appears to be a bandwagon thing. But the *Complete Idiot's* guides can be clear and more comprehensible if you are, um, well, a complete idiot.

### Investing Online ***

S Eckett

*FT Pitman 1997*

Encyclopaedic in coverage and an excellent reference tool with a focus on global investing.

## Short-term trading

### Long-term Secrets to Short-term Trading ***

L Williams

*Wiley 1999*

Larry Williams is a proven trader. An excellent book, because he clearly knows his stuff and trades off it.

## Day-trading

### How to Get Started in Electronic Day Trading ***

David S Nassar

*McGraw-Hill 1999*

Nassar owns a day-trading firm, and this book is written from the perspective of a man who knows his business.

### Electronic Day Traders' Secrets **

M Friedfertig and G West

*McGraw-Hill 1999*

This book has a series of interviews with days traders from Friedfertig's own brokerage company. A lot of trading psychology here, but light on strategies.

### Day Trade Online *
**C Farrell**
*Wiley 1999*
Farrell is a young man who trades for a living. Some good content in here, but layout, design and substance lacking in other respects.

### The Day Trader's Advantage *
**H Abell**
*Dearborn Financial 1996*

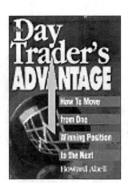

A little dated from the ubiquitous Abell, who seems to be a full-time author producing what feels like one book per month. Focuses on the trading psychology aspects of day-trading.

### The Electronic Day Trader ***
**M Friedfertig and G West**
*McGraw-Hill 1999*
A very popular title indeed for day-traders from a day-trading brokerage owner.

### The 22 Rules of Day Trading Online **
**D Nassar**
*McGraw-Hill 1999*
After the success of his earlier day-trading book, David Nassar returns with a different format.

### The Compleat Day Trader *
**J Bernstein**
*McGraw-Hill 1999*
A very good seller, with an unusual title. Covers not only day-trading but also risk management.

### High Impact Day Trading **
**Robert Barnes**
*Irwin 1996*
This book highlights the author's Mountain Valley system, going for longer moves and ignoring shorter ones. It has proved a very popular title.

## Trading psychology

### The Bhagavad Gita ★★★
*Various editions*
Although written more than 2,000 years ago, and not directly about trading, I found it to be one of the most useful 'trading' books I have ever read. It largely discusses discipline – how and why – and the benefits of discipline. Since a lack of mental discipline is one of the major downfalls of traders, this is likely to be a very profitable read.

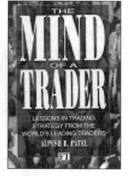

### The Mind of a Trader ★★★
**Alpesh B Patel**
*FT Pitman 1997*
Advice on becoming a better trader from the world's leading traders, including Pat Arbor, former Chairman of the Chicago Board of Trade, and Bill Lipschutz, former Global Head of Forex at Salomon Brothers, who made on average $250,000 each and every trading day he was there, for eight years!

### The Disciplined Trader ★★
**Mark Douglas**
*Prentice Hall 1990*
An extremely good book. Written in a very intelligent fashion and gets away from 'Mickey Mouse'-fashion psychology. Deserves a far higher profile than it has to date received.

### The Inner Game of Trading ★★
**Robert Koppel and Howard Abell**
*Irwin Professional 1997*
Includes interviews with some leading traders, but its value comes from the analysis of psychological difficulties traders are likely to encounter. Definitely recommended.

## Classics

### Reminiscences of a Stock Operator ✱✱✱
**Edwin Le Fevre**
*Wiley 1994 (reprint edition)*
An undoubted classic. The fictionalized trading biography of Jesse Livermore, one of the greatest speculators ever seen. While dated (it was written in 1923), it nevertheless provides some insight into the difficulties encountered by traders. A very enjoyable read.

### Extraordinary Popular Delusions and the Madness of Crowds and Confusion de Confusiones ✱✱
**Charles Mackay and Joseph de la Vega**
*Wiley 1995*
Explores crowd psychology and how that affects market movement. While its examinations are 300 years old, it is highly relevant today. Short and interesting.

### The Art of Speculation ✱✱
**Philip L Carret**
*Wiley 1997*
Apparently highly regarded by Victor Niederhoffer. However, in spite of that, I would recommend it as a good read.

### Manias, Panics and Crashes ✱✱
**Charles Kindleberger**
*Wiley 1996*
Why do the economists, statisticians and government nerds always get it wrong? This book does not provide any answers, but it does provide some insights.

## Stocks

### Getting Started in Stocks ✱✱
**Alvin D Hall**
*Wiley 1997 (3rd edition)*
A very good primer for stocks. Hall has a clear style and injects humour now and again to alleviate the rigour.

### Winning on Wall Street ✷

**Martin Zweig**

*Warner Books 1997 (revised edition)*

Zweig is famous for his market reports and for being one of Schwager's market wizards. I found a copy of this book for $11.99 – you can't go wrong.

## Futures

### Getting Started in Futures ✷✷

**Todd Lofton**

*Wiley 1997 (3rd edition)*

Very clear and easy to understand as well as giving lots of information for delving deeper.

### A Complete Guide to the Futures Markets ✷✷✷

**Jack Schwager**

*Wiley 1984*

This book covers fundamental analysis and technical analysis as well as spreads and options. Characteristic of Schwager's books, it is very thorough.

## Commodities trading

### Mastering Commodity Futures and Options ✷✷

**George Kleinman**

*FT Pitman 1997*

This book is very well-presented indeed. A little like a textbook in style, but covers the ground very well for both beginner and intermediate user.

### The CRB Commodity Yearbook ✷✷

**Knight-Ridder**

*Knight-Ridder annual*

A very useful reference guide to commodities. Filled with data, charts, tables and articles on trends and strategies. If you are serious about commodities you should have this.

## Soybean Trading and Hedging **
## Wheat Trading and Hedging **
## Corn Trading and Hedging **
## Investing in Wheat, Soybeans, Corn **

**William Grandmill**

*Irwin Professional 1988, 1989, 1990, 1991 (respectively)*

A series of books by the appropriately named Grandmill for commodity traders. Grandmill provides details of the commodities, and his own systems for picking entry and exit points. If you think it is best to become an expert in one area of commodity trading then books such as these should be a good starting point to developing your skills and understanding.

## Options

## Traded Options **

**Peter Temple**

*Rushmere Wynne 1995*

For those trading options on LIFFE. Thorough and explains all the basics, from what options are to buying software.

## Getting Started in Options ***

**Michael Thomsett**

*Wiley 1993*

Again, very clear and easy to understand. An excellent start for beginners.

## McMillan on Options ***

**Lawrence McMillan**

*Wiley 1996*

Brands itself as the 'Bible' of the options markets. Why do publishers refer to their books as the 'Bible' of something? I wonder if they mean only a minority of people will ever read the book but more are supposed to and it competes with equivalent books for the rest. Anyway, that aside, McMillan goes beyond explaining the basics about options and actually applies a degree of critique. Should consider if you are a beginner.

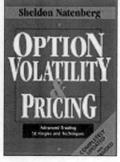

## Option Volatility & Pricing Strategies *
**Sheldon Natenberg**
*Probus 1994*
Natenberg is a leader in this field. This book is definitely for the more advanced trader wanting to dig into option mechanics.

## The Options Markets *
**John Cox and Mark Rubinstein**
*Prentice Hall 1985*
This is a classic text on options. The book is about valuing options – these authors, of course, created the famous Cox–Rubinstein option pricing model.

## All About Options **
**Russell Wasendorf and Thomas McCafferty**
*Probus 1993*
The good thing about this book is that it covers both strategies and some of the background mechanics behind options, such as what happens on the trading floor.

## Advanced Options Trading **
**Robert Daigler**
*Probus 1993*
This book moves beyond basics and discusses some strategies generally used only by the professionals. That does not mean a private investor using them will have hit upon some sector – so beware. But if you are interested in knowing more than just the basics, this book is better than most.

## Trading Options on Futures *
**John Labuszewski**
*Wiley 1998*
This covers treasuries, currencies and commodities. I think if you are trading options on futures there is more to it than understanding options and understanding futures. The whole is greater than the sum of the parts, and therefore a book such as this is added value in being exclusively written for one trading sector.

## Make Money with S&P Options *
## How to Make Money with Corn Options *
## Make Money with Soybean Options *
**William Grandmill**
*Irwin 1989, 1990, 1990 (respectively)*
If you are concentrating on one of these areas and feeling you need something

specifically addressing your trading needs, then these books were written with you in mind. Grandmill is a prolific writer and knows what he is talking about.

### Trading and Investing in Bond Options *

**M Anthony Wong**

*Wiley 1991*

This title covers strategies and pricing models and details the peculiarities of trading this market using options.

### Options on Foreign Exchanges *

**David DeRosa**

*Probus 1992*

Not to leave out the currency-option boys and girls, this market specialist covers valuation of options and pricing of currencies, as well as how the various markets work. Probably useful for the beginner and intermediate-level trader in forex options.

### Commodity Options **

**Larry Spears**

*Marketplace Books 1985*

This one is for beginners who may not have settled on a particular commodity and want an overview.

## Technical analysis

### Technical Analysis Explained **

**Martin Pring**

*McGraw-Hill 1991*

The first half of this book is more relevant than the second. While a little disappointing, nevertheless provides insights not available elsewhere.

### The Investor's Guide to Technical Analysis **

**Elli Gifford**

*FT Pitman 1995*

While the book uses UK companies to illustrate points, it is nevertheless useful to traders in any country. Thorough, comprehensive, and easy to read and understand. Good as a starter and for more advanced study; however, it is not mathematical.

### Technical Analysis from A to Z **

**Steven B Achelis**

*Probus 1995*

A good introductory guide which is comprehensive. Lots of pics of indicators.

### The Visual Investor **

**John Murphy**

*Wiley 1996*

Former CNBC presenter provides a good primer on technical analysis. He draws on one of the key aspects of technical analysis – it is visual.

### Encyclopedia of Technical Market Indicators **

**R Colby and T Meyers**

*Business One Irwin 1988*

As one would expect of a book claiming to be an encyclopedia this is an exhaustive study. It will be most useful if you want a good overview before settling down on a few chosen indicators.

### Martin Pring on Market Momentum *

**Martin Pring**

*McGraw-Hill 1993*

Aimed at the user who has chosen momentum as one technical indicator from his arsenal and wants to learn more, this book is typical Pring; clear and useful. Unfortunately Pring maintains his habit of stylized artificial charts instead of giving more real market illustrations to make his points.

### Momentum Direction and Divergence *

**William Blau**

*Wiley 1995*

Definitely for the advanced user. If, after learning about oscillators, you want to take things further and uncover some mathematics to better understand their weaknesses then this is a good book.

### Stock Market Trading Systems **

**Gerald Appel and Fred Hitschler**

*Dow Jones Irwin 1980*

This is a classic and discusses the price ROC and moving average trading systems among others. It is always best to go to the original source to gain insights which later secondary texts are likely to miss.

## The Moving Average Convergence-Divergence Method ✱✱✱
**Gerald Appel**
*Signalert 1979*
Appel is the creator of this highly popular trading method, and this book explains it straight from the source's mouth. Useful if you plan to place large weight on this indicator in your own trading.

## Volume Cycles in the Stock Market ✱✱
**Richard Arms**
*Equis 1994*
Arms is a well-known technical analyst and this book delves in depth into volume. If volume analysis is something you intend using then this a very good source of information.

## How to Use the Three-Point Reversal Method of Point and Figure Stock Market Trading ✱✱
**A.W. Cohen**
*Chartcraft 1984*
Despite the cumbersome title this is a useful book on this popular method of drawing charts.

## Understanding Fibonacci Numbers ✱✱
**Edward Dobson**
*Traders Press 1984*
Not too difficult to understand if Fibonacci fascinates.

## New Strategy of Daily Stock Market Timing for Maximum Profit ✱✱
**Joseph Granville**
*Prentice Hall 1976*
Another one of the technical analysis gods. This book discusses on-balance volume in particular. Granville created that indicator, so who better to learn more about it from?

## Japanese Candlestick Charting Techniques ✱✱✱
**Steven Nison**
*New York Institute of Finance 1991*
Steve Nison is regarded as the expert on Japanese candlesticks. This book is very clear and very easy to understand. Nison uses actual charts and not stylized fictional ones. He also focuses on how and when the chart indications fail. The book helps an understanding of the rationale behind technical analysis, why it works, and why it does not. Excellent.

### New Concepts in Technical Trading Systems **
**Welles J Wilder**
*Trend Research 1978*
Wilder is very highly regarded in the technical analysis world. Here he explains and interprets numerous indicators, including RSI.

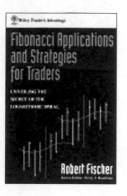

### Fibonacci Applications and Strategies for Traders *
**Robert Fischer**
*Wiley 1993*
Take Fibonacci study further with this book. While you do not necessarily need such detailed knowledge, if you are going to use it, you may as well know all there is.

### Volume and Open Interest **
**Kenneth Shaleen**
*Irwin 1996*
A good starter to investigating these two popular statistics in technical analysis. Probably unavoidable if you are trading futures.

### Point and Figure Charting **
**Carroll Aby**
*Traders Press 1996*
Both a beginners' guide and a reference book for this method of plotting prices.

## Traders' profiles

### The Mind of a Trader ***
**Alpesh B Patel**
*FT Pitman 1997*
As noted at the beginning of this appendix, the world's leading traders share their insights, not merely in a question and answer format but in an easy-to-understand category-based layout. You can see at any point what exactly is being discussed and, with a summary at the end plus author comment, the conclusions are made clear.

### Market Wizards
### New Market Wizards ***
**Jack Schwager**
*Harper Business 1993, Wiley 1995 (respectively)*

An absolute must. Fascinating, although since it's in a question and answer format you are left to draw many of your own conclusions.

## 100 Minds that Made the Market *
**Kenneth Fisher**
*Business Classics 1991*
Biographical in nature and the profiles are somewhat short, but nevertheless a good bedtime or holiday read.

## The Super Traders *
**Alan Rubenfeld**
*Irwin 1992*
Nine profiles of traders from diverse backgrounds. While a little bit too biographical, nevertheless makes for a good read.

# Floor trading insights

## Tricks of the Floor Trader * * *
**Neal Weintraub**
*Irwin 1996*
One of the few books of its kind. Gives the outsider a view of what the insider does. Provides knowledge which is useful to know.

TRICKS OF THE
**Floor Trader**
INSIDER TRADING TECHNIQUES
FOR THE OFF-THE-FLOOR TRADER

Neal T. Weintraub

## The Trader's Edge * *
**Grant Noble**
*Probus 1995*
Some very useful insights into what they do on the floor. A good insider's view and useful pointers on some of the advantages.

## Trading Rules * *
**William Eng**
*FT Pitman 1995*
While some of the rules will be familiar, others provide valuable enough information to justify buying this easy-to-understand book.

# Exchanges of the world

| Country | Exchange | Address |
|---|---|---|
| Argentina | **Buenos Aires Cereal Exchange** (Bolsa de Cereales de Buenos Aires) | Avenida Corrientes 127, Buenos Aires *Tel*: +54 1 311 9540 *Fax*: +54 1 311 9540 *E-mail*: bolcerc@datamarkets.com.ar |
| | **Mercado Abierto Electronico SA** | 25 de Mayo 565, 4 Piso, Buenos Aires *Tel*: +54 1 312 8060 *Fax*: +54 1 313 1445 |
| | **Cordoba Stock Exchange** (Bolsa de Comercio de Cordoba) | Rosario de Santa Fe 231, 1 Piso, Cordoba *Tel*: +54 51 22 4230 *Fax*: +54 51 22 6550 *E-mail*: bolsacba@nt.com.ar |
| | **Mendoza Stock Exchange** (Bolsa de Comercio de Mendoza) | Paseo Sarmiento 199, Mendoza *Tel*: +54 61 20 23 59 *Fax*: +54 61 20 40 50 |
| | **La Plata Stock Exchange** (Bolsa de Comercio de La Plata) | Calle 48, No. 515, 1900 La Plata, Buenos Aires *Tel*: +54 21 21 47 73 *Fax*: +54 21 25 50 33 |
| | **Rosario Board of Trade** (Bolsa de Comercio de Rosario) ROFEX | Cordoba 1402, Pcia Santa Fe, Rosario *Tel*: +54 341 425 9610 *Fax*: +54 341 421 5097 *E-mail*: info@rofex.com.ar *URL*: http://www.rofex.com.ar |
| | **Rosario Stock Exchange** (Mercado de Valores de Rosario SA) | Cordoba Esquina Corrientes, Pcia Santa Fe, Rosario *Tel*: +54 41 21 34 70 *Fax*: +54 41 24 10 19 *E-mail*: titulos@bcr.com.ar |
| | **Buenos Aires Stock Exchange** (Bolsa de Comercio de Buenos Aires) | Sarmiento 299, Buenos Aires *Tel*: +54 1 313 3334 *Fax*: +54 1 312 9332 *E-mail*: cau@sba.com.ar *URL*: http://www.merval.sba.com.ar |

|  | *Country* | *Exchange Address* |
|---|---|---|
| **Argentina** | **Buenos Aires Futures Market** (Mercado a Termino de Buenos Aires SA) | Bouchard 454, 5to Piso, Buenos Aires<br>*Tel*: +54 1 311 47 16<br>*Fax*: +54 1 312 47 16 |
|  | **Merfox** (Mercados de Futuros y Opciones SA) | Samiento 299, 4/460, Buenos Aires<br>*Tel*: +54 1 313 4522<br>*Fax*: +54 1 313 4472 |
|  | **Rosario Futures Exchange** (Mercado a Termino de Rosario) | Cordoba 1402, Pcia Santa Fe, Rosario<br>*Tel*: +54 41 21 50 93<br>*Fax*: +54 41 21 50 97<br>*E-mail*: termino@bcr.com.ar |
| Armenia | **Yerevan Stock Exchange** | 22 Sarian Street, Yerevan Centre<br>*Tel*: +374 2 525 801<br>*Fax*: +374 2 151 548 |
| Australia | **Australian Stock Exchange** | Exchange Centre, 20 Bond Street, Sydney<br>*Tel*: +61 29 227 0000<br>*Fax*: +61 29 235 0056<br>*E-mail*: info@asx.com.au<br>*URL*: http://www.asx.com.au |
|  | **Sydney Futures Exchange** SFE | 30–32 Grosvenor Street, Sydney<br>*Tel*: +61 29 256 0555<br>*Fax*: +61 29 256 0666<br>*E-mail*: sfe@hutch.com.au<br>*URL*: http://www.sfe.com.au |
| Austria | **Wiener Borse AG** (Wiener Borse) | PO Box 192, Strauchgasse 1–2, Vienna<br>*Tel*: +43 1 53165 0<br>*Fax*: +43 1 532 97 40<br>*E-mail*: info@wbag.at<br>*URL*: http://www.wbag.at |
| Bahrain | **Bahrain Stock Exchange** | PO Box 3203, Manama<br>*Tel*: +973 261260<br>*Fax*: +973 256362<br>*E-mail*: bse@bahrainstock.com<br>*URL*: http://www.bahrainstock.com |
| Bangladesh | **Dhaka Stock Exchange** | Stock Exchange Building, 9E & 9F, Motijheel C/A, Dhaka<br>*Tel*: +880 2 956 4601<br>*Fax*: +880 2 956 4727<br>*E-mail*: info@dse.bdnet.net |

| Country | Exchange | Address |
|---------|----------|---------|
| Barbados | **Securities Exchange of Barbados** | 5th Floor, Central Bank Building, Church Village, St Michael<br>*Tel*: +1809 / 1246 246 436 9871<br>*Fax*: +1809 / 1246 246 429 8942<br>*E-mail*: sebd@caribf.com |
| Belgium | **Antwerp Stock Exchange** (Effectenbeurs van Antwerpen) | Korte Klarenstraat 1, Antwerp<br>*Tel*: +32 3 233 80 16<br>*Fax*: +32 3 232 57 37 |
| | **Brussels Stock Exchange** (Société de la Bourse de Valeurs Mobilieres de Bruxelles) | Palais de la Bourse, Brussels<br>*Tel*: +32 2 509 12 11<br>*Fax*: +32 2 509 12 12<br>*E-mail*: dan.maerten@pophost.eunet.be<br>*URL*: http:// www.stockexchange.be |
| | **Belgian Futures & Options Exchange** BELFOX | Palais de la Bourse, Rue Henri Mausstraat, 2, Brussels<br>*Tel*: +32 2 512 80 40<br>*Fax*: +32 2 513 83 42<br>*E-mail*: marketing@belfox.be<br>*URL*: http:// www.belfox.be |
| | **European Association of Securities Dealers Automated Quotation** EASDAQ | Rue des Colonies, 56 box 15, 1000 Brussels<br>*Tel*: +32 2 227 6520<br>*Fax*: +32 2 227 6567<br>*E-mail*: info@easdaq.com<br>*URL*: http:// www.easdaq.com |
| Bermuda | **Bermuda Stock Exchange** BSE | *E-mail*: info@bse.com<br>*URL*: http:// www.bsx.com |
| Bolivia | **Bolivian Stock Exchange** (Bolsa Boliviana de Valores SA) | Av. 16 de Julio No 1525, Edif Mutual La Paz, 3er Piso,<br>Casillia 12521,<br>La Paz<br>*Tel*: +591 2 39 29 11<br>*Fax*: +591 2 35 23 08<br>*E-mail*: bbvsalp@wara.bolnet.bo<br>*URL*: http:// bolsa-valores-bolivia.com |
| Country | Exchange | Address |
| Botswana | **Botswana Stock Exchange** | 5th Floor, Barclays House, Khama Crescent, Gaborone<br>*Tel*: +267 357900<br>*Fax*: +267 357901<br>*E-mail*: bse@info.bw |

| Country | Exchange | Address |
|---------|----------|---------|
| Brazil | **Minas, Espirito Santo, Brasilia Stock Exchange** (Blsa de Valores Minas, Espirito Santo, Brasilia) | Rua dos Carijos, 126–3 Andar, Belo Horizonte<br>*Tel*: +55 31 219 9000<br>*Fax*: +55 21 273 1202 |
| | **Rio de Janeiro Stock Exchange** (Bolsa de Valores de Rio de Janeiro) | Praca XV de Novembro No 20, Rio de Janeiro<br>*Tel*: +55 21 271 1001<br>*Fax*: +55 21 221 2151<br>*E-mail*: info@bvrj.com.br<br>*URL*: http://www.bvrj.com.br |
| | **São Paolo Stock Exchange** (Bolsa de Valores de São Paolo) | Rua XV de Novembro 275, Sao Paolo<br>*Tel*: +55 11 233 2000<br>*Fax*: +55 11 233 2099<br>*E-mail*: bovespa@bovespa.com.br<br>*URL*: http://www.bovespa.com.br |
| | **Bahia, Sergipe, Alagoas Stock Exchange** (Bolsa de Valores Bahia, Sergipe, Alagoas) | Rua Conselheiro Dantas, 29-Comercio, Salvador<br>*Tel*: +55 71 242 3844<br>*Fax*: +55 71 242 5753 |
| | **Far-South Stock Exchange** (Bolsa de Valores do Extremo Sul) | Rua dos Andradas, 1234–8 Andar, Porte Alegre<br>*Tel*: +55 51 224 3600<br>*Fax*: +55 51 227 4359 |
| | **Parana Stock Exchange** (Bolsa de Valores do Parana) | Rua Marechal Deodoro, 344-6 Andar, Curitiba<br>*Tel*: +55 41 222 5191<br>*Fax*: +55 41 223 6203 |
| | **Regional Stock Exchange** (Bolsa de Valores Regional) | Avenida Dom Manuel, 1020, Fortaleza<br>*Tel*: +55 85 231 6466<br>*Fax*: +55 85 231 6888 |
| | **Santos Stock Exchange** (Bolsa de Valores de Santos) | Rua XV de Novembro, 111, Santos<br>*Tel*: +55 132 191 5119<br>*Fax*: +55 132 19 1800 |
| | **Brazilian Futures Exchange** (Bolsa Brasileira de Futuros) | Praca XV de Novembro, 20, 5th Floor, Rio de Janeiro<br>*Tel*: +55 21 271 1086<br>*Fax*: +55 21 224 5718<br>*E-mail*: bbf@bbf.com.br |
| | **Pernambuco and Paraiba Stock Exchange** (Bolsa de Valores de Pernambuco e Paraiba) | Avenida Alfredo Lisboa, 505, Recife<br>*Tel*: +55 81 224 8277<br>*Fax*: +55 81 224 8412 |

| Country | Exchange | Address |
|---------|----------|---------|
| Brazil | **Commodities & Futures Exchange** (Bolsa de Mercadoris & Futuros) BM&F | Praca Antonio Prado, 48, São Paulo *Tel*: +55 11 232 5454 *Fax*: +55 11 239 3531 *E-mail*: webmaster@bmf.com.br *URL*: http://www.bmf.com.br |
| Bulgaria | **Sofia Commodity Exchange** SCE | 1 Bulgaria Sq, Sofia 1463 *Tel*: +359 2 543 031 *Fax*: +359 2 543 072 *E-mail*: sce@online.bg *URL*: http://www.online.bg/sce |
| | **Bulgarian Stock Exchange** | 1 Macedonia Square, Sofia *Tel*: +359 2 81 57 11 *Fax*: +359 2 87 55 66 *E-mail*: bse@bg400.bg *URL*: http://www.online.bg/bse |
| Canada | **Winnipeg Stock Exchange** | 620 – One Lombard Place, Winnipeg *Tel*: +1 204 987 7070 *Fax*: +1 204 987 7079 *E-mail*: vcatalan@io.unwinnipef.ca |
| | **Alberta Stock Exchange** | 21st Floor, 300 Fifth Avenue SW, Calgary *Tel*: +1 403 974 7400 *Fax*: +1 403 237 0450 *URL*: http://www.ase.ca |
| | **Toronto Stock Exchange** TSE | The Exchange Tower, 2 First Canadian Place, Toronto *Tel*: +1 416 947 4700 *Fax*: +1 416 947 4662 *E-mail*: skee@tse.com *URL*: http://www.tse.com |
| | **Vancouver Stock Exchange** VSE | Stock Exchange Tower, 609 Granville Street, Vancouver *Tel*: +1 604 689 3334 *Fax*: +1 604 688 6051 *E-mail*: information@vse.ca *URL*: http://www.vse.ca |
| | **Winnipeg Commodity Exchange** WCE | 500 Commodity Exchange Tower, 360 Main St., Winnipeg *Tel*: +1 204 925 5000 *Fax*: +1 204 943 5448 *E-mail*: wce@wce.mb.ca *URL*: http://www.wce.mb.ca |

| Country | Exchange Address |
|---|---|
| **Canada** | | |
| **Toronto Futures Exchange** TFE | The Exchange Tower, 2 First Canadian Place, Toronto *Tel*: +1 416 947 4487 *Fax*: +1 416 947 4272 |
| **Montreal Exchange** (Bourse de Montreal) ME | The Stock Exchange Tower, 800 Square Victoria, C.P. 61, Montreal *Tel*: +1 514 871 2424 *Fax*: +1 514 871 3531 *E-mail*: info@me.org *URL*: http://www.me.org |
| Cayman Islands | **Cayman Islands Stock Exchange** CSX | 4th Floor, Elizabethan Square, P.O Box 2408 G.T., Grand Cayman *Tel*: +1345 945 6060 *Fax*: +1345 945 6061 *E-mail*: CSX@CSX.COM.KY *URL*: http://www.csx.com.ky |
| Chile | **Santiago Stock Exchange** (Bolsa de Comercio de Santiago) | La Bolsa 64, Casilla 123-D, Santiago *Tel*: +56 2 698 2001 *Fax*: +56 2 672 8046 *E-mail*: ahucke@comercio.bolsantiago.cl *URL*: http://www.bolsantiago.cl |
| **Bolsa Electronica de Chile** | Huerfanos 770, Piso 14, Santiago *Tel*: +56 2 639 4699 *Fax*: +56 2 639 9015 *E-mail*: info@bolchile.cl *URL*: http://www.bolchile.cl |
| China | **Shenzhen Mercantile Exchange** | 1/F Bock B, Zhongjian Overseas Decoration , Hua Fu Road, Shenzhen *Tel*: +86 755 3343 502 *Fax*: +86 755 3343 505 |
| **Shenzhen Stock Exchange** | 203 Shangbu Industrial Area, Shenzhen *Tel*: +86 755 320 3431 *Fax*: +86 755 320 3505 |
| China | **Shanghai Cereals and Oils Exchange** | 199 Shangcheng Road, Pudong New District, Shanghai *Tel*: +86 21 5831 1111 *Fax*: +86 21 5831 9308 *E-mail*: liangzhu@public.sta.net.cn |

| Country | Exchange | Address |
|---------|----------|---------|
| China | **China-Commodity Futures Exchange, Inc of Hainan** CCFE | Huaneng Building, 36 Datong Road, Haikou, Hainan Province *Tel*: +86 898 670 01 07 *Fax*: +86 898 670 00 99 *E-mail*: ccfehn@public.hk.hq.cn |
| | **China Zhengzhou Commodity Exchange** CZCE | 20 Huanyuan Road, Zhengzhou *Tel*: +86 371 594 44 54 *Fax*: +86 371 554 54 24 |
| | **Wuhan Securities Exchange Centre** WSEC | 2nd Floor, Jianghchen Hotel, Wuhan *Tel*: +86 27 588 4115 *Fax*: +86 27 588 6038 |
| | **Guandong United Futures Exchange** | JingXing Hotel, 91 LinHe West Road, Guangzhou *Tel*: +86 20 8755 2109 *Fax*: +86 20 8755 1654 |
| | **Beijing Commodity Exchange** BCE | 311 Chenyun Building, No. 8 Beichen East Road, Chaoyang District, Beijing *Tel*: +86 1 492 4956 *Fax*: +86 1 499 3365 *E-mail*: sunli@intra.cnfm.co.cn |
| | **Shanghai Stock Exchange** | 15 Huang Pu Road, Shanghai *Tel*: +86 216 306 8888 *Fax*: +86 216 306 3076 |
| Colombia | **Bogota Stock Exchange** BSE | Carrera 8, No. 13-82 Pisos 4-9, Apartado Aereo 3584, Santafe de Bogota *Tel*: +57 243 6501 *Fax*: +57 281 3170 *E-mail*: bolbogot@bolsabogota.com.co *URL*: http://www.bolsabogota.com.co |
| | **Medellin Stock Exchange** (Bolsa de Medellin SA) | Apartado Aereo 3535, Medellin *Tel*: +57 4 260 3000 *Fax*: +57 4 251 1981 *E-mail*: 104551.1310@compuserve.com |
| | **Occidente Stock Exchange** (Bolsa de Occidente SA) | Calle 10, No. 4-40 Piso 13, Cali *Tel*: +57 28 817 022 *Fax*: +57 28 816 720 *E-mail*: bolsaocc@cali.cetcol.net.co *URL*: http://www.bolsadeoccidente.com.co |

| Country | Exchange | Address |
|---------|----------|---------|
| Costa Rica | **National Stock Exchange** (Bolsa Nacional de Valores, SA) BNV | Calle Central, Avenida 1, San Jose *Tel*: +506 256 1180 *Fax*: +506 255 0131 |
| Côte D'Ivoire (Ivory Coast) | **Abidjan Stock Exchange** (Bourse des Valeurs d'Abidjan) | Avenue Marchand, BP 1878 01, Abidjan 01 *Tel*: +225 21 57 83 *Fax*: +225 22 16 57 |
| Croatia (Hrvatska) | **Zagreb Stock Exchange** (Zagrebacka Burza) | Ksaver 208, Zagreb *Tel*: +385 1 428 455 *Fax*: +385 1 420 293 *E-mail*: zeljko.kardum@zse.hr *URL*: http://www.zse.hr |
| Cyprus | **Cyprus Stock Exchange** CSE | 54 Griva Dhigeni Avenue, Silvex House, Nicosia *Tel*: +357 2 368 782 *Fax*: +357 2 368 790 *E-mail*: cyse@zenon.logos.cy.net |
| Czech Republic | **Prague Stock Exchange** PSE | Rybna 14, Prague 1 *Tel*: +42 2 2183 2116 *Fax*: +42 2 2183 3040 *E-mail*: marketing@pse.vol.cz *URL*: http://www.pse.cz |
| Denmark | **Copenhagen Stock Exchange & FUTOP** (Kobenhavns Fondsbors) | Nikolaj Plads 6, PO Box 1040, Copenhagen K *Tel*: +45 33 93 33 66 *Fax*: +45 33 12 86 13 *E-mail*: kfpost@xcse.dk *URL*: http://www.xcse.dk |
| Ecuador | **Quito Stock Exchange** (Bolsa de Valores de Quito, CC) | Av Amazonas 540 y Carrion, 8vo Piso *Tel*: +593 2 526 805 *Fax*: +593 2 500 942 *E-mail*: bovalqui@ecnet.ec *URL*: http://www.ccbvq.com |
|  | **Guayaquil Stock Exchange** (Bolsa de Valores de Guayaquil, CC) | Av. 9 de Octubre, 110 y Pinchina, Guayaquil *Tel*: +593 4 561 519 *Fax*: +593 4 561 871 *E-mail*: bvg@bvg.fin.ec *URL*: http://www.bvg.fin.ec |

| Country | Exchange | Address |
|---------|----------|---------|
| Egypt | **Cairo & Alexandria Stock Exchanges** CASE | 4(A) El Cherifeen Street, Cairo *Tel*: +20 2 392 1402 *Fax*: +20 2 392 8526 *E-mail*: info@egyptse.com *URL*: http://www.egyptse.com |
| | **Alexandria Stock Exchange** | 11 Talaat Harp Street, Alexandria *Tel*: +20 3 483 7966 *Fax*: +20 3 482 3039 |
| El Salvador | **El Salvador Stock Exchange** (Mercado de Valores de El Salvador, SA de CV) | 6 Piso, Edificio La Centroamericana, Alameda Roosevelt No 3107, San Salvador *Tel*: +503 298 4244 *Fax*: +503 223 2898 *E-mail*: ggbolsa@gbm.net |
| Estonia | **Tallinn Stock Exchange** | Ravala 6, Tallinn *Tel*: +372 64 08 840 *Fax*: +372 64 08 801 *E-mail*: tse@depo.ee *URL*: http://www.tse.ee |
| Finland | **Helsinki Stock Exchange** HSE | Fabianinkatu 14, Helsinki *Tel*: +358 9 173 301 *Fax*: +358 9 173 30399 *E-mail*: mika.bjorklund@hex.fi *URL*: http://www.hse.fi |
| | **Finish Options Exchange** (Suomen Optioporssi Oy) FOEX | Erottajankatu 11, Helsinki *Tel*: +358 9 680 3410 *Fax*: +358 9 604 442 *E-mail*: info@foex.fi *URL*: http://www.foex.fi |
| France | **MATIF** (Marche á Terme International de France) MATIF | 176 rue Montmartre, Paris *Tel*: +33 33 1 40 28 82 82 *Fax*: +33 33 1 40 28 80 01 *E-mail*: larrede@matif.fr *URL*: http://www.matif.fr |
| | **Paris Stock Exchange** (Bourse de Paris) | 39 rue Cambon, Paris *Tel*: +33 1 49 27 10 00 *Fax*: +33 1 49 27 13 71 *E-mail*: 100432.201@compuserve.com |
| | **MONEP** (Marche des Options Négociables de Paris) MONEP | 39, rue Cambon, Paris *Tel*: +33 1 49 27 18 00 *Fax*: +33 1 9 27 18 23 *URL*: http://www.monep.fr |

| Country | Exchange | Address |
|---|---|---|
| Germany | **Stuttgart Stock Exchange** (Baden-Wurttembergische Wertpapierbörse zu Stuttgart) | Königstrasse 28, Stuttgart *Tel*: +49 7 11 29 01 83 *Fax*: +49 7 11 22 68 11 9 |
| | **Deutsche Terminbörse** DTB | Boersenplatz 4, Frankfurt-am-Main *Tel*: +49 69 21 01 0 *Fax*: +49 69 21 01 2005 *URL*: http://www.exchange.de |
| | **Bavarian Stock Exchange** (Bayerische Börse) | Lenbachplatz 2(A), Munich *Tel*: +49 89 54 90 45 0 *Fax*: +49 89 54 90 45 32 *E-mail*: bayboerse@t-online.de *URL*: http://www.bayerischeboerse.de |
| | **Berlin Stock Exchange** (Berliner Wertpapierbörse) | Fasanenstrasse 85, Berlin *Tel*: +49 30 31 10 91 0 *Fax*: +49 30 31 10 91 79 |
| | **Bremen Stock Exchange** (Bremer Wertpapierbörse) | Obernstrasse 2–12, Bremen *Tel*: +49 4 21 32 12 82 *Fax*: +49 4 21 32 31 23 |
| | **Düsseldorf Stock Exchange** (Rheinisch-Westfalische Börse zu Düsseldorf) | Ernst-Schneider-Platz 1, Düsseldorf *Tel*: +49 2 11 13 89 0 *Fax*: +49 2 11 13 32 87 |
| | **Hamburg Stock Exchange** (Hanseatische Wertpapierbörse Hamburg) | Schauenburgerstrasse 49, Hamburg *Tel*: +49 40 36 13 02 0 *Fax*: +49 40 36 13 02 23 *E-mail*: wertpapierboerse.hamburg@t-online.de |
| | **Hanover Stock Exchange** (Niedersachsische Börse zu Hanover) | Rathenaustrasse 2, Hanover *Tel*: +49 5 11 32 76 61 *Fax*: +49 5 11 32 49 15 |
| | **German Stock Exchange** (Deutsche Börse AG) FWB | Börsenplatz 4, Frankfurt-am-Main *Tel*: +49 69 21 01 0 *Fax*: +49 69 21 01 2005 *URL*: http://www.exchange.de |
| Ghana | **Ghana Stock Exchange** | 5th Floor, Cedi House, Liberia Road, PO Box 1849, Accra *Tel*: +233 21 669 908 *Fax*: +233 21 669 913 *E-mail*: stockex@ncs.com.gh *URL*: http://ourworld.compuserve.com/homepages/khaganu/stockex.htm |

| Country | Exchange | Address |
|---|---|---|
| Greece | **Athens Stock Exchange** ASE | 10 Sophocleous Street, Athens *Tel*: +30 1 32 10 424 *Fax*: +30 1 32 13 938 *E-mail*: mailto:aik@hol.gr *URL*: http://www.ase.gr |
| | **Athens Derivatives Exchange** ADEX | 23–25 Lekka Str, Athens *Tel*: +30 321 7244 *Fax*: +30 321 7302 *E-mail*: secretariat@adex.ase.gr *URL*: http://www.adex.ase.gr |
| Honduras | **Honduran Stock Exchange** (Bolsa Hondurena de Valores, SA) | 1er Piso Edificio Martinez Val, 3a Ave 2a Calle SO, San Pedro Sula *Tel*: +504 53 44 10 *Fax*: +504 53 44 80 *E-mail*: bhvsps@simon.intertel.hn |
| Hong Kong | **Hong Kong Stock Exchange** SEHK | 1st Floor, One and Two Exchange Square, Central *Tel*: +852 2522 1122 *Fax*: +852 2810 4475 *E-mail*: info@sehk.com.hk *URL*: http://www.sehk.com.hk |
| | **Chinese Gold and Silver Exchange Society** | Gold and Silver Commercial Building, 12–18 Mercer Street *Tel*: +852 544 1945 *Fax*: +852 854 0869 |
| | **Hong Kong Futures Exchange Ltd** HKFE | 5/F, Asia Pacific Finance Tower, Citibank Plaza, 3 Garden Road *Tel*: +852 2842 9333 *Fax*: +852 2810 5089 *E-mail*: prm@hkfe.com *URL*: http://www.hfke.com |
| Hungary | **Budapest Stock Exchange** | Deak Ferenc utca 5, Budapest *Tel*: +36 1 117 5226 *Fax*: +36 1 118 1737 *URL*: http://www.fornax.hu/fmon |
| | **Budapest Commodity Exchange** BCE | POB 495, Budapest *Tel*: +36 1 269 8571 *Fax*: +36 1 269 8575 *E-mail*: bce@bce-bat.com *URL*: http://www.bce-bat.com |

| Country | Exchange | Address |
|---|---|---|
| Iceland | **Iceland Stock Exchange** | Kalkofnsvegur 1, Reykjavik<br>*Tel*: +354 569 9775<br>*Fax*: +354 569 9777<br>*E-mail*: gw@vi.is |
| India | **The OTC Exchange of India**<br>OTCEI | 92 Maker Towers F, Cuffe Parade, Bombay<br>*Tel*: +91 22 21 88 164<br>*Fax*: +91 22 21 88 012<br>*E-mail*: otc.otcindia@gems.vsnl.net.in |
| | **Calcutta Stock Exchange** | 7 Lyons Range, Calcutta |
| | **Bangalore Stock Exchange** | *Tel*: +91 33 209 366<br>Stock Exchange Towers, 51, 1st Cross, JC Road, Bangalore<br>*Tel*: +91 80 299 5234<br>*Fax*: +91 80 22 55 48 |
| | **Pune Stock Exchange** | Shivleela Chambers, 752 Sadashiv Peth,<br>Kumethekar Road, Pune<br>*Tel*: +91 212 441 679 |
| | **Magadh Stock Exchange** | Industry House, Su=inha Library Road, Patna<br>*Tel*: +91 612 223 644 |
| | **Delhi Stock Exchange** | 3&4/4B Asaf Ali Road, New Delhi<br>*Tel*: +91 11 327 90 00<br>*Fax*: +91 11 327 13 02 |
| | **The Stock Exchange – Ahmedabad** | Kamdhenu Complex, Ambawadi, Ahmedabad<br>*Tel*: +91 79 644 67 33<br>*Fax*: +91 79 21 40 117<br>*E-mail*: supvsr@08asxe |
| | **Gauhati Stock Exchange** | Saraf Building, Annex, AT Road, Gauhati<br>*Tel*: +91 361 336 67<br>*Fax*: +91 361 543 272 |
| | **Jaipur Stock Exchange** | Rajasthan Chamber Bhawan, MI Road, Jaipur<br>*Tel*: +91 141 56 49 62<br>*Fax*: +91 141 56 35 17 |
| | **Madhya Pradesh Stock Exchange** | 3rd Floor, Rajani Bhawan, Opp High Court, MG Road, Indore<br>*Tel*: +91 731 432 841<br>*Fax*: +91 731 432 849 |

| Country | Exchange | Address |
|---|---|---|
| India | **The Stock Exchange, Mumbai** | Phiroze Jeejeebhoy Towers, Dalal Street, Bombay<br>*Tel*: +91 22 265 5860<br>*Fax*: +91 22 265 8121<br>*URL*: http://www.bseindia.com |
| | **Bhubaneswar Stock Exchange Association** | A-22 Falcon House, Jharapara, Cuttack Road, Bhubaneswar<br>*Tel*: +91 674 482 340<br>*Fax*: +91 674 482 283 |
| | **Kanara Stock Exchange** | 4th Floor, Ranbhavan Complex, Koialbail, Mangalore<br>*Tel*: +91 824 32606 |
| | **Ludhiana Stock Exchange** | Lajpat Rai Market, Near Clock Tower, Ludhiana<br>*Tel*: +91 161 39318 |
| | **Madras Stock Exchange** | Exchange Building, PO Box 183, 11 Second Line Beach, Madras<br>*Tel*: +91 44 510 845<br>*Fax*: +91 44 524 4897 |
| | **Uttar Pradesh Stock Exchange** | Padam Towers, 14/113 Civil Lines, Kanpur<br>*Tel*: +91 512 293 115<br>*Fax*: +91 512 293 175 |
| | **Coimbatore Stock Exchange** | Chamber Towers, 8/732 Avanashi Road, Coimbatore<br>*Tel*: +91 422 215 100<br>*Fax*: +91 422 213 947 |
| | **Hyderabad Stock Exchange** | 3–6–275 Himayatnagar, Hyderabad<br>*Tel*: +91 842 23 1985 |
| | **Cochin Stock Exchange** | 38/1431 Kaloor Road Extension, PO Box 3529, Emakulam, Cochin<br>*Tel*: +91 484 369 020<br>*Fax*: +91 484 370 471 |
| Indonesia | **Jakarta Stock Exchange** (PT Bursa Efek Jakarta) | Jakarta Stock Exchange Building, 13th Floor, Jl Jenderal Sudiman, Kav 52-53, Jakarta<br>*Tel*: +62 21 515 0515<br>*Fax*: +62 21 515 0330<br>*E-mail*: webmaster@jsx.co.id<br>*URL*: http://www.jsx.co.id |

| Country | Exchange | Address |
|---------|----------|---------|
| Indonesia | **Indonesian Commodity Exchange Board** (Badan Pelaksana Bursa Komoditi) | Gedung Bursa, Jalan Medan Merdeka Selatan 14, 4th Floor, Jakarta Pusat<br>*Tel*: +62 21 344 1921<br>*Fax*: +62 21 3480 4426 |
| | **Surabaya Stock Exchange** (PT Bursa Efek Surabaya) | 5th Floor, Gedung Madan Pemuda, 27–31 Jalan Pemuda, Surabaya<br>*Tel*: +62 21 526 6210<br>*Fax*: +62 21 526 6219<br>*E-mail*: heslpdesk@bes.co.id<br>*URL*: http://www.bes.co.id |
| | **Capital Market Supervisory Agency** (Baden Pelaksana Pasar Modal) BAPEPAM | Jakarta Stock Exchange Building, 13th Floor, Jl Jenderal Sudiman, Kav 52-53, Jakarta<br>*Tel*: +62 21 515 1288<br>*Fax*: +62 21 515 1283<br>*E-mail*: bapepam@indoexchange.com<br>*URL*: http://www.indoexchange.com/bapepam |
| Iran | **Tehran Stock Exchange** | 228 Hafez Avenue, Tehran<br>*Tel*: +98 21 670 309<br>*Fax*: +98 21 672 524<br>*E-mail*: stock@neda.net<br>*URL*: http://www.neda.net/tse |
| Ireland | **Irish Futures & Options Exchange** IFOX | Segrave House, Earlsfort Terrace, Dublin 2<br>*Tel*: +353 1 676 7413<br>*Fax*: +353 1 661 4645 |
| | **Irish Stock Exchange** | 28 Anglesea Street, Dublin 2<br>*Tel*: +353 1 677 8808<br>*Fax*: +353 1 677 6045 |
| Israel | **Tel Aviv Stock Exchange Ltd** TASE | 54 Ahad Haam Street, Tel Aviv<br>*Tel*: +972 3 567 7411<br>*Fax*: +972 3 510 5379<br>*E-mail*: ofers@tase.co.il<br>*URL*: http://www.tase.co.il |
| Italy | **Italian Derivatives Market** IDEM | Piazza Affari 6, Milan<br>*Tel*: +39 2 72 42 61<br>*Fax*: +39 2 72 00 43 33<br>*E-mail*: postoffice@borsaitalia.it<br>*URL*: http://www.borsaitalia.it |
| | **Italian Financial Futures Market** (Mercato Italiano Futures) MIF | Piazza del Gesu' 49, Rome<br>*Tel*: +39 6 676 7514<br>*Fax*: +39 6 676 7250 |

| Country | Exchange | Address |
|---------|----------|---------|
| Italy | **Italian Stock Exchange**<br><br>(Consiglio de Borsa) | Piazza degli Affari, 6, Milan<br>*Tel*: +39 2 724 261<br>*Fax*: +39 2 864 64 323<br>*E-mail*: postoffice@borsaitalia.it<br>*URL*: http://www.borsaitalia.it |
| Jamaica | **Jamaica Stock Exchange** | 40 Harbour Street, PO Box 1084, Kingston<br>*Tel*: +1809 809 922 0806<br>*Fax*: +1809 809 922 6966<br>*E-mail*: jse@infochan.com<br>*URL*: http://www.jamstockex.com |
| Japan | **Tokyo Commodity Exchange**<br>(Tokyo Kogyoin Torihikijo)<br>TOCOM | 10–8 Nihonbashi, Horidome-cho, Chuo-ku, 1-chome, Tokyo<br>*Tel*: +81 3 3661 9191<br>*Fax*: +81 3 3661 7568 |
| | **Kansai Agricultural Commodities Exchange**<br>KANEX | 1–10–14 Awaza, Nishi-ku, Osaka<br>*Tel*: +81 6 531 7931<br>*Fax*: +81 6 541 9343<br>*E-mail*: kex-1@kanex.or.jp<br>*URL*: http://www.kanex.or.jp |
| | **Kammon Commodity Exchange**<br>(Kammon Shohin Torihikijo) | 1–5 Nabe-cho, Shimonoseki<br>*Tel*: +81 832 31 1313<br>*Fax*: +81 832 23 1947 |
| | **Osaka Textile Exchange**<br>(Osaka Seni Torihikijo) | 2–5–28 Kyutaro-machi, Chuo-ku, Osaka<br>*Tel*: +81 6 253 0031<br>*Fax*: +81 6 253 0034 |
| | **Tokyo Stock Exchange**<br>(Tokyo Shoken Torihikijo)<br>TSE | 2–1 Nihombashi-Kabuto-Cho, Chuo-ku, Tokyo<br>*Tel*: +81 3 3666 0141<br>*Fax*: +81 3 3663 0625<br>*URL*: http://www.tse.or.jp |
| | **Kobe Raw Silk Exchange**<br>(Kobe Kiito Torihiksho)<br>KSE | 126 Higashimachi, Chuo-ku, Kobe<br>*Tel*: +81 78 331 7141<br>*Fax*: +81 78 331 7145 |
| | **Kobe Rubber Exchange**<br>(Kobe Gomu Torihiksho)<br>KRE | 49 Harima-cho, Chuo-ku, Kobe<br>*Tel*: +81 78 331 4211<br>*Fax*: +81 78 332 1622 |

| Country | Exchange | Address |
|---------|----------|---------|
| Japan | **Nagoya Stock Exchange** (Nagoya Shoken Torihikijo) NSE | 3–17 Sakae, 3-chome, Naka-ku, Nagoya *Tel*: +81 81 52 262 3172 *Fax*: +81 81 52 241 1527 *E-mail*: nse@po.iijnet.or.jp *URL*: http://www.iijnet.or.jp/nse-jp/ |
| | **Nagoya Textile Exchange** | 2–15 Nishiki 3 Chome, Naka-ku, Naka-ku, Nagoya *Tel*: +81 52 951 2171 *Fax*: +81 52 961 6407 |
| | **Osaka Securities Exchange** (Osaka Shoken Torihikijo) OSE | 8–l6, Kitahama, 1-chome, Chuo-ku, Osaka *Tel*: +81 6 229 8643 *Fax*: +81 6 231 2639 *E-mail*: osakaexc@po.iijnet.or.jp *URL*: http://www.ose.or.jp |
| | **Tokyo Grain Exchange** (Tokyo Kokumotsu Shohin Torihikijo) TGE | 1–12–5 Nihonbashi, Kakigara-cho, 1-Chome, Chuo-ku, Tokyo *Tel*: +81 3 3668 9321 *Fax*: +81 3 3661 4564 *E-mail*: webmas@tge.or.jp *URL*: http://www.tge.or.jp |
| | **Tokyo International Financial Futures Exchange** TIFFE | 1–3–1 Marunouchi, Chiyoda-ku, Tokyo *Tel*: +81 3 5223 2400 *Fax*: +81 3 5223 2450 *URL*: http://www.tiffe.or.jp |
| | **Japan Securities Dealing Association** (Nihon Shokengyo Kyokai) | Tojyo Shoken Building, 5-8 Kayaba-cho, 1-chome, Nihonbashi, Tokyo *Tel*: +81 3 3667 8451 *Fax*: +81 3 3666 8009 |
| | **Kyoto Stock Exchange** KANEX | 66 Tachiurinishi-machi, Higashinotoin-higashiiru, Shijo-dori Shimogyo-ku, Kyoto *Tel*: +81 75 221 1171 *Fax*: +81 75 221 8356 |
| | **Hiroshima Stock Exchange** KANEX | 14–18 Kanayama-cho, Naka-ku, Hiroshima *Tel*: +81 82 541 1121 *Fax*: +81 82 541 1128 |
| | **Fukuoka Stock Exchange** KANEX | 2–14–2 Tenjin, Chuo-ku, Fukuoka *Tel*: +81 92 741 8231 *Fax*: +81 92 713 1540 |
| | **Maebashi Dried Cocoa Exchange** (Maebashi Kanken Torihikijo) | 1–49–1 Furuichi-machi, Maebashi *Tel*: +81 272 52 1401 *Fax*: +81 272 51 8270 |

| Country | Exchange | Address |
|---------|----------|---------|
| Japan | **Sapporo Securities Exchange** (Sapporo Shoken Torihikijo) | 5–14–1 Nishi-minami, I-jo, Chuo-ku, Sapporo<br>*Tel*: +81 11 241 6171<br>*Fax*: +81 11 251 0840 |
| | **Niigata Securities Exchange** (Niigata Shoken Torihikijo) | 1245 Hachiban-cho, Kamiokawame-don, Niigata<br>*Tel*: +81 25 222 4181<br>*Fax*: +81 25 222 4551 |
| | **Cubu Commodity Exchange** | 3–2–15 Nishiki, Naka-ku, Nagoya<br>*Tel*: +81 52 951 2170<br>*Fax*: +81 52 961 1044 |
| | **Yokohama Raw Silk Exchange** (Yokohama Kiito Torihikijo) | Silk Centre, 1 Yamashita-cho, Naka-ku, Yokohama<br>*Tel*: +81 45 641 1341<br>*Fax*: +81 45 641 1346 |
| Jordan | **Amman Financial Market** | PO Box 8802, Ammam<br>*Tel*: +962 6 607171<br>*Fax*: +962 6 686830<br>*E-mail*: afm@go.com.jo<br>*URL*: http://accessme.com/AFM/ |
| Kenya | **Nairobi Stock Exchange** | PO Box 43633, Nairobi<br>*Tel*: +254 2 230692<br>*Fax*: +254 2 224200<br>*E-mail*: nse@acc.or.ke |
| Korea (South) | **Korea Stock Exchange** KSE | 33 Yoido-dong, Youngdeungpo-gu, Seoul<br>*Tel*: +82 2 3774 9000<br>*Fax*: +82 2 786 0263<br>*E-mail*: world@www.kse.or.kr<br>*URL*: http://www.kse.or.kr |
| Kuwait | **Kuwait Stock Exchange** | PO Box 22235, Safat, Kuwait<br>*Tel*: +965 242 3130<br>*Fax*: +965 242 0779 |
| Latvia | **Riga Stock Exchange** | Doma Iaukums 6, Riga<br>*Tel*: + 7 212 431<br>*Fax*: + 7 229 411<br>*E-mail*: rfb@mail.bkc.lv<br>*URL*: http://www.rfb.lv |
| Lithuania | **National Stock Exchange of Lithuania** | Ukmerges St 41, Vilnius<br>*Tel*: +370 2 72 14 07<br>*Fax*: +370 2 742 894<br>*E-mail*: office@nse.lt<br>*URL*: http://www.nse.lt |

| Country | Exchange | Address |
| --- | --- | --- |
| Luxembourg | **Luxembourg Stock Exchange** (Société Anonyme de la Bourse de Luxembourg) | 11 Avenue de la Porte-Neuve<br>*Tel*: +352 47 79 36-1<br>*Fax*: +352 47 32 98<br>*E-mail*: info@bourse.lu<br>*URL*: http://www.bourse.lu |
| Macedonia | **Macedonia Stock Exchange** MSE | *Tel*: +389 91 122 055<br>*Fax*: +389 91 122 069<br>E-mail: mse@unet.com.mk<br>URL: http://www.mse.org.mk |
| Malaysia | **The Kuala Lumpur Options & Financial Futures Exchange** KLOFFE | 10th Floor, Wisma Chase Perdana, Damansara Heights,<br>Jalan Semantan,<br>Kuala Lumpur<br>*Tel*: +60 3 253 8199<br>*Fax*: +60 3 255 3207<br>*E-mail*: kloffe@kloffe.com.my<br>*URL*: http://www.kloffe.com.my |
| | **Kuala Lumpur Commodity Exchange** KLCE | 4th Floor, Citypoint, Komplex Dayabumi,<br>Jalan Sulta Hishamuddin,<br>Kuala Lumpur<br>*Tel*: +60 3 293 6822<br>*Fax*: +60 3 274 2215<br>*E-mail*: klce@po.jaring.my<br>*URL*: http://www.klce.com.my |
| | **Malaysia Monetary Exchange BHD** | 4th Floor, City Point, PO Box 11260, Dayabumi Complex,<br>Jalan Sultan<br>Hishmuddin, Kuala Lumpur<br>*E-mail*: mme@po.jaring.my<br>*URL*: http://www.jaring.my/mme |
| | **Kuala Lumpur Stock Exchange** KLSE | 4th Floor, Exchange Square, Off Jalan Semantan,<br>Damansara Heights,<br>Kuala Lumpur<br>*Tel*: +60 3 254 64 33<br>*Fax*: +60 3 255 74 63<br>*E-mail*: webmaster@klse.com.my<br>*URL*: http://www.klse.com.my |
| Malta | **Malta Stock Exchange** | 27 Pietro Floriani Street, Floriana, Valletta 14<br>*Tel*: +356 244 0515<br>*Fax*: +356 244 071<br>*E-mail*: borza@maltanet.omnes.net |

| Country | Exchange | Address |
|---------|----------|---------|
| Mauritius | **Mauritius Stock Exchange** | Stock Exchange Commission, 9th Floor, SICOM Building, Sir Celicourt Anselme Street, Port Louis<br>*Tel*: +230 208 8735<br>*Fax*: +230 208 8676<br>*E-mail*: svtradha@intnet.mu<br>*URL*: http://lynx.intnet.mu/sem/ |
| Mexico | **Mexican Stock Exchange** (Bolsa Mexicana de Valores, SA de CV) | Paseo de la Reforma 255, Colonia Cuauhtemoc, Mexico DF<br>*Tel*: +52 5 726 66 00<br>*Fax*: +52 5 705 47 98<br>*E-mail*: cinform@bmv.com.mx<br>*URL*: http://www.bmv.com.mx |
| Morocco | **Casablanca Stock Exchange** (Société de la Bourse des Valeurs de Casablanca) | 98 Boulevard Mohammed V, Casablanca<br>*Tel*: +212 2 27 93 54<br>*Fax*: +212 2 20 03 65 |
| Namibia | **Namibian Stock Exchange** | Kaiserkrone Centre 11, O Box 2401, Windhoek<br>*Tel*: +264 61 227 647<br>*Fax*: +264 61 248 531<br>*E-mail*: tminney@nse.com.na<br>*URL*: http://www.nse.com.na |
| Netherlands | **Financiele Termijnmarkt Amsterdam NV** FTA | Nes 49, Amsterdam<br>*Tel*: +31 20 550 4555<br>*Fax*: +31 20 624 5416 |
| | **AEX-Options Exchange** AEX | Beursplein 5, PO Box 19163, Amsterdam<br>*Tel*: +31 20 550 4444<br>*Fax*: +31 20 550 4950<br>*URL*: http://www.aex-optiebeurs.ase.nl |
| | **AEX-Stock Exchange** AEX | Beursplein 5, PO Box 19163, Amsterdam<br>*Tel*: +31 20 550 4444<br>*Fax*: +31 20 550 4950<br>*URL*: http://www.aex.nl/ |
| | **AEX-Agricultural Futures Exchange** | Beursplein 5, PO Box 19163, Amsterdam<br>*Tel*: +31 20 550 4444<br>*Fax*: +31 20 623 9949 |

| Country | Exchange | Address |
|---|---|---|
| New Zealand | **New Zealand Futures & Options Exchange Ltd** NZFOE | 10th Level, Stock Exchange Centre, 191 Queen Street, Auckland 1 *Tel*: +64 9 309 8308 *Fax*: +64 9 309 8817 *E-mail*: info@nzfoe.co.nz *URL*: http://www.nzfoe.co.nz |
| | **New Zealand Stock Exchange** NZSE | 8th Floor, Caltex Tower, 286-292 Lambton Quay, Wellington *Tel*: +64 4 4727 599 *Fax*: +64 4 4731 470 *E-mail*: info@nzse.org.nz *URL*: http://www.nzse.co.nz |
| Nicaragua | **Nicaraguan Stock Exchange** (Bolsa de Valores de Nicaragua, SA) | Centro Financiero Banic, 1er Piso, Km. 5 1/2 Carretera Masaya *E-mail*: info@bolsanic.com *URL*: http://bolsanic.com/ |
| Nigeria | **Nigerian Stock Exchange** | Stock Exchange House, 8th & 9th Floors, 2/4 Customs Street, Lagos *Tel*: +234 1 266 0287 *Fax*: +234 1 266 8724 *E-mail*: alile@nse.ngra.com |
| Norway | **Oslo Stock Exchange** (Oslo Bors) OSLO | PO Box 460, Sentrum, Oslo *Tel*: +47 22 34 17 00 *Fax*: +47 22 41 65 90 *E-mail*: informasjonsavdelingen@ose.telemax.no *URL*: http://www.ose.no |
| Oman | **Muscat Securities Market** | PO Box 3265, Ruwi *Tel*: +968 702 665 *Fax*: +968 702 691 |
| Pakistan | **Karachi Stock Exchange** | Stock Exchange Building, Stock Exchange Road, Karachi *Tel*: +92 21 2425502 *Fax*: +92 21 241 0825 *URL*: http://www.kse.com.pk |
| | **Lahore Stock Exchange** | PO Box 1315, 19 Khayaban e Aiwan e Iqbal, Lahore *Tel*: +92 42 636 8000 *Fax*: +92 42 636 8484 |
| | **Islamabad Stock Exchange** | Stock Exchange Building, 101–E Fazal-ul-Haq Road, Blue Area *Tel*: +92 51 27 50 45 *Fax*: +92 51 27 50 44 *E-mail*: ise@paknet1.ptc.pk |

| Country | Exchange | Address |
|---------|----------|---------|
| Palestine | **Palestine Securities Exchange** | PO Box 128, Nablus<br>*Tel*: + 9 375 946<br>*Fax*: + 9 375 945<br>*E-mail*: anafin@netvision.net.il |
| Panama | **Panama Stock Exchange** (Bolsa de Valores de Panama, SA) | Calle Elvira Mendex y Calle 52, Edif Valarino, Planta Baja<br>*Tel*: +507 2 69 1966<br>*Fax*: +507 2 69 2457<br>*URL*: http://www.urraca.com/bvp/ |
| Paraguay | **Ascuncion Stock Exchange** (Bolsa de Valores y Productos de Ascuncion) | Estrella 540, Ascuncion<br>*Tel*: +595 21 442 445<br>*Fax*: +595 21 442 446<br>*E-mail*: bolsapya@pla.net.py<br>*URL*: http://www.pla.net.py/bvpasa |
| Peru | **Lima Stock Exchange** (La Bolsa de Valores de Lima) | Pasaje Acuna 191, Lima<br>*Tel*: +51 1 426 79 39<br>*Fax*: +51 1 426 76 50<br>*E-mail*: web_team@bvl.com.pe<br>*URL*: http://www.bvl.com.pe |
| Philippines | **Manila International Futures Exchange** MIFE | 7/F Producer's Bank Centre, Paseo de Roxas, Makati<br>*Tel*: +63 2 818 5496<br>*Fax*: +63 2 818 5529 |
| | **Philippine Stock Exchange** | Philippine Stock Exchange Centre, Tektite Road, Ortigas Centre, Pasig<br>*Tel*: +63 2 636 01 22<br>*Fax*: +63 2 634 51 13<br>*E-mail*: pse@mnl.sequel.net<br>*URL*: http://www.pse.com.ph |
| Poland | **Warsaw Stock Exchange** | Gielda papierow, Wartosciowych w Warszawie SA, Ul Nowy Swiat 6/12, Warsaw<br>*Tel*: +48 22 628 32 32<br>*Fax*: +48 22 628 17 54<br>*E-mail*: gielda@kp.atm.com.pl<br>*URL*: http://www.atm.com.pl/gpw/ |
| | **Warsaw Commodity Exchange** (Warszawska Gielda Towarowa) WGT | *E-mail*: wgt@wgt.com.pl<br>*URL*: http://www.wgt.com.pl |

| Country | Exchange | Address |
|---|---|---|
| Portugal | **Oporto Derivatives Exchange** (Bolsa de Derivados do Oporto) BDO | Av. da Boavista 3433, Oporto *Tel*: +351 2 618 58 58 *Fax*: +351 2 618 56 66 |
| | **Lisbon Stock Exchange** (Bolsa de Valores de Lisboa) BVL | Edificio da Bolsa, Rua Soeiro Pereira Gomes, Lisbon *Tel*: +351 1 790 99 04 *Fax*: +351 1 795 20 21 *E-mail*: webmaster@bvl.pt *URL*: http://www.bvl.pt |
| Romania | **Bucharest Stock Exchange** BSE | Doamnei no. 8, Bucharest *E-mail*: bse@delos.ro *URL*: http://www.delos.ro/bse/ |
| | **Romanian Commodities Exchange** (Bursa Romana de Marfuri SA) | Piata Presei nr 1, Sector 1, Bucharest *Tel*: +40 223 21 69 *Fax*: +40 223 21 67 |
| Russian Federation | **Sibiu Monetary-Financial and Commodities Exchange** (Bursa Monetar-Financiara si de Marfuri Sibiu) SMCFE | Piata 1 Decembrie 1918, nr. 69 *Tel*: +40 69 211798 *Fax*: +40 69 211153 *E-mail*: office@bmfms.ro *URL*: http://www.bmfms.ro |
| | **Moscow Interbank Currency Exchange** MICEX | 21/1, Sadovaya-Spasskay, Moscow *Tel*: +7 095 705 9627 *Fax*: +7 095 705 9622 *E-mail*: inmicex@micex.com *URL*: http://www.micex.com/ |
| | **Russian Exchange** RCRME | Myasnitskaya ul 26, Moscow *Tel*: +7 095 262 06 53 *Fax*: +7 095 262 57 57 *E-mail*: assa@vc-rtsb.msk.ru *URL*: http://www.re.ru |
| | **St Petersburg Futures Exchange** SPBFE | 274 Ligovski av., St Petersburg *Tel*: +7 812 294 15 12 *Fax*: +7 812 327 93 88 *E-mail*: seva@spbfe.futures.ru |

| Country | Exchange | Address |
|---------|----------|---------|
| Russian Federation | **Vladivostock Stock Exchange** VSE | 21 Zhertv Revolyutsii Str, Vladivostock *Tel*: +7 4232 22 78 87 *Fax*: +7 4232 22 80 09 |
| | **National Association** of Securities Market Participants (NAUF) | Floor 2, Building 5, Chayanova Street 15, Moscow *Tel*: +7 095 705 90 *Fax*: +7 095 976 42 36 *E-mail*: naufor@rtsnet.ru *URL*: http://www.rtsnet.ru |
| | **St Petersburg Stock Exchange** SPSE | 274 Ligovsky pr, St Petersburg *Tel*: +7 812 296 10 80 *Fax*: +7 812 296 10 80 *E-mail*: root@lse.spb.su |
| | **Siberian Stock Exchange** | PO Box 233, Frunze St 5, Novosibirsk *Tel*: +7 38 32 21 06 90 *Fax*: +7 38 32 21 06 90 *E-mail*: sibex@sse.nsk.su |
| | **Stock Exchange 'Saint-Petersburg'** SPBEX | VO 26 linia 15, Saint-Petersburg *Tel*: +7 812 322 44 11 *Fax*: +7 812 322 73 90 *E-mail*: spbex@spbex.ru *URL*: http://www.spbex.ru |
| | **Moscow Central Stock Exchange** | 9(B) Bolshaya Maryinskaya Stre, Moscow *Tel*: +7 095 229 88 82 *Fax*: +7 0995 202 06 67 |
| | **Moscow International Stock Exchange** MISE | Slavyanskaya Pl 4, Bld 2, Moscow *Tel*: +7 095 923 33 39 *Fax*: +7 095 923 33 39 |
| | **Moscow Commodity Exchange** | Pavilion No. 4, Russian Exhibition Centre, Moscow *Tel*: +7 095 187 83 07 *Fax*: +7 095 187 9982 |
| Saudi Arabia | **Saudi Arabian Monetary Authority** SAMA | PO Box 2992, Riyadh *Tel*: +966 1 466 2300 *Fax*: +966 1 466 3223 |
| Singapore | **Stock Exchange of Singapore** | No. 26–01/08, 20 Cecil Street, The Exchange *Tel*: +65 535 3788 *Fax*: +65 535 6994 *E-mail*: webmaster@ses.com.sg *URL*: http://www.ses.com.sg |

| Country | Exchange | Address |
|---------|----------|---------|
| Singapore | **Singapore International Monetary Exchange Ltd** SIMEX | 1 Raffles Place, No. 07–00, OUB Centre Tel: +65 535 7382 Fax: +65 535 7282 E-mail: simex@pacific.net.sg URL: http://www.simex.com.sg |
|  | **Singapore Commodity Exchange Ltd** SICOM | 111 North Bridge Road, #23–04/, Peninsula Plaza Tel: +65 338 5600 Fax: +65 338 9116 E-mail: sicom@pacific.net.sg |
| Slovak Republic | **Bratislava Stock Exchange** (Burza cenny ch papierov v Bratislave) BSSE | Vysoka 17, Bratislava Tel: +42 7 5036 102 Fax: +42 7 5036 103 E-mail: kunikova@bsse.sk URL: http://www.bsse.sk |
| Slovenia | **Ljubljana Stock Exchange, Inc** LJSE | Sovenska cesta 56, Ljubljana Tel: +386 61 171 02 11 Fax: +386 61 171 02 13 E-mail: info@jse.si URL: http://www.ljse.si |
|  | **Commodity Exchange of Ljubljana** | Smartinskal 52, PO Box 85, Ljubljana Tel: +386 61 18 55 100 Fax: +386 61 18 55 101 E-mail: infos@bb-lj.si URL: http://www.eunet.si/commercial/bbl/bbl-ein.html |
| South Africa | **Johannesburg Stock Exchange** JSE | 17 Diagonal Street, Johannesburg Tel: +27 11 377 2200 Fax: +27 11 834 3937 E-mail: r&d@jse.co.za URL: http://www.jse.co.za |
|  | **South African Futures Exchange** SAFEX | 105 Central Street, Houghton Estate 2198, Johannesburg Tel: +27 11 728 5960 Fax: +27 11 728 5970 E-mail: jani@icon.co.za URL: http://www.safex.co.za |
| Spain | **Bilbao Stock Exchange** (Sociedad Rectora de la Bolsa de Valoes de Bilbao) | Jose Maria Olabarri 1, Bilbao Tel: +34 4 423 74 00 Fax: +34 4 424 46 20 E-mail: bolsabilbao@sarenet.es URL: http://www.bolsabilbao.es |

| Country | Exchange | Address |
|---------|----------|---------|
| Spain | **Spanish Financial Futures Market** (MEFF Renta Fija) MEFF RF | Via Laietana, 58, Barcelona *Tel*: +34 3 412 1128 *Fax*: +34 3 268 4769 *E-mail*: marketing@meff.es *URL*: http://www.meff.es |
| | **Citrus Fruit and Commodity Market of Valencia** (Futuros de Citricos y Mercaderias de Valencia) | 2, 4 Libreros, Valencia *Tel*: +34 6 387 01 88 *Fax*: +34 6 394 36 30 *E-mail*: futuros@super.medusa.es |
| | **Valencia Stock Exchange** (Sociedad Rectora de la Bolsa de Valoes de Valencia) | Libreros 2 y 4, Valencia *Tel*: +34 6 387 01 00 *Fax*: +34 6 387 01 14 |
| | **Barcelona Stock Exchange** | Paseo Isabel II No 1, Barcelona *Tel*: +34 3 401 35 55 *Fax*: +34 3 401 38 59 *E-mail*: agiralt@borsabcn.es *URL*: http://www.borsabcn.es |
| | **Madrid Stock Exchange** (Bolsa de Madrid) | Plaza de la Lealtad 1, Madrid *Tel*: +34 1 589 26 00 *Fax*: +34 1 531 22 90 *E-mail*: internacional@bolsamadrid.es *URL*: http://www.bolsamadrid.es |
| | **Spanish Options Exchange** (MEFF Renta Variable) MEFF RV | Torre Picasso, Planta 26, Madrid *Tel*: +34 1 585 0800 *Fax*: +34 1 571 9542 *E-mail*: mefrv@meffrv.es *URL*: http://www.meffrv.es |
| Sri Lanka | **Colombo Stock Exchange** CSE | 04-01 West Bloc, World Trade Centre, Echelon Square, Colombo 1 *Tel*: +94 1 44 65 81 *Fax*: +94 1 44 52 79 *E-mail*: cse@sri.lanka.net *URL*: http://www.lanka.net/cse/ |

| Country | Exchange | Address |
| --- | --- | --- |
| Swaziland | **Swaziland Stock Market** | Swaziland Stockbrokers Ltd, 2nd Floor Dlan'ubeka House, Walker St,<br>Mbabane<br>*Tel*: +268 46163<br>*Fax*: +268 44132<br>*URL*: http://mbendi.co.za/exsw.htm |
| Sweden | **The Swedish Futures and Options Market**<br>(OM Stockholm AB)<br>OMS | Box 16305, Brunkebergstorg 2, Stockholm<br>*Tel*: +46 8 700 0600<br>*Fax*: +46 8 723 1092<br>*URL*: http://www.omgroup.com |
| | **Stockholm Stock Exchange Ltd**<br>(Stockholm Fondbors AB) | Kallargrand 2, Stockholm<br>*Tel*: +46 8 613 88 00<br>*Fax*: +46 8 10 81 10<br>*E-mail*: info@xsse.se<br>*URL*: http://www.xsse.se |
| Switzerland | **Swiss Options & Financial Futures Exchange AG**<br>SOFFEX | Selnaustrasse 32, Zurich<br>*Tel*: +41 1 229 2111<br>*Fax*: +41 1 229 2233<br>*E-mail*: webmaster@swx.ch<br>*URL*: http://www.bourse.ch |
| | **Swiss Exchange**<br>SWX | Selnaustrasse 32, Zurich<br>*Tel*: +41 1 229 21 11<br>*Fax*: +41 1 229 22 33<br>*URL*: http://www.bourse.ch |
| Taiwan | **Taiwan Stock Exchange** | Floors 2–10, City Building, 85 Yen Ping Road South, Taipei<br>*Tel*: +886 2 311 4020<br>*Fax*: +886 2 375 3669<br>*E-mail*: intl-aff@tse.com.tw<br>*URL*: http://www.tse.com.tw |
| Thailand | **The Stock Exchange of Thailand**<br>SET | 2nd Floor, Tower 1, 132 Sindhorn Building, Wireless Road, Bangkok<br>*Tel*: +66 2 254 0960<br>*Fax*: +66 2 263 2746<br>*E-mail*: webmaster@set.or.th<br>*URL*: http://www.set.or.th |
| Trinidad and Tobago | **Trinidad and Tobago Stock Exchange** | 65 Independence Street, Port of Spain<br>*Tel*: +1809 809 625 5108<br>*Fax*: +1809 809 623 0089 |

| Country | Exchange | Address |
|---------|----------|---------|
| Tunisia | **Tunis Stock Exchange** (Bourse des Valeurs Mobilières de Tunis) | Centre Babel – Bloc E, Rue Jean-Jacques Rousseau, Montplaisir, Tunis *Tel*: +216 1 780 288 *Fax*: +216 1 789 189 |
| Turkey | **Istanbul Stock Exchange** (Istanbul Menkul Kiymetler Borasi) ISE | Istinye, Istanbul *Tel*: +90 212 298 21 00 *Fax*: +90 212 298 25 00 *E-mail*: info@ise.org *URL*: http://www.ise.org |
| United Kingdom | **London International Financial Futures & Options Exchange** LIFFE | Cannon Bridge, London *Tel*: +44 20 7623 0444 *Fax*: +44 20 7588 3624 *E-mail*: exchange@liffe.com *URL*: http://www.liffe.com |
| | **The Baltic Exchange** | *Tel*: +44 20 7623 5501 *Fax*: +44 20 7369 1622 *E-mail*: enquiries@balticexchange.co.uk *URL*: http://www.balticexchange.co.uk |
| | **London Metal Exchange** LME | 56 Leadenhall Street, London *Tel*: +44 20 7264 5555 *Fax*: +44 20 7680 0505 *E-mail*: lsnow@lmetal.netkonect.co.uk *URL*: http://www.lme.co.uk |
| | **London Commodity Exchange** LCE | 1 Commodity Quay, St. Katharine Docks, London *Tel*: +44 20 7481 2080 *Fax*: +44 20 7702 9923 *URL*: http://www.liffe.com |
| | **The London Securities and Derivatives Exchange** OMLX | 107 Cannon Street, London *Tel*: +44 20 7283 0678 *Fax*: +44 20 7815 8508 *E-mail*: petter.made@omgroup.com *URL*: http://www.omgroup.com/ |
| | **International Petroleum Exchange of London Ltd** IPE | International House, 1 St. Katharine's Way, London *Tel*: +44 20 7481 0643 *Fax*: +44 20 7481 8485 *E-mail*: busdev@ipe.uk.com *URL*: http://www.ipe.uk.com |

| Country | Exchange | Address |
|---|---|---|
| United Kingdom | **London Stock Exchange** LSE | Old Broad Street, London *Tel*: +44 20 7797 1000 *Fax*: +44 20 7374 0504 |
| | **Tradepoint Investment Exchange** | 35 King Street, London *Tel*: +44 20 7240 8000 *Fax*: +44 20 7240 1900 *E-mail*: g171@dial.pipex.com *URL*: http://www.tradepoint.co.uk |
| United States | **International Securities Exchange** ISE | 110 Wall Street, New York *Tel*: +1 212 269 4914 *Fax*: +1 212 269 4923 *E-mail*: gkatz@iseoptions.com *URL*: http://www.iseoptions.com |
| | **Minneapolis Grain Exchange** MGE | 400 S. Fourth St., Minneapolis *Tel*: +1 612 338 6216 *Fax*: +1 612 339 1155 *E-mail*: mgex@ix.netcom.com *URL*: http://www.mgex.com |
| | **Nasdaq Stock Market** | 1735 K Street NW, Washington DC *Tel*: +1 202 728 8000 *Fax*: +1 202 293 6260 *E-mail*: fedback@nasdaq.com *URL*: http://www.nasdaq.com |
| | **Chicago Board Options Exchange** CBOE | 400 S. LaSalle Street, Chicago *Tel*: +1 312 786 5600 *Fax*: +1 312 786 7409 *E-mail*: investor_services@cboe.com *URL*: http://www.cboe.com |
| | **Chicago Board of Trade** CBOT | 141 West Jackson Boulevard, Chicago *Tel*: +1 312 435 3500 *Fax*: +1 312 341 3306 *E-mail*: comments@cbot.com *URL*: http://www.cbt.com |
| | **Chicago Stock Exchange** CHX | One Financial Place, 440 S. LaSalle St, Chicago *Tel*: +1 312 663 222 *Fax*: +1 312 773 2396 *E-mail*: marketing@chicagostockex.com *URL*: http://www.chicagostockex.com |

| Country | Exchange | Address |
|---|---|---|
| United States | **Chicago Mercantile Exchange** CME | 30 S. Wacker Drive, Chicago *Tel*: +1 312 930 1000 *Fax*: +1 312 930 3439 *E-mail*: info@cme.com *URL*: http://www.cme.com |
| | **Coffee, Sugar & Cocoa Exchange Inc.** CSCE | 4 World Trade Center, New York *Tel*: +1 212 938 2800 *Fax*: +1 212 524 9863 *E-mail*: csce@ix.netcom.com *URL*: http://www.csce.com |
| | **MidAmerica Commodity Exchange** MIDAM | 141 W. Jackson Boulevard, Chicago *Tel*: +1 313 341 3000 *Fax*: +1 312 341 3027 *E-mail*: comments@cbot.com *URL*: http://www.midam.com |
| | **New York Cotton Exchange** NYCE | 4 World Trade Center, New York *Tel*: +1 212 938 2702 *Fax*: +1 212 488 8135 *URL*: http://www.nyce.com |
| | **Pacific Stock Exchange, Inc** PSE | 301 Pine Street, San Francisco *Tel*: +1 415 393 4000 *Fax*: +1 415 393 4202 *URL*: http://www.pacificex.com |
| | **Philadelphia Board of Trade** | 1900 Market Street, Philadelphia *Tel*: +1 215 496 5357 *Fax*: +1 215 496 5653 |
| | **New York Stock Exchange** NYSE | 11 Wall Street, New York *Tel*: +1 212 656 3000 *Fax*: +1 212 656 5557 *URL*: http://www.nyse.com |
| | **Boston Stock Exchange, Inc** BSE | 38th Floor, One Boston Place, Boston *Tel*: +1 617 723 9500 *Fax*: +1 617 523 6603 *URL*: http://www.bostonstock.com |
| | **American Stock Exchange** AMEX | 86 Trinity Place, New York *Tel*: +1 212 306 1000 *Fax*: +1 212 306 1802 *E-mail*: jstephan@amex.com *URL*: http://www.amex.com |

| Country | Exchange | Address |
|---------|----------|---------|
| United States | **The Cincinnati Stock Exchange** | 400 South LaSalle Street, Chicago<br>*Tel*: +1 312 786 8803<br>*Fax*: +1 312 939 7239<br>*URL*: http://www.cincinnatistock.com |
| | **Philadelphia Stock Exchange** PHLX | 1900 Market Street, Philadelphia<br>*Tel*: +1 215 496 5000<br>*Fax*: +1 215 496 5653<br>*URL*: http://www.phlx.com |
| | **Kansas City Board of Trade** KCBT | 4800 Main St., Suite 303, Kansas City<br>*Tel*: +1 816 753 7500<br>*Fax*: +1 816 753 3944<br>*E-mail*: kcbt@kcbt.com<br>*URL*: http://www.kcbt.com |
| | **New York Mercantile Exchange** NYMEX | 4 World Trade Center, New York<br>*Tel*: +1 212 938 222<br>*Fax*: +1 212 938 2985<br>*E-mail*: marketing@nymex.com<br>*URL*: http://www.nymex.com |
| Venezuela | **Maracaibo Stock Exchange** (Bolsa de Valores de Maracaibo) | Calle 96, Esq Con Avda 5, Edificio Banco Central de Vene, Piso 9,<br>Maracaibo<br>*Tel*: +58 61 225 482<br>*Fax*: +58 61 227 663 |
| | **Venezuela Electronic Stock Exchange** (de Venezuela) | Cámara de Comercio de Valencia, Edif. Cámara de Comercio, Av.<br>Bolívar, Valencia, Edo. Carabobo, Apartado 151<br>*Tel*: +58 57.5109<br>*Fax*: +58 57.5147<br>*E-mail*: set@venezuelastock.com<br>*URL*: http://www.venezuelastock.com |
| | **Caracas Stock Exchange** (Bolsa de Valores de Caracas) | Edificio Atrium, Piso 1 Calle Sorocaima, Urbanizacion, El Rosal,<br>Caracas<br>*Tel*: +58 2 905 5511<br>*Fax*: +58 2 905 5814<br>*E-mail*: anafin@true.net<br>*URL*: http://www.caracasstock.com |

| Country | Exchange | Address |
|---------|----------|---------|
| Yugoslavia | **Belgrade Stock Exchange** (Beogradska Berza) | Omladinskih 1, 3rd Floor, PO Box 214, Belgrade<br>*Tel*: +381 11 19 84 77<br>*Fax*: +381 11 13 82 42<br>*E-mail*: beyu@eunet.yu |
| Zimbabwe | **Zimbabwe Stock Exchange** | 5th Floor, Southampton House, Union Avenue, Harare<br>*Tel*: +263 4 736 861<br>*Fax*: +263 4 791 045 |

# Glossary

**Abandoned option**  Where an option is neither sold nor exercised but allowed to lapse at expiry.

**Accumulation**  A technical analysis term describing a stock whose price is moving sideways.

**Acid test ratio**  A measure of financial strength. Also known as the quick ratio. Cash plus short-term investments plus accounts receivable divided by current liabilities for the same period. All other things being equal, a relatively high figure may indicate a healthy company.

**Active channels**  A feature of Internet Explorer 4. Internet sites that are selected as channels provide special IE4 content. Gates wants to lead internet tv – hence the term channels.

**Active market**  Securities trading with a relatively high degree of liquidity, the major benefit of which is narrow spreads. A term of art rather then precision.

**Aftermarket**  Also known as "secondary market," refering to the trading in a security after its initial public offering.

**All or none**  Order instructing the broker to buy or sell the entire amount of the order in one transaction or not at all.

**American depositary receipt (ADR)**  Effectively like owning in dollars stocks of non-US-listed companies. A popular form of owning shares of foreign companies.

**American option**  An option that is exerciseable at any time within its life. Can be traded outside Europe and are.

**American Stock Exchange (AMEX)**  Located in New York, this is the third-largest US stock exchange. Shares trade in the same "auction" manner used by the larger New York Stock Exchange unlike the Nasdaq's "market-making" methods.

**Arbitrage**  The purchase in one market of an instrument and the sale in another market of it or a closely linked instrument in order to profit from the small price differentials between the products in the two markets. Arbitrage profits usually only exist for a small time because someone usually scoops on them since they are "locked in."

**Arbitrageur** A trader engaged in arbitrage. They seek to make a lot of small, quick profits.

**Ask** The lowest price at which a dealer or market maker will sell a security (also, "bid," "offer").

**Assign** To oblige a call option writer to sell shares to the option holder, or to oblige a put option writer to buy shares from a put option holder.

**At the close** Order instructing to be filled as close as possible to the, um, close of a particular security, or to be canceled otherwise.

**At the market** An order to buy or sell at the best price obtainable in the market.

**At the open** Order instructing the transaction to be filled in one of the first trades for a particular security, or to be canceled otherwise.

**Averaging** Where a price moves against a trader and he trades more of the stock to enlarge his position but to lower his overall entry price. It will mean he will have a lower exit price at which he can make a profit.

**Away from the market** Trade orders that cannot be executed because they are above or below the current bid or ask. For example, a limit order to buy 50 shares of AOL at $105 when the best offer is $109 will not be filled and is said to be "away from the market."

**Backbone** A high-speed connection within a network that connects all the other circuits. Another name for a "hub." A central connection from which "spokes" or connections radiate.

**Bandwidth** The capacity of a network to carry data. If your pipes are clogged (low bandwidth) then things take forever to load. It's an issue not of length but of width.

**Basis point** Used to calculate differences in interest rate yields, e.g. the difference between 5.25 percent and 6.00 percent is 75 basis points.

**BBS** A bulletin board system. A little like an electronic notice board. You "post" messages to the board and everyone who subscribes to the board can view them.

**Bear(ish)** An individual who thinks prices will fall.

**Bear market** A market in which prices are falling.

**Bear spread** An option position where it is intended to profit from a falling market. Usually the position involves the purchase of a put at one strike price and the sale of a put at a lower strike price.

**Beta** This measure the stock's volatility to the market as a whole. A beta value greater than 1.0 represents greater volatility than the general market; less than 1.0 represents less volatility than the general market.

**Bid** An offer to purchase at a specific price.

**Big Board** Nickname for the New York Stock Exchange. Greatly adds to your smugability if you only ever refer to the NYSE as the Big Board. The ignorant will instantly fall admiringly at your feet. That a person of flesh and blood could know so much!?

**Black-Scholes Pricing Modelability** A mathematical model used to calculate the price in theory of an option. The main input variables are: the risk-free interest rate, volatility, dividends, time to expiry, the strike price, underlying price.

**Block** As in "the sale of a block of shares." A transaction involving a large number of shares or other security. Often blocks are bought or sold at a discount to the current market as an accepted cost of trading a large number of shares.

**Boiler room** Derogatory term to describe a brokerage firm where investors are aggressively solicited over the telephone with high-pressure telephone sales tactics. Smug traders, stay well clear.

**Bounce** What happens to mail which for some reason (e.g. wrong e-mail address) cannot be delivered.

**Breadth** Comparison of issues traded on a stock exchange on a given day to the total number of issues listed for trading. The broader a market move the more significant it is.

**Break** A sudden fall in price.

**Breakout** When the price moves out of its recent range. Sometimes signals further moves in the direction of the breakout.

**Broker** An individual who executes customers' orders.

**Bucket shop** Slang term for a disreputable brokerage firm that regularly engages in illegal practices, such as selling customers stock it may own at a higher than market price without disclosing the fact.

**Bull(ish)** An individual who believes prices will rise.

**Bull market** A market in which prices are rising.

**Bull spread** An option position where it is intended to profit from a rising market. Usually the position involves the purchase of a call at one strike price and the sale of a call at a higher strike price.

**Buy in** A person having to buy a security because of an inability to deliver the shares from a previous sale of said shares. Often associated with short sellers.

**Call option (calls)** The right, but not the obligation, existing only for a fixed period of time, to purchase a fixed quantity of stock at a fixed price.

**Cash flow per share** The trailing 12-month cash flow divided by the 12-month average shares outstanding. All other things being equal, a relatively high figure, growing steadily, is sign of a growing and healthy company and may indicate a rising share price.

**Churning** Illegal practice by a broker to cause excessive transactions in a client's account to benefit the broker through increased transaction fees.

**Clerk** An employee of an exchange's member firm, who is registered to work on the exchange floor.

**Closed** When referring to a position this means one has made an equal and opposite trade to one already held and so has no more exposure to the market on that trade.

**Co-mingling** Illegal act of combining client assets with those of the brokerage to boost the fiduciary's financial standing.

**Contrarian** An individual who generally believes it is usually better not to do what the majority is doing, because the majority does not make money.

**Cookie** According to conspiracy theorists, a cookie is a small piece of software that is downloaded from a web-site to your computer's hard drive that tells the web-master all your hidden and deepest secrets. According to everyone else, a cookie is a small piece of software that is downloaded from a web-site to your computer's hard drive that tells the web-master your username, password, viewing preference, and one or two other things. It means you do not have to enter the same information over and over again.

**Crossed market** The highest bid is greater than the lowest offer due to buyer and seller imbalance. Usually only lasts a few seconds until the market "sorts itself out."

**Current ratio** The ratio of total current assets divided by the total current liabilities for the same period. A measure of financial strength. All other things being equal, a relatively high figure would indicate a healthy company.

**Cyberspace** William Gibson's name in his fantasy novel Neuromancer (William Gibson, 1994) to describe what is now known as the internet.

**Daisy chain** Creating the illusion of trading activity in a stock through collusion of a number of brokers. Yes, it is illegal.

**Day trade(r)**  A position that is closed the same day it was opened.

**Deep discount**  Often, internet brokers that charges commissions far less than full service or discount brokers; as cheap as you can get.

**Delta**  The change of the options price for a change in the underlying price. A delta of 0.5 means a 10-point move in the underlying causes a five-point move in the option.

**Depreciation**  Not a measure of spousal dissatisfaction. An accounting measure used to reduce the value of capital expenditure for the purposes of reclaiming tax.

**Diversification**  Reducing risk by spreading investments among different interments. Not putting all your eggs in a few baskets.

**Dividend ex-date**  This is the date from which a purchaser of the stock will not be entitled to receive the last announced dividend. Appropriately, when a stock goes ex-dividend its price falls by approximately the value of the dividend.

**Dividend growth rate**  A measure of corporate growth. The annual positive change in dividend paid to stockholders. All other things being equal, an increase should indicate a growing company and should be reflected in rising share price.

**Dividend rate**  This is the total expected dividends for the forthcoming 12 months. It is usually the value of the most recent dividend figure multiplied by the number of times dividends are paid in a year, plus any extra dividend payments.

**Dividend yield**  This is calculated by dividing the annual dividend by the current price and expressing the figure as a percentage.

**Domain**  Part of a web or e-mail address. Separated from the rest of the address by dots.

**Dotted quad**  A set of four numbers separated by dots that constitutes an internet address, e.g. 123.32.433.234.

**Down tick**  A trade in a security that was executed at a lower price than the previous trade; same as "minus tick."

**Drawdown**  The reduction in trading capital as a result of losses.

**Dynamic HTML**  This makes web designers very excited. It means bits of web pages can be made to do things like change color when you point to them. These bits are therefore dynamic and not static (unlike their designers, who are definitely not dynamic).

**Encryption**  These scramble data and so keep them private from those who want to sneak a peek or drop an eave (eavesdroppers).

**EPS** Earnings per share. A measure of corporate growth. The value of corporate earning divided by the number of shares outstanding. All other things being equal, a growing figure reflects a healthy growing company and should be reflected in the share price.

**European option** An option that is only exercisable at expiry.

**Exercise** Where the holder of an option uses his right to buy or sell the underlying security. Also means to workout.

**Expiry** The date up to which a trader can exercise his option.

**Flame** An e-mail that is abusive or argumentative. Usually includes the words "You are a . . ." somewhere in the message.

**Flamefest** The same as a flame orgy.

**Flat** (1) A market where the price of a stock and/or its volume have not changed significantly over a period of time; (2) to no longer hold a position in a particular security or account.

**Floor broker** A member who executes orders for clearing members.

**Floor trader** An individual who trades on the floor of an exchange either for himself or a company.

**Free speech** An issue relating to the internet about which the US Congress spends inordinate quantities of time. Essentially, the concern is to give rights to those who would deny them to others, including those who granted them.

**Freeriding** Rapid buying and selling of a security by a broker without putting up funds for the purchase. Yup, it is illegal.

**Front running** Buying or selling securities ahead of a large order so as to benefit from the subsequent price move.

**FTP (file transfer protocol)** The protocol for sending files through the internet.

**Fundamental analysis** Forecasting prices by using economic or accounting data. For example, one might base a decision to buy a stock on its yield.

**Futures** A standardized contract for the future delivery of goods, at a pre-arranged date, location, price.

**Gap** Where a price opens and trades higher than its previous close.

**Geek** Also known as a net nerd. They were the kids everyone hated at school, who wore thick black-rimmed spectacles and were extremely uncool. They would also get sand kicked in their faces and were so unpopular no one would be seen dead with them – sometimes not even their parents. Now the sand has settled, and it has become clear that because they were unpopular they spent all their time studying, and can now be considered some of the wealthiest people on the planet, with the fastest flashiest cars. They definitely had the last laugh.

**Gross margin**  A measure of company profitability. The previous 12-month total revenue less cost of goods sold divided by the total revenue. All other things being equal, a decrease in gross margins could indicate troubled times ahead.

**Hedge**  Protection against current or anticipated risk exposure, usually through the purchase of a derivative. For example, if you hold DM and fear that the price will decline in relation to the dollar you may go long dollar. You would then make some profit on your long position to offset your losses in holding DM.

**Hit the bid**  When a seller places market orders with the intention of selling to the highest bidder, regardless of price.

**Implied volatility**  Future price volatility as calculated from actual, not theoretical, options prices. The volatility is implied in the prices.

**In and out**  Term for day trading in a security.

**Income per employee**  The income after taxes divided by the number of employees. A measure of corporate efficiency. All other things being equal, a greater the figure, or a growing figure, indicates a more efficient company and should be reflected in a rising share price.

**Initial margin requirement**  Amount of cash and securities a customer must have in his/her account before trading on margin.

**Initial public offering (IPO)**  First sale of stock by a company to the public.

**Insider**  Person such as a corporate officer or director with access to privileged company information.

**Insider share purchases**  The number of shares in the company purchased by its insiders – officers and directors – over a stated period of time. All other things being equal, a relatively large move may indicate a forthcoming upward move in the stock price.

**INSTINET**  A "fourth stock market" allowing members to display bid and ask quotes and bypass brokers in securities transactions. Owned by Reuters.

**Institutional net shares purchased**  This is the difference between institutional share purchases less institutional share sales in the company over a stated period of time. All other things being equal, a relatively large move may indicate a forthcoming upward move in the stock price.

**Institutional percent owned** This is the percentage of shares owned by all the institutions taken together. It is a percentage of the total shares outstanding. All other things being equal, a relatively large move may indicate a forthcoming upward move in the stock price.

**Intranet** This is a collection of computers connected to one another and usually located in a company or other organization. Unlike the internet, the network is private and not principally intended for the public.

**Java** An island or a coffee bean or a programming language developed by Sun Microsystems. It allows users to do lots of clever things with web pages.

**LAN (local area network)** A network of computers operating up to a few thousand meters from each other.

**Level I quotes** Basic service of the Nasdaq stock market that displays current bid and ask quotes.

**Level II quotes** Service of the Nasdaq stock market that displays current bid and ask quotes and the bids and asks from all market makers in a particular stock.

**Level III quotes** Service of the Nasdaq stock market that allows a market maker or registered broker–dealer to enter a bid or ask on the electronic trading system.

**Limit** The maximum permitted price move up or down for any given day, under exchange rules.

**Liquid market** A market which permits relatively easy entry and exit of large orders because there are so many buyers and sellers. Usually a characteristic of a popular market.

**Long** A position, opened but not yet closed, with a buy order.

**Long-term debt to total equity** A measure of financial strength. The long-term debt of the company divided by the total shareholder equity for the same period. All other things being equal, a relatively high figure may indicate an unhealthy company.

**Margin** A sum placed with a broker by a trader to cover against possible losses.

**Margin call** A demand for cash to maintain margin requirements.

**Mark to market** Daily calculation of paper gains and losses using closing market prices. Also used to calculate any necessary margin that may be payable.

**Market capitalization** This is the product of the number of shares outstanding and the current price.

**Market order** See At the market

**MIME** Multi-purpose internet mail extensions. This enables you to attach files to e-mail.

**Momentum** An indicator used by traders to buy or sell. It is based on the theory that the faster and further prices move in a particular direction, the more likely they are to slow and turn.

**Moving average** A system used by traders to determine when to buy and sell. An average (simple, exponential, or other) is taken of the closing (or opening, or other) prices over a specific number of previous days. A plot is made based on the average. As each day progresses, the moving average has to be recalculated to take account of the latest data and remove the oldest data.

**Net** After expenses, or short for the internet.

**Net profit margin** A measure of profitability. Income after taxes divided by the total revenue for the same period. All other things being equal, downward pressure on the net profit margin could provide advance warning of impending share price decline.

**Netiquette** Proper net behavior. For instance, swearing is neither appropriate etiquette nor is it netiquette.

**Network** A group of computers connected to each other so that their users can access each others' machines.

**Offer** A price at which a seller is willing to sell.

**Off-line browser** A browser that permits viewing of sites previously downloaded without being connected to the net.

**Open position** A position that has not yet been closed and therefore the trader is exposed to market movements.

**Overbought/oversold** A term used to mean, broadly, that a stock is likely not to advance further and may decline (overbought) or advance (oversold).

**Position** Trades which result in exposure to market movements.

**Price, 52-week high** This is the highest price the stock traded in the last 52 weeks. It may not necessarily be a closing high, it could be an intra-day high.

**Price, 52-week low** This is the lowest price the stock traded in the past 52 weeks. Could be an intra-day low price.

**Price to book ratio** The current price divided by the latest quarterly book value per share. All other things being equal, a relatively low figure may indicate the stock is undervalued.

**Price to cash flow ratio**  The current price divided by the cash flow per share for the trailing 12 months. All other things being equal, a relatively low figure may indicate the stock is undervalued.

**Price to earnings ratio**  The current share price divided by earnings per share before extraordinary items, usually taken over the previous 12 months. All other things being equal, a relatively low figure may indicate the stock is undervalued.

**Protocols**  A set of rules with which two computers must comply in order to communicate.

**Push technology**  The internet can be quite a passive experience, needing the user to log onto a site to determine if changes have occurred, or to download information. With push technology, the browser can be set to automatically download data from a set site.

**Put option**  A right, but not the obligation, existing for a specified period of time, to sell a specific quantity of stock or other instrument at a specified price.

**Pyramiding**  The increase in size of an existing position by opening further positions, usually in decreasing increments.

**Quick ratio**  A measure of financial strength. Cash plus short-term investments plus accounts receivable divided by current liabilities for the same period. All other things being equal, a relatively high figure may indicate a healthy company. See also Acid test ratio.

**Return on assets**  A measure of management effectiveness. Income after taxes divided by the total assets. All other things being equal, a relatively high or growing figure may indicate a company doing well.

**Return on equity**  A measure of management effectiveness. Income available to shareholders divided by the total common equity. All other things being equal, a relatively high or growing figure may indicate a company doing well.

**Return on investments**  A measure of management effectiveness. Income after taxes divided by the average total assets long-term debt. All other things being equal, a relatively high or growing figure may indicate a company doing well.

**Revenue percent change year on year**  A measure of growth. The revenue of the most recent period less the revenue of the previous period divided by the revenue of the previous period. All other things being equal, a growing figure indicates a growing company and should be reflected in a rising share price.

**Sales per employee**  A measure of company efficiency. The total sales divided by the total number of full-time employees. All other things being equal, the greater this figure the more efficient the company.

**Sales percent change** A measure of corporate growth. The value of sales for the current period less the value of sales for the preceding period divided by the value of sales for the preceding period, expressed as a percentage. All other things being equal, a growing figure indicates a growing company and should be reflected in a rising share price.

**Scalper** A trader also seeks to enter and exit the market very quickly and thereby make a lot of small profits.

**Seat** Exchange membership that permits floor trading.

**Server** A computer that shares its resources with others. The resources may be disk space, or files, or something else.

**Shares outstanding** The number of shares issued less those held in treasury.

**Short** An open position created by a sell order, in the expectation of a price decline and so the opportunity to profit by purchasing the instrument (so "closing out") at a lower price.

**Short-term debt** The value of debt due in the next 12 months.

**SMTP (simple mail transfer protocol)** The standard set of rules for transferring e-mail messages from one computer to another.

**Speculator** An individual who purchases financial instruments in order to profit. Often used to refer to a non-professional. Sometimes used derogatorily.

**Spread** The simultaneous purchase of one contract and the sale of a similar, but not identical, contract. Depending on the exact combination, a profit can be made from either a rising or falling market.

**Stop order (stop-loss orders)** An order left with a broker instructing him to close out an existing position if the market price reaches a certain level. Can be used to take profits or stop losses.

**TCP/IP (transmission control protocol/internet protocol)** A set of rules used to connect to other computers.

**Technical analysis** Method used to forecast future prices using the price data alone (for example, by plotting them on a chart and noting direction) or using the price as an input in mathematical formulae and plotting the results. See also Fundamental analysis.

**Technical rally or decline** A price movement resulting from factors unrelated to fundamentals or supply and demand.

**Tick** The smallest possible price move.

**Total debt to equity ratio** A measure of financial strength. The total debt divided by total shareholder equity for the same period. All other things being equal, a relatively low figure is a sign of a healthy company.

**Total operating expenses** A measure of the cost of running the company. All other things being equal, a lower figure is preferable to a higher one.

**Trendline** A line on a price chart indicating market price direction. The line connects at least three price points which touch the line, with no prices breaking the line.

**Volatility** A statistical indication of probable future price movement size (but not direction) within a period of time. For example 66 percent probability of a 15 pence move in three months.

**Webcasting** This is the internet trying to be older – like TV or radio. Instead of viewing pages, you view a stream of data in the form of radio or video. Unfortunately, the infrastructure is lacking to make this a popular alternative to TV and radio.

**Whipsaw** A price move first in one direction, and, shortly thereafter, in another direction thereby catching traders wrong-footed. Such markets may be termed "choppy." Such effects often give rise to false buy and sell signals, leading to losses.

# Index*

*entries in bold are definitions